THE
POLITICAL
ECOLOGY
OF DISEASE
IN TANZANIA

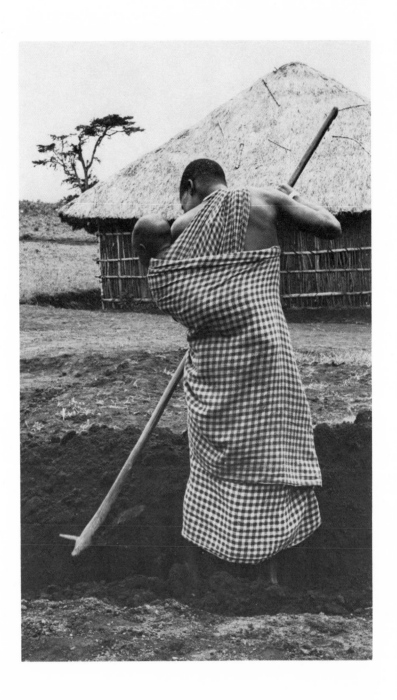

Meredeth Turshen

THE
POLITICAL
ECOLOGY
OF DISEASE
IN TANZANIA

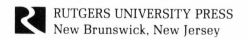
RUTGERS UNIVERSITY PRESS
New Brunswick, New Jersey

Jacket photo courtesy UNICEF photo
ICEF Series 5181-90 UNICEF Basic
Health Tanzania ICEF 5181/Lynn
Millar/66

Frontispiece courtesy of International
Labour Office, Bureau International du
Travail (IT-Tanzania-Agr-1)

Library of Congress Cataloging in Publication Data

Turshen, Meredeth
   The political ecology of disease in Tanzania.

   Bibliography: p.
   Includes index.
   1. Public health—Tanzania—History. 2. Medical
care—Tanzania—History. 3. Diseases—Tanzania—
Causes and theories of causation—History. 4. Medical
policy—Tanzania—History. 5. Medical economics—
Tanzania—History. 6. Social medicine—Tanzania—
History. 7. Women—Tanzania—History. 8. Tanzania—
Economic policy. I. Title
RA552. T34T87 1984   362.1'09678   83–15967
ISBN 0–8135–1030–9

For my brothers and sisters

CONTENTS

TABLES

Map precedes page 1

PREFACE

My motive for writing this book is the wish to understand why the health of colonized people deteriorated under colonial rule and how colonialism restructured African societies so that the factors responsible for ill health persisted after independence. The need to reexamine colonial medical history stemmed from my dissatisfaction with perceptions of the causes and cures of disease embedded in historical accounts. Most analyses separate ecological change from malnutrition, political struggle from epidemics, and social upheaval from health and healing. None consider the relation of ecological, political, and social aspects of disease to the economic transformations wrought by colonialism and capitalism in Africa. Although the medical model is now being challenged, it persists in assumptions—usually couched in terms of culture or life style—that people are to blame for their own illnesses and in beliefs that medical services improve health.

In studying Tanzania I sought to identify the colonial policies that had the greatest impact on the health of African people. Policies that affected food and nutrition would, I knew, be more germane to health status than would the colonial medical services. The health of Tanzanian women, who are central to the society's food system, was a special concern and focus of my research. To explain changes in family health, I had to look beyond domestic structures to colonial labor policies, new capitalist land tenure arrangements, and the creation of an export economy. One especially puzzling paradox was the steady growth of population after World War I, despite persuasive evidence of declining health. More rewarding than conventional studies of women's fertility for an understanding of changes in population dynamics were reports of new labor demands in

a colonial plantation economy dependent on migrant workers. I looked for repercussions of this economic transformation in labor supply areas and in plantation centers;
specifically I examined changes in social relations of
production—the new organization of work, the different
distribution of products, and the changed rapport between
men and women—and in levels of agricultural productivity
that would affect food supplies, as well as in patterns of
death and the provision of curative medical services.

After reading the colonial record, one is tempted to identify imperialism as the source of all current difficulties—a
temptation not surprising for someone who is highly critical of capitalist society. Similarly, one tends to overcom-
pensate for Victorian racism by portraying life in the precolonial era as golden. Both inclinations are misplaced;
neither helps find a way out of the development dilemma.

Unprecedented famines are predicted for the decade of
the 1980s in Africa, predictions that unhappily appear to be
accurate. Following so soon after the catastrophic drought
of 1968–1974, which claimed one hundred thousand lives
in the Sahel, the current exigency raises troubling questions
about the political ecology of Africa, that is, the peculiar interplay of physical changes occurring in a deteriorating
landscape and economic policies reflected in national and
international politics. My purpose, in addressing the issues
of political ecology, is to establish the economic, social,
and political determinants of ill health and the dynamics of
underdevelopment. Perhaps with these coordinates it will
be possible to map the way forward.

ACKNOWLEDGMENTS

Since I began the studies that led to my writing this book, I have met many people who stimulated and supported me. It is with pleasure that I thank some of them publicly and ask those whose names are omitted not to think that I have forgotten them. Many Tanzanians spent hours discussing the problems of their country with me; they have my deepest gratitude, but as they bear no responsibility for my views they shall remain anonymous. For their intellectual and moral support and for reading and commenting on various drafts, I should like to express my appreciation to Carol Wolkowitz, Raphie Kaplinsky, Elinor Kamath, Joe Eyer, Oscar Gish, Fred Bienefeld, Steven Feierman, Dorothy Remy, Judy Freidman, Malcolm Segall, and Teddy Brett. For their guidance of my doctoral studies, which this book draws upon, I should like to thank Bob Benewick, Bruce Graham, Geoff Lamb, and John Powles. Thanks go to my coeditors at the *Review of African Political Economy*, especially Peter Lawrence and Lionel Cliffe; thanks, too, to members of the East Coast Health Discussion Group—Evan Stark, Kim Hopper, and Len Rodberg. Similarly, my thanks to the Capitol Kapitalistate Collective, particularly Cathy Schoen, Barbara Smith, and Michel Cretin. I owe a special debt to Ron Frankenberg for his careful reading of a complete draft.

Part of the research was accomplished under a fellowship from the Population Council while I was on leave from the World Health Organization, and I would like to thank both organizations for making my studies possible. I would also like to thank Ingrid Palmer and Lourdes Beneria for their assistance with the research I did on women in Tanzania for the International Labour Organisation. Several institutions have assisted me in my work: the Institute for Development Studies of the University of Sussex and the

Research and Training Institute at Ilonga, Tanzania. This book would not have been published without the assistance of my editors, Marlie Wasserman, Joan Bothell, and Leslie Mitchner. Finally, special thanks go to certain individuals who played an important role in shaping my ideas—Pierre Chaulet, Sally Cornwell, and René Thomson.

THE
POLITICAL
ECOLOGY
OF DISEASE
IN TANZANIA

TANZANIA
REGIONS AND DISTRICTS

————	Main roads
＋＋＋＋	Railways
＋＋＋	TAN-ZAM railway
————	Region boundaries
- - - -	District boundaries
▬▬▬	International boundaries

KENYA

LAKE NATRON

Olduvai

MONDULI

Monduli

ARU HAI ROMBO
MERU Moshi
Arusha
MOSHI

KILIMANJARO

Same
PARE

LAKE MANYARA

ARUSHA

MASAI

Kondoa
KONDOA

TANGA

LUSHOTO

Lushoto
KOROGWE
Korogwe

TANGA
Tanga

PEMBA

INDIAN OCEAN

4°

Kiberashi

Handeni
HANDENI

Pangani
PANGANI

DODOMA

Dodoma

Mpwapwa

Gulwe
MPWAPWA

Kilosa
KILOSA

BAGAMOYO

Bagamoyo

COAST

ZANZIBAR

DODOMA

Morogoro

Ruvu

DAR ES SALAAM
DAR ES SALAAM

MOROGORO

KISARAWE

Mikumi

Msanga

Kisiju

ringa

RUFIJI

MAFIA

8°

NGA

KILOMBERO

Utete

o Hill

Mahenge

Malinyi

MOROGORO

ULANGA

LINDI

Kilwa Masoko

NACHINGWEA

KILWA

pemba

Liwale

Lindi
LINDI

Mtwara

SONGEA

Nachingwea
NACHINGWEA
Masasi

MTWARA

NEWALA

Songea

MTWARA
MASASI Newala

ga

RUVUMA

Tunduru
TUNDURU

Bay

36°

MOZAMBIQUE

40°

INTRODUCTION

The delivery of health care to the rural areas of underdeveloped countries is today the subject of much discussion and, in the last three decades, the object of many programs. The subject is important because many people in the Third World are still debilitated by disease and because most of them live in rural areas. With a few notable exceptions such as the People's Republic of China (Sidel and Sidel 1982) and the Socialist Republic of Vietnam (McMichael 1976), underdeveloped countries have achieved little success in extending health facilities to rural areas.

The global decline in death rates and increase in population are thought to indicate an improvement in health, which has apparently occurred in spite of the slow development and faulty functioning of the health service network. Even if health is improving overall, it is doing so more slowly in some countries (for example, Haiti) than in others (Cuba), suggesting a political dimension to the problem.

Since World War II, governments in underdeveloped countries have initiated innumerable rural health service programs, often with the assistance of bilateral and multilateral aid agencies, both governmental and nongovernmental. Few of these programs have succeeded (World Bank 1980: 6–7). Public health specialists have rarely analyzed the failures in terms of the theoretical assumptions on which the programs rest, and public health administration theory still relies on the empiricism of trial and error. The difficulties facing poor countries that wish to reorient health policy in favor of the rural majority have been misunderstood and underestimated. The problems are usually defined either by the medical profession (and health ministries staffed and advised by physicians), who think that better health for the masses is primarily a matter of more money for medical personnel, or by health economists, who maintain that the obstacles are poor planning and scarce resources (see, for example, World Bank 1980).

This view is not limited to the old guard of the medical profession; it is shared by liberal, enlightened physicians in the field of international health. Bryant, for example, in a study for the Rockefeller Foundation regarded as a classic in the field, states, "Limitations of resources must top any list of obstacles to providing health care. The interlocking shortages of money, personnel, and materials make it impossible to penetrate some areas of need and reduce other efforts to thinly patched frameworks" (1969: 314). Scarcity of money is the major constraint in providing adequate health care and the lack of resources is, in Bryant's words, "beyond our influence." Although it is not clear whether "our influence" refers to the medical profession or to aid agencies, it is wrong to imply that the current level of resources is not amenable to radical change. To dismiss the subject without analyzing it is to miss the whole question of the locus of economic and political power—in the world as well as in the health sector. Since Bryant's statement starts from a false premise that contains unexamined and ideologically biased assumptions, it necessarily arrives at false conclusions; thus ineffective solutions are proposed for wrongly formulated problems.

In this view the solution to the health problems of underdeveloped countries lies essentially in behavioral change. The question is how medicine can penetrate communities in order to manipulate and change behavior. Adherents of this position ignore the underlying causes of disease and death embedded in political and economic systems; instead they seek the causes of conditions like malnutrition, gastroenteritis, and pneumonia in the way people live (May 1958). We are left with the classic triad, the "vicious circle" of poverty, ignorance, and disease.[1] In a modern restate-

---

1. The second factor in the triad is much more difficult to evaluate: ignorance by whose standard and by what measurement? Ignorance is a relative term: used in the colonial context, it implied lack of formal education in a school system and lack of knowledge of Western science and technology. This usage betrays a cultural bias in the definition of knowledge, as there are more types than this one. The consequences to traditional medicine, to mention just one example of non-Western knowledge, are discussed in chapter 8.

ment of the Malthusian position, Bryant says, "These problems, in turn, are worsened by high rates of population
growth, which result in crowding in the home and less food
and attention for each child" (1969:x–xi).

The distribution of health care is a question not so much
of resources as of who controls those resources. Some advanced capitalist countries—the United States, Sweden,
and the United Kingdom—with a high per person expenditure on health care, have not achieved better health for all
of their citizens or health care systems that reach adequately all of their people (Anderson 1972). At the same
time, a very few poor socialist countries—the Socialist Republic of Vietnam and the People's Republic of China—
have improved the health of their people. It is not merely a
matter of money or management.

Capitalist management techniques by themselves do not
bring about equitable distribution of health care, nor can an
increase in expenditure necessarily do so. Even if an equitable system could be designed, the question of its scientific
and technical content would still remain. Agencies like the
World Health Organization (WHO) used to believe the solution to the problems of ill health in underdeveloped countries to be the transfer of modern Western medical science
and technology. There is general agreement that the underdeveloped countries of Africa, Asia, and Latin America suffer grave ill health and high death rates: the alleviation of
that burden through medical aid is held by humanists to be
a duty of the technologically advanced countries and by
economists to be in their long-term self-interest. Brock
Chisholm, the first director-general of WHO, saw as his organization's task the realization of this technology transfer.
In his annual report for 1951 he wrote: "Today in the eyes
of humanity it has become the duty of those countries more
richly endowed with more resources and more skilled in
their use and conservation to help those less developed to
provide the scientific and medical means of improving the
health of their peoples" (Chisholm 1952:1). This position
has come under heavy attack from a number of angles. Crit-
ics like myself have challenged the relevance of the scientific approach adopted in industrialized and urbanized societies to the health problems of underdeveloped countries
with large rural populations; the suitability of the technology, especially the capital-intensive technology, to poverty-
stricken countries; the contribution of postwar science and

technology to the solution of health problems in the advanced capitalist countries themselves; and the position that science and technology are neutral or value-free (Turshen and Thébaud 1981). We have indicted bilateral aid for its role as a weapon of foreign policy and multilateral aid for its capitalist ideological bias, which we believe works against the independence and progress of underdeveloped countries (see also Hayter 1971; Payer 1982). Health aid is often a purveyor of Western science and technology: most experts sent under bilateral and multilateral auspices to underdeveloped countries were until recently from Western Europe and North America. The situation in international organizations improved gradually in the 1960s as membership widened and as other countries increasingly became able to provide assistance, but even many of these countries use Western science and technology.

More fundamental still than issues of management, increased resources, and the transfer of medical science and technology is the question of improved health as a natural concomitant of economic development. Classical liberal economics places hope for better health in economic growth. Hughes notes, "It is widely held among economists that by concentrating first on the development of a viable economy, gross national product will rise, nutrition should improve, sanitation becomes less of a problem, and better health results" (1972:8). These assumptions must be challenged. First, a "viable" economy may have more than one definition; second, gross national product is a measure of a limited type of economic growth rather than of development; third, the improvement of nutrition entails a distribution of gross national product that is not automatic in every economic system; and fourth, the amelioration of sanitary arrangements requires deliberate action and does not occur spontaneously.

Even if the necessary mechanisms for redistribution were built into the economy, how is development to occur? Given the colonial and neocolonial structure of the world political and economic system, economic growth is impeded by subordination of the neocolony to the requirements of the United States and Western Europe, resulting in the creation of an increasingly dependent economy. The successful attraction of foreign capital, its investment in enterprises located in underdeveloped countries, and the production of commodities within the confines of the international market will not bring development. In Africa, the reason for this is to be found in the particularities of capitalist development there: Europeans initiated the process from outside at the time when capitalism had reached the advanced stage of imperialism. In contrast, the national capitalist systems that emerged in Europe, North America, and Japan were driven by indigenous forces (editorial, *Review of African Political Economy* 1974:3). But Africa is not merely the reflection of imperialism: the dynamic of African societies is a result of complex internal and external forces that limit and distort the development of the forces of production under capitalism. Thus Africa's continuing chronic poverty is not an innate or inherent problem but a product of colonial history, present dependence, and changed social relations of production.

This analysis has direct bearing on an understanding of health problems and the formulation of health policies in Africa. It means that the health sector was subject to limitation and distortion under colonial rule and that widespread ill health and especially chronic malnutrition were not natural or internal problems. It also means that improvement in health is contingent upon overcoming dependency and upon the transformation of the social system. Specifically, it means that malnutrition will not be eliminated until there is an end to neocolonial exploitation of agricultural production in Africa. The Sahel famine shows that natural phenomena alone do not account for the problems. Meillassoux (1974:29–30), writing about the famine, argues that the extraction of surplus for export, in conjunction with the limited means of production and the need to perpetuate the subsistence economy, results in the exhaustion of the factors of production. Only limited provision could be made to meet predicted shortages in the inevitable periods of drought that have always struck these regions; the agricultural economy became extremely fragile under colonialism and later neocolonialism, and the people's livelihood especially vulnerable to severe climatic disruption (Comité Information Sahel 1974).

Apologists for colonial regimes often look myopically at the medical services, proclaim their humanity, and even argue that their philosophy ran counter to that of imperialism: had their activities not been hampered by budgetary limitations, they would ultimately have created an African medical service (Beck 1970:202–203). Such claims are not supported by the evidence. While medical authorities did not produce the worst atrocities committed in the imperialist cause, they did participate in them and support them (Paul 1977).

The imbalance in existing medical services in the East African nation of Tanzania, the subject of this study, is in part a legacy of colonial government. The health system created under the colonial rule first of Germany (1884–1918)[2] and then of Great Britain (1919–1961) was unsuited to the physical realities of geography and population distribution, to the financial realities of a poor country, and to the medical realities of the actual disease burden. Furthermore, the health system was embedded in a capitalist structure that distorted development, thereby increasing poverty and disease, and that twisted the educational system, thereby reproducing inappropriate health care. This structure was responsible for many of the difficulties in reorienting health care in accordance with the socialist aims of the Tanzanian government after independence in 1961 (and especially after a move toward socialism beginning in 1967).

By analyzing the development of health care in Tanzania[3] from precolonial times through German and British colonial rule to the present, this book intends to challenge, not only conventional explanations of the rationale for colonial medical services and inflated claims for their

2. The dates of German ascension in East African are given variously as 1884, when the German explorer Karl Peters signed treaties for Germany; 1886, when the sultan of Zanzibar who controlled the coast made concessions; 1888, when Britain and Germany reached agreement on their spheres of influence; and 1891, when Germany declared its protectorate in East Africa.

3. Tanzania is the name adopted by the independent government of Tanganyika in 1964 after union with Zanzibar. The period covered in this study includes the precolonial past before a nation-state existed, the German colonial era when the country was called German East Africa (and was administered with Rwanda and Burundi), and the British colonial era when it was administered first under a League of Nations mandate and after World War II as a United Nations trust territory called Tanganyika. The current name—rather than the names imposed by colonial authorities—is used throughout but should be understood to refer to the mainland only unless stated otherwise.

achievements, but also accepted definitions of health and disease. The first aim is to analyze the health effects of changed social relations of production and reproduction under the capitalist system; in this analysis health is shown to be the product of labor, health levels are linked to stages of development, and changes in African health status are keyed to the transformation of social relations in land. The second aim is to uncover human agency in outbreaks of disease in several epochs of Tanzanian history to demonstrate that epidemics are what Stark (1977) termed "social events" in which labor power is reorganized. The third aim is to show that medical services are the state's response to labor's demand for improved living and working conditions. It is my hope that the accumulated evidence will confirm the premise that health, illness, and medical care are embedded in historically specific struggles, so that Africans and other Third World peoples can progress toward the alleviation of human suffering in their countries.

1

THE UNNATURAL HISTORY
OF DISEASE

Olduvai Gorge in northern Tanzania is the discovery site of many human fossils, including some of our earliest ancestors. Scientists speculate that conditions there must have been particularly favorable for human development because the descendants of these people adapted to a wide range of physical environments. Looking at the semiarid scrublands that cover much of the countryside now, it is hard to imagine a prehistoric Garden of Eden. Today, the inhabitants of that region, like people everywhere in Tanzania, are poor and disease-ridden. Common illnesses include tuberculosis, malaria, bilharzia, and sleeping sickness. The children in particular suffer from malnutrition, diarrheal diseases, and respiratory infections.

The colonialists, generalizing from their own experience of an alien climate in which they suffered greatly, assumed that Africa had always been an unhealthy place to live. White mortality in the late eighteenth and early nineteenth centuries was extremely high; among the troops in West Africa, for example, according to Philip Curtin, 50 percent of the enlisted men succumbed. But recent studies, such as those of Kjekshus, challenge the colonial assumption that a heavy burden of disease is natural to Africa. How and why did conditions change?

In the precapitalist era, health conditions in Tanzania were probably comparable to those in Europe, although different diseases were prevalent (Dubos 1968). Bubonic plague, for example, which was the scourge of Europe in the fourteenth century, was unknown in Africa. The burden of infection was considerably lighter among pastoralists and hunter-gatherers than among settled agriculturalists. Birth spacing was probably wider (three to four years as

9

compared with two to three), and population sizes and densities would usually not have been sufficient to sustain many infectious diseases (Lee and DeVore 1968). Nutrition was better in part because shifting agriculturalists could move to fertile soil whenever their old farms became exhausted. In these mainly egalitarian societies, whatever food was available would have been shared equitably by all.

Precapitalist medical technology was also probably comparable in Europe and Africa (Dubos 1959). Some historians attribute at least half the deaths of Europeans recorded in West Africa in the early nineteenth century to the dangerous practices of European doctors, whose treatments included bleeding, cupping, and leeching, and the use of arsenic and mercury as medicines. Only in the last quarter of the nineteenth century did European medicine acquire scientific foundations, which gave it a technical advantage over some aspects of African medical practice.

By the end of the nineteenth century, to judge by declining infant mortality rates in England, Norway, and elsewhere, health conditions were improving in Europe. In East Africa, the situation was worsening, as evidenced by unprecedented epidemics of jiggers, smallpox, syphilis, rinderpest, and sleeping sickness. By the mid twentieth century, the contrast between European and African health conditions was startling.

The colonial medical services, conditioned by the same capitalist forces that shaped colonial governments, looked for proximate sources of tropical diseases and found them in the poor hygiene of Africans, their lack of immunity to diseases they had no prior experience of, and a poor diet that lowered general resistance to disease. They studied the "natural history of disease." They did not consider that these diseases surged against changing political boundaries, as a century of exploration and wars of conquest ended in the imperialist division of Africa; that they spread in the wake of the slave trade, which had depopulated some areas and debilitated the people of others; and that they became endemic under new economic conditions, as colonialism displaced the precapitalist organization of life. This is the "unnatural history of disease," the study of the economic, social, and political roots of disease. It is not merely the extension of causality beyond the immediate biological event to the environment in a historical perspective, but a radically different approach to disease causation that leads to new conclusions about the nature and development of ill health.

To demonstrate the importance of this approach, and to understand the fallacies of the other, it is necessary to trace the development of epidemiology from its origins in the study of acute infections like cholera to its present application in the study of chronic diseases like cancer. Once we have seen the failure of current applications, it becomes possible to question the standard approach not only to chronic diseases but also, retrospectively, to acute infections and more especially to tropical diseases like trypanosomiasis (sleeping sickness).

The Failure of Epidemiology

Epidemiology, the study of disease causation, was originally an inquiry into the way infectious diseases spread, that is, a study of epidemics. Epidemiology evolved in the nineteenth century with the rise of the germ theory of disease, generally credited to Louis Pasteur and Robert Koch. This theory identified discrete, specific, and external causal agents for disease processes that were usually acute and short-lived, giving support to the idea of specific therapies and coinciding with the ascendance of the liberal view that progress lay in the mechanical domination of nature. Germ theory was grounded in the science of biology, and epidemiological studies proceeded with the observation of individual cases and the history and behavior of specific microorganisms. Epidemiology identified the triad of disease agent, host, and environment and studied their interaction.

Epidemiology is a public health discipline but it continues to use the scientific paradigm of clinical medicine to explain disease processes within the host. This Cartesian paradigm takes individual physiology (as contrasted with broader social conditions) as the norm for pathology and locates sickness in the individual's body (as opposed to the body politic). Treatment consists in readjustment of the body until the physiological norm is restored, a mechanistic approach that reduces the body to a machine whose organs can be discretely examined and regulated. This reductionist paradigm reflects the philosophy of the Enlightenment. It is not an adequate representation of the disease process, and it tends to confuse the cause of a disease with its treatment (Lewontin 1983).

From the end of the nineteenth century, as bacteriologists identified more agents of disease and as the accuracy and efficacy of specific therapies improved, the underlying theory was reinforced and the scope of epidemiology expanded. Infectious diseases like tuberculosis, in which epidemics are not characteristic, were exposed. Though public health dogma holds that chronic diseases are different from infectious diseases, epidemiologists next applied their techniques to noninfectious diseases, believing that their methods would elucidate the characteristics and distribution of lung disease, diabetes, and cancer, the chronic and degenerative conditions that are the principal causes of death in industrialized countries today. They expanded the number of variables considered in disease causation and used a multifactorial model in their studies.

Yet it is questionable whether epidemiological methodology is adequate to explain widely dissimilar diseases under contrasting circumstances of industrialization and underdevelopment. Epidemiologists are unable to account for epidemics of cancer and heart and lung disease, or to provide clinical research with a useful model of causation (McKeown 1976). Although some medical scientists now appreciate the environmental origins of most cancers and admit the contribution of stress, diet, and exercise to cardiovascular disease, their epidemiological studies are handicapped by the limitations of biology. They are unable to deal theoretically (as distinct from statistically) with biological phenomena at levels of organization above a single organism (Powles 1973). As the study of disease causation leads researchers into the realm of economic, social, and political factors, biological methods are no longer adequate as analytical tools (Enzensberger 1974). They cannot explain the essentially social relation between civil society and the individuals of which it is composed (Turshen 1977). In this case, the whole is greater than the accumulated characteristics of its parts, because modern society is composed of classes, not single individuals. The aggregation of individual characteristics by epidemiologists using sophisticated statistics and computerized techniques does not produce a dynamic etiological picture of disease.

Epidemiology incorporates a secular ideology that was

widely accepted in nineteenth-century Britain and France. Because epidemiologists maintain that their work is value-free and that science is neutral, the set of beliefs upon which their science rests should be made explicit. Their underlying philosophy of how individuals relate to one another is materialistic and empirical, the philosophy of classical bourgeois liberalism, conceived by Hobbes and elaborated by Bentham and Mill. As befits the world view that informs capitalism, this philosophy is rigorously rationalist and secular, drawing its force and methods from science (chiefly mathematics and physics), and marked by a belief in progress and a pervasive individualism. In this view, society consists of self-contained individuals, like atoms, with built-in passions and drives, each seeking to maximize his or her satisfactions and minimize his or her dissatisfactions, with equal opportunity of competition, and recognizing no natural limits or rights of interference with his or her urges. It is the aggregate of agreements individuals enter into with one another—which Rousseau called the social contract—that constitutes society (Hobsbawm 1962). In epidemiology these assumptions mask the class nature of disease with empiricism and a pragmatic determinism.

Epidemiologists have adopted two models of society drawn from sociology and based on the philosophy of classical liberalism. The structural-functional model, which describes social institutions in terms of their functions and individuals in terms of their social roles and status within those institutions, can be traced from writers like David Mechanic (1962, 1963) back through Talcott Parsons (1952, 1963) and R. K. Merton (1957) to Emile Durkheim (1938, 1951) and Max Weber (1968). This school embodies a teleological determinism that is static and conservative. The sociobiological model, which describes human behavior in terms of biological evolution and the development of non-human organisms, can be traced from E. O. Wilson (1975) back through Ashley Montagu (1956) and Konrad Lorenz (1966, 1971) to Thomas Huxley (1959) and Charles Darwin (1904). This school believes in biological determinism and natural selection, which puts a premium on selfishness.

The liberal philosophical system and the sociological schools based upon it ignore the economic basis of human behavior, neglect the unequal power relations between classes of individuals, and reject historical evidence of the political evolution of class society. Uninformed by the sciences of history, economics, and politics, the system cannot be used to analyze complex relations between classes of people and their environment, which are at the base of the so-called diseases of civilization. Yet epidemiology, perhaps more than any other science, because it deals with the dissemination of disease within a population, must have a conception of group process, social organization, and the cultural pattern of the people affected.

The purpose of epidemiological studies is to learn the etiology of disease in order to prevent its occurrence. Today we know that when the disease agent is discrete, specific, and external, and the disease process short and acute, prevention may be effected by conferring immunity on the individual or by cleansing the environment of the offending organisms. But current epidemics of chronic and degenerative diseases are products of specific historical stages in industrialization and urbanization. The body and mind cannot be made immune to the daily onslaughts of pollution and stress, and the relations between classes of people and an overdeveloped environment cannot be ameliorated by sanitary engineers. Similarly, malnutrition and tropical diseases are products of specific historical stages of colonialism and underdevelopment; they cannot be prevented by immunizations or the eradication of vectors that carry disease. Only changes in the social relations of production and reproduction will improve health in the Third World.

This review of disease investigation explains why colonial medical authorities attributed tropical diseases to an unsanitary environment and lack of host resistance to infectious agents. These were the factors the dominant theory of causation took into consideration. The review raises several basic questions about epidemiological theory and method. Do we understand the cause of a disease (for example, tuberculosis) when the disease agent (tubercle bacillus) is identified? John Snow's mid nineteenth-century work on cholera in London—recognized as the first epidemiological study—revealed how that infection spread, not what its nature is. Can epidemiology explain the spread of diseases more complex than cholera—for example, the so-called tropical diseases?[1] The recent recrudescence of malaria in

1. Many diseases—like malaria and yellow fever—now called tropical were found in the temperate climates of Europe and North America well into the twentieth century. The label "tropical" reinforces the impression

the Third World and the admission by public health authorities of their failure to eradicate that disease call into question the predictive value of their science. Do biochemical and immunological studies of host resistance contribute to the eradication of disease any more than new drugs do? When disease causation is located in modes of production (that is, the social system by which work is organized to provide the means of subsistence) or, more specifically, in the forces of production (the level of development) and the social relations of production (the rapport between producers and owners), public health programs based on epidemiological research cannot eradicate disease in the absence of larger social changes affecting the structure of society.

The physical and chemical laws that govern the mechanics of disease at the level of the individual are not in question here (though they are being questioned by others [see Rose 1982a, 1982b]). The problem is that such laws operate within boundaries and under conditions that determine which of the "natural store" of possible diseases will be expressed in a given period. The traditional epidemiological triad of interacting agent, host, and environment does not take under consideration those boundaries and conditions, which are largely defined by modes of production. For the past twenty-five years, epidemiologists have been broadening the definitions of elements in the triad to include more factors (for example, multiple disease agents and psychosocial environment), but these accretions have not changed the basic character of the model.

The model does not explain why epidemics occur at certain historical moments, and whereas it may enable authorities to control or even eradicate a specific infection, it does not reveal the conditions that produce disease and therefore cannot prevent the occurrence of illness. The eradication of a specific infection like smallpox does not necessarily lead to improved health. This observation is at the crux of the distinction between the natural and the unnatural history of disease. Disease agents such as bacteria and viruses may occur spontaneously in nature, but there is nothing natural or spontaneous about epidemics.

---

that natural conditions like climate rather than economic conditions or political circumstances are responsible for the persistence of these diseases in the Third World.

A Critical Theory of Disease Causation

The argument presented thus far takes issue with specific aspects of epidemiological models and methods.[2] Internal critiques of epidemiological methodology usually imply acceptance of the empiricist perspective. But in this section I reject the perspective itself and attempt to outline foundations for a critical theory of disease causation, though I do not here offer a full-scale substitute model.

A critical theory of disease causation is premised on a different construction of social reality, one not rooted in classical bourgeois liberalism or serving the capitalist system. In this new construction, individuals exist in social relations rather than in isolation or in competition, and these relations are changing rather than fixed or static. Individuals are not passive objects to be acted upon; they are actors with choices that are free (as opposed to being teleologically or biologically determined). Society does not consist of the aggregate of these individuals but expresses the sum of interrelations, in other words, the sum of relations in which these individuals stand (Marx 1973:265). This construction of social reality implies a different notion of causality. According to empiricism, cause and effect exist in a one-way relationship and causes have a natural origin. In a Marxist construction of social reality, objective conditions (for example, natural resources, tools, factories) cannot be causes; only human agency is causal. Nature is neither given nor predetermined; it is transformed by individual creative activity (Gould 1981).

If only human action has causal efficacy, then germs cannot be said to cause disease, and the empiricist model of infectious disease etiology, which is central to epidemiology, is inaccurate. To understand the etiology of any disease, whether infectious or chronic, one must study people as instrumental in historical and social relations. One advantage of this perspective is that it permits medical scientists to take directly into account relations of class, race, and gen-

2. Beginning in 1975, a group of American health activists initiated a discussion of epidemiology in relation to Marxist theory. We called ourselves the East Coast Health Discussion Group and published our ideas in the H(ealth) M(arxist) O(rganization) packets. For a review of our contribution see Stark 1982.

der. Instead of being reduced to population characteristics or statistical variables, the class, race, and gender of individuals are understood as social relations at specific historical moments in particular societies.

In the chapters that follow, the disease experience in Tanzania is reconstructed on the basis of the social ontology outlined here; that is, human agency or instrumentality is traced in the etiology of epidemics or, more generally, in the underdevelopment of African health in Tanzania.

This reconstruction employs an interdisciplinary approach. The division of knowledge into disciplines handicaps problem solving in public health. Social and cultural descriptions often ignore political and economic conditions, and vice versa. Several of the disciplines are influenced by political trends. Historical material is sometimes biased, a product of the political system that produced it. In the case of anthropology, British policy demanded a practical anthropology that would facilitate the implementation of indirect rule in Africa and would help preserve, understand, and use African institutions in controlling subject populations. Anthropologists helped gather intelligence that allowed efficient rule in the colonial interest; they accepted as given the imperialist framework and its concomitant myths—for example, that there was a harmony of interest between ruler and ruled, exploiter and exploited (see Goddard 1969; Stauder 1974). In the case of ethnography, fieldworkers interested in medicine compiled lists of drugs used by Africans and of diseases in which they were applied; they based their judgment of whether a drug was effective on scientific assessment of the treatment (for example, chemical analysis of drugs), ignoring the cultural and social aspects of medical care. Because they omitted to investigate the ideas underlying therapeutic acts and to describe the circumstances in which the acts were performed, their studies are of limited use (see Ackernecht 1946).

Relating information from several separate academic disciplines—ecology, agronomy, medicine, public health, population studies, and history—is a corrective to the biases and political determinants of any one of them. Ecology is the branch of biology that deals with the relations of living organisms to their surroundings, their habits, and their modes of life. Political ecology, in the usage adopted here, gives central importance to human agency in the transformation of the complex, interacting web that characterizes the environment of East Africa. History must be included because there is no adequate explanation of the current development dilemma in Africa without reference to Africa's past. Colonial accounts of the last century are not enough; they must be reinterpreted in the light of the oral history and anthropological fieldwork that give Africans the central role in their own stories.

This interdisciplinary approach also uses dialectics to make sense of contradictions, which seem to abound in descriptions of Africa. For example, political economists have shown that Tanzanians were exploited and oppressed under the capitalist system in the British colonial period (Kaniki 1980). At the same time, according to historians, the African population doubled in the period of British rule (Iliffe 1979). These contradictory observations are reconciled in the dialectical analysis of the antagonistic relation between capital and labor (see chapter 3), an antagonism between two classes—bourgeoisie and proletariat—intrinsic to the capitalist system. In describing the introduction of capitalism to Tanzania (see chapter 2), the growing class nature of Tanzanian society is shown. Thus there is no need to debate whether classes, in Marx's definition of the term, exist in Africa (Cohen and Daniel 1981). Marx's (1967) concept of class is predicated on the social relations of production; in the capitalist system, the principal relation is between those who own or control the means of production and the producers (owners of labor power). A third class, the peasantry, preceded the capitalist mode of production in Europe; the creation of this class in Tanzania is the subject of chapter 4.

Controversy also surrounds the issue of how race relates to class (Mhlongo 1981). The issue is important in Tanzania, where Arabs lived with Africans in the precolonial era and where imperialism brought, not only Europeans to own production and control the newly created state apparatus, but also Asians as indentured labor. The resolution adopted here is to give primacy to class as determined by social relations of production and to see race as increasing the complexity of basic class divisions (Cohen 1981).

Similar theoretical difficulties are raised by gender relations. One needs to explain the particular oppression of women, their subordinate political position, and their economic exploitation. Yet to make sense of the realities of women's lives in a sophisticated way requires the use of Marx's theory of class, which differentiates the nature of constraints on a woman of the ruling class like Jihan Sadat from the actual existence of a poor village woman living in rural Egypt.

With the research tools sketched above, it is possible to analyze the internal situation in a country like Tanzania and learn how the history of disease is embedded in the changing economic, social, and political system. Internal analysis is insufficient, however, because the national system is subject to international control. In the period of colonial rule, Tanzanians confronted first German and then British capital. After the country achieved political independence in 1961, it confronted international capital through relations with many more states, multilateral organizations, and multinational firms. The global structure of postcolonial relations is characterized by the domination of the capitalist mode of production and by uneven development in which the expansion of production increases the gap between the industrial countries of the North and the underdeveloped countries of the South (Brewer 1980). Marxist theories of imperialism are used to analyze that gap, manifest in the increasing immiseration of the Tanzanian people.

2

THE IMPOSITION OF
COLONIALISM

In the social ontology of Marx, nature is not a given; it is a product of human activity and therefore constantly changing. A description of the human ecology of Tanzania in 1984 cannot convey accurately the conditions that existed in 1884, when Karl Peters acquired the first 140,000 square kilometers of territory for Germany. Tanzania today is a country of physical extremes—altitudes, temperatures, vegetation, rainfall, and population density all vary widely, not only from one part of the country to another but even within districts. The extent to which this environmental diversity is a product of uneven development in the colonial period is not fully known (Ford 1971; Iliffe 1979; Kjekshus 1977); the subject is explored in chapter 5.

The interplay between ecology and health is complex; for example, in the humid and populous Usambara mountains of the northeast, respiratory infections are common among poor people who cannot afford adequate shelter and sufficient fuel to protect them from cold and damp weather. More typical of Tanzania are hot and dry conditions. Though Svendsen (1969:8) attributes the precarious nutritional status of the people of Ugogo, the arid central plateau, to erratic and insufficient rainfall, Kjekshus (1977:120) describes Ugogo as rich and prosperous in the nineteenth century and Iliffe (1979:315) remarks that a reactionary British administration deliberately isolated the people of Ugogo from territorial affairs in the interwar years, suggesting economic and political dimensions to the problem of hunger in Ugogo.

Tanzania covers a total area of 945,200 square kilometers. The nation has few permanent rivers; about 90 percent of the country has no permanent streams (Brooke 1967). Most of the central plateau is without running water throughout the dry season; only half the country is supplied with natural water throughout the year. One-third of the total area of Tanzania is uninhabited, much of it because of inadequate rainfall. Over about one-fourth of the country, annual rainfall is less than the 750 millimeters needed to support agriculture (Svendsen 1969:8). Even where rainfall is greater, the dry season can be severe; as a result parts of the country are regularly subjected to drought.

Water is among the central environmental factors affecting human health; it is needed for human consumption, crop production, and livestock development. Many diseases—for example, cholera—are carried by contaminated water. Malaria mosquitoes breed in swampy stagnant water, and schistosomiasis is present in the snail-infested waters of Lake Victoria. Many more diseases—such as skin diseases and eye infections—are associated with lack of water. In 1969 only 9 percent of Tanzania's rural population of 11.8 million were served by improved water supplies (that is, clean, potable water in adequate quantities), though by 1977, 36 percent of the rural population had improved water supplies, including improved shallow wells (World Bank 1977b, part B, paragraph 14).

Tanzania's mainland population is seventeen million (1978 census). In only one-tenth of the country does population density exceed ten per square kilometer, and only 7 percent of the population live in urban areas. The low population density poses formidable physical difficulties to the provision of services. In addition, people are distributed unevenly around the country: population is concentrated around the perimeter while the center is very sparsely inhabited. Whereas some observers believe that population was shaped by nature—Iliffe, for example, says, "Men followed the dictates of the land" (1979:6)—a Marxist reading of political ecology indicates that the slave trade and the colonial and neocolonial experiences all affected population distribution, stimulated migration, and exacerbated physical differences.

The population is usually said to be divided into *tribes*. Europeans use this term too loosely, however; it is applied to aggregates of autonomous villages (like the people of Undendeuli) and to societies with a relatively centralized administrative and judicial apparatus (like the people of Ungoni). In some cases the development of formal chieftainships took place as part of the struggle against colonial domination; but in most cases, British authorities created tribal structures and stimulated tribal identities in a system of indirect rule. The political and social purpose was to create effective units of government, to enable the state to penetrate African society more deeply, and to standardize life—in short, to establish social control (Iliffe 1979). The economic purpose was to reorganize labor, a motive that emerges clearly in an examination of population trends (see chapter 3). Gulliver (1969:13, 24) says that *tribe* must be understood as an essentially dynamic concept of groups that emerge, function for a time, and dissolve. Feierman (1982, personal communication), however, maintains that the very concept is an ideological creation of colonial rule and does not reflect African reality. The colonial stereotype of tribal man and tribal woman masked social and political policies. Nonetheless, in discussions of the colonial past, the term is impossible to avoid. For practical purposes, we will usually refer to place names and use them to cover the inhabitants.

Colonialists counted between 80 and 120 societies in Tanzania, the number varying with different definitions of the term. (Languages were almost as numerous, though most are part of the Bantu group, and Swahili is the lingua franca.) No single nation was dominant in colonial censuses: the people of Usukuma (southeast of Lake Victoria) were the most numerous, though those of three smaller areas—Uchagga (Mount Kilimanjaro), Buhaya (west of Lake Victoria), and Unyakyusa (northwest of Lake Nyasa)—early exposed to education through missionary efforts, became prominent in government and trade.

Cultural diversity affects health and health services, especially health education. Diseases associated with a dying pastoralism are different from those found among prosperous cash crop farmers. Health workers must learn and understand disparate customs regarding hygiene, birth rituals, and diet, which influence health; their task is complicated by the need to use the vernacular among unilingual peoples.

The Slave Trade

The reconstruction of early Tanzanian history is a difficult
task. There are no written records of the interior and few of
the coast. Colonial reports cover a later period and are culturally biased, often distorting or ignoring the history of
Africans. The task is further complicated by the division
of data into academic disciplines, which divorce the study
of social and cultural life from that of political and economic conditions.

Recent collections of Tanzanian oral histories are more
helpful. They indicate that by the time the Portuguese navi-
gator Vasco da Gama discovered the East African coast at
the end of the fifteenth century, several stable agricultural
societies had evolved in areas of high rainfall. On the sa-
vanna between these mountainous areas, pastoral groups
like the Masai traded livestock with cereal-producing agriculturalists. This trade took place at fixed intervals (four to
ten days) and at designated localities, without reliance on
traders (Kjekshus 1977:112–116). The international centers
of trade were on islands off the coast, where Arabs traded
gold and ivory supplied from Zimbabwe and Mozambique
to the Arabian peninsula and India. The Portuguese captured and dominated this trade in the sixteenth and seven-
teenth centuries. Long-distance caravan routes from the
coast to the string of lakes that divides Tanzania from Zaire
were established by ivory traders in the eighteenth century
and integrated with the older iron and salt trade networks
of the interior. The pace of change quickened as international contacts increased in the nineteenth century. The
overall picture of this precolonial period is one of growing
prosperity and economic, social, and political evolution for
some Africans and, from the eighteenth century, of slavery,
death, or social disintegration for others.

There is little evidence that slaves were shipped from the
mainland before 1698, when Oman conquered the southern
Tanzanian island of Kilwa (Iliffe 1979:42). After the Omani
accession to power in the Indian Ocean, Zanzibar became
an increasingly important focal point of the ivory and slave
trade. From the almost incidental impressment of porters
who carried ivory from the interior to the coast, the slave
trade grew into a thriving Omani business. The first major
impetus to increase the volume of the East African slave

trade came in the mid eighteenth century from the French, who imported slaves to work the sugar plantations they established on the islands of Mauritius and Reunion; the high death rate among slaves required a steady supply. By 1810, between six and ten thousand slaves were being sold annually at Kilwa and Zanzibar. A second impetus came after 1830, when the Omani established clove and copra plantations on Zanzibar and Pemba (Alpers 1975:234–238). By the 1860s, as many as twenty thousand slaves were being sold each year in the slave markets (Iliffe 1979:49). A very conservative guess is that one million able-bodied workers were traded through Zanzibar, Kilwa, and other coastal slave markets between 1750 and 1875.

Nonetheless, the East African slave trade was always less important numerically than the West African trade, and the worst period in the east was less intense than the least active period in the west (Kuczynski 1949:122). The irony of the slave trade in East Africa is that it reached its peak in the age of humanitarianism. Though Britain passed the Abolition Act in 1807, ended the transatlantic slave trade by British subjects in 1811, and outlawed slavery in British colonies in 1837, and President Lincoln signed the Emancipation Proclamation in 1863 ending slavery in the United States, the export of slaves from East Africa was not prohibited by the British until 1873; it did not completely cease until Britain assumed colonial power in Tanzania in 1919 and abolished the institution of slavery.

When considering the effect of the slave trade on Tanzanian society, it is necessary to adjust for the Victorian view of black Africa. With the end of the West African trade in the 1820s, antislavery groups had turned their attention to the East African trade and had tended to exaggerate its magnitude, in part to garner support for their cause and in part to justify the civilizing mission of Christianity and colonialism.

The slave trade is usually assessed on the basis of the number of Africans captured and sold, but in terms of its impact on health conditions in Tanzania, the evolution of areas that were raided is more important. The way in which the demand for slaves was met is a matter of some controversy. The Victorians painted an alarming scene: slave raiding amounted to warfare. To procure five thousand slaves, six times that number were slain or died by the roadside of injuries, starvation, or disease, more than a hundred villages were destroyed, and the areas scoured by slavers were abandoned. European reporters insisted on the cruelty, brutality, and barbarity of slave raiding; even if we discount for racial prejudices, their accounts are still suspect because they were based on hearsay. None was an eyewitness report.

Verney Lovett Cameron (1877), a British explorer, is one source of the number of deaths incurred in raids. Though he never witnessed a raid, he did encounter Portuguese slavers in Zaire. In Katanga, he met a band of fifty-two female captives and worked out a formula according to which ten villages had been destroyed and fifteen hundred persons killed, injured, or driven into the bush without resources, in order to obtain these women. He simply assumed they were captured in bloody raids; he could not know whether they had actually been bought for local currency, captured in a war, or traded for cloth, guns, or alcohol. Communication was difficult and words sometimes passed through four interpreters. Though British explorers usually spoke Hindi or Arabic, they rarely knew Swahili, so the local African languages had to be first translated into Swahili and then rendered into Hindi or Arabic for the Englishmen. In addition, these early travelers saw themselves as observers and failed to recognize the impact of their own presence and participation on events.

The dates of these accounts are important. Until the death in 1856 of Sayyid Said, the powerful Omani ruler of Zanzibar, Arab penetration may have been orderly and Africans may have been able to accommodate these new trading partners in positive ways that stimulated development. Said's death was a turning point, because it left a power vacuum that European nations vied to fill in the following twenty-five years; their struggle had a disastrous impact on African economies, culminating in ecological collapse in the last decade of the nineteenth century.

No European explorer witnessed events in the interior before 1857, when Richard Burton and John Speke traveled across the country to Ujiji on Lake Tanganyika. Speke returned in 1861 with Charles Grant, and five years later David Livingstone began his last journey from Mikindani around the southern end of Lake Nyasa, eventually meeting the American journalist Henry Stanley at Ujiji in 1871.

Burton appears to have witnessed the instability that pre-ceded European colonization. He wrongly assumed that what he saw was old and customary, that he was reporting on a fixed and static way of life. In particular he is the source of much exaggeration regarding African warfare. "All African wars," Burton wrote, "are for one of two ob-jects, cattle lifting and kidnapping. . . . Slaves, however, are much more frequently the end and aim of feud and foray. The process of kidnapping, an inveterate custom in these lands, is in every way agreeable to the mind of the man-hunter. . . . A poor and powerful chief will not allow his neighbors to rest wealthier than himself; a quarrel is soon found, the stronger attacks the weaker, hunts and harries his cattle, burns his villages, carries off his subjects and sells them to the first passing caravan" (1860:515–516). That the African motive for raids was the same pressing need for labor as British plantation owners had experienced elsewhere did not occur to Burton; Victorians never granted Africans the same needs as Europeans.

The critical question for the well-being of East Africans is whether they were progressively better organized over the course of the century to meet the demands of the slave trade with a minimum of disruption, or whether raiding sowed increasing anarchy as the Omani and then Europe-ans, fortified with powerful firearms, penetrated the interior and finally gained ascendancy. The answer determines two related issues: did nineteenth-century East Africans enjoy a measure of prosperity, and did the population grow?

In a controversial reinterpretation of history, Kjekshus (1977) concludes—mainly on the basis of Abdul Sheriff's (1971) doctoral dissertation and Kuczynski's (1949) demo-graphic survey—that nineteenth-century European reports exaggerated both African warfare and slave raiding and that the demographic pattern was one of slow or no growth un-til 1890, when a long decline began. He maintains that the period as a whole was one of relative stability and prosper-ity in East Africa, with a thriving cattle economy and suc-cessful agricultural systems, industrial supports, markets, and trading networks.

The data assembled to support this nationalist history are contentious. The main agricultural societies Kjekshus de-scribes—in Buhaya, Unyakyusa, Uchagga, Usambara, Upare, and Matengo—were stable mountain cultures with strong, centralized political systems. They were probably prosperous in the early nineteenth century and their populations may have grown; making use of their mountain geography, they organized to protect themselves from foreign incursion. However, they probably represented less than one-seventh of the Tanzanian population; while no nineteenth-century data are available, their importance in terms of territory and population was small in the colonial period (Tanganyika 1963). And by the 1860s, even they were not immune to the growing importance of foreign trade and military power.

More representative and numerically important are the pastoral and semipastoral economies of the Masai and the people of Usukuma, Ugogo, Unyamwezi, Uzinza, Uha, Ujiji, Ufipa, Ukimbu, Usangu, Uhehe, Ungoni, and Uzigua. With the exception of the Masai and the people of Ungoni, these were decentralized or loosely organized societies; their impermanent settlements were far more pervious to the long-distance caravans that criss-crossed their extensive lands. Unyamwezi, a large area around Tabora in the center of the country, supplied many slaves, as did the southern part of the country bordered by the Ruvuma River (Alpers 1975:235). Historians surmise that as lands nearer the coast became depopulated, slavers moved further into the interior in search of defenseless people.

Feierman (1982, personal communication) points out that Kjekshus relies on the impressionistic reports of travelers (like Burton and Speke), selecting only those that report densely populated valleys and villages; but other diarists in equal numbers recorded depopulation. Feierman also points out that the very act of self-defense gave rise to unhealthy conditions that would have increased death rates—the concentration of people in stockaded villages exposed them to epidemics, as did the assemblage of armies and caravans.

The slave trade may have been one of the most important precursors of deteriorating health conditions in Africa. And while rising standards of living in Europe were inducing improved health conditions there in the nineteenth century, at least some of the wealth that raised living standards came from the slave trade that was responsible for worsening conditions in Africa. As to its physical impact on Africans, frankly the contradictory histories of the East African slave trade do not allow a firm determination; its economic importance lies in the new social and class relations it engendered.

European Conquest

The territory now known as Tanzania was conquered by Germany in the 1880s, but African resistance continued for fifteen years. Kjekshus (1977:187–190), for example, enumerates fifty-four battles fought between 1889 and 1896 by Africans in revolt against German attempts to establish hegemony. These wars were very destructive of land and life; the penalty Africans paid for their failure to negotiate was famine. The struggles of this period created the epidemics of the decade and the ecological catastrophe that has had such long-lasting effects.

Africans also experienced changes in social relations. According to Iliffe (1979:119–120), the penetration of European missionaries and militia from the 1880s on forced Africans to rearrange relations of power and privilege within and between societies. Africans were required to supply labor and building materials, as well as auxiliary soldiers. From 1898, with the imposition of tax, the immigration of European farmers, and compulsory cultivation of export crops on communal farms, African social relations changed decisively. The collection of taxes required a hierarchy not previously known in stateless societies; settlement by European farmers introduced concepts of private property, displaced Africans from their hereditary lands, and fundamentally transformed relations of production; and the cultivation of export crops upset the balance of population and food resources.

Although slavery was abolished, near-slavery was substituted in the form of involuntary servitude. In the German colonial period Africans from all parts of the country were forced to serve in the army and to work on road gangs, as porters transporting goods on their heads across the country, in railway construction, in mines, and on plantations. Labor recruiters were posted in various districts: in 1913 they numbered over a thousand in Tabora District alone. Between 1908/1909 and 1911/1912 the supply of labor to northeastern Tanzania doubled, and total paid labor rose by twenty thousand each year. The German colonial secretary acknowledged in 1907 that working conditions were appalling: he strongly criticized the abuse of corporal punishment. Despite ordinances passed in 1909 to suppress the worst of the excesses, during the 1909/1911 period, 27 Europeans were actually convicted of brutalizing Africans by the Dar es Salaam Provincial Court alone, and in 1911/1912, 5,944 Africans were sentenced to corporal punishment by the local courts of German East Africa (Iliffe 1969:91, 106, 132). Even when payment was made for this work, wage labor was but a euphemism for forced labor, and in this way a system of free wage labor was prevented from developing. Coerced labor thus helped block the development of capitalism.

The Maji Maji War[1] of 1905–1906 was started by laborers on the southern coast who were forced to grow cotton for the German textile industry. Thousands of farmers with makeshift arms were killed and more died in the savage reprisals that continued for two years. Hundreds of leaders were publicly executed and thousands more Africans perished in the famines that followed the German army's deliberate destruction of crops and other food resources.

Recovery was slow and hardly completed when World War I was declared. Colonial Tanzania was the main theater of the East African campaign, which ravaged the countryside and touched off widespread famine. Germany fought Britain, which invaded from Kenya and Uganda to the north and northwest, and Belgium, which invaded from its base in Zaire to the west. The Germans, Belgians, and British mustered in Africans as soldiers and porters; these raw recruits sustained injuries at an alarming rate, but they suffered even more from malaria and dysentery. Medical supplies were prevented from reaching the German army by the British blockade of the coast. According to a German army surgeon, the death rate was appalling (Taute 1939).

After Germany's defeat, the newly established League of Nations created a British mandate in all of the territory except two western regions (now Rwanda and Burundi), which were awarded to Belgium. Britain named its mandate Tanganyika.

---

1. *Maji* is Swahili for water but in the context of the war meant medicine. In the ceremony to initiate new recruits, *maji* symbolically conferred invincibility on warriors, expressed as the power to turn bullets into water.

Colonial Administration

Under German administration Tanzania had a system of direct rule. The country was divided into nineteen civil and two military districts, each under a district administrator. Each district area was divided into groups of villages consisting of twenty-eight to thirty thousand people in the charge of officials of the central government (*akidas*), and over each village was placed a *jumbe*. The *akidas* and *jumbes* were Swahili/Muslim agents who had been employed by Arabs and now shifted to German service (Gwassa 1969:130; Rodney 1980:130).

Under British rule, the country was administered through the crown colony system and governed through indirect rule. Authority flowed from the seat of government in London through the secretary of state for the colonies to the governor of the territory and his councils, and from there to the provincial commissioners and district commissioners down to the local administrative officers (Chidzero 1961). The governor was the chief legislative and executive authority, the appointed representative of the crown; he appointed the members of the Executive Council, an advisory body over which he presided. Members of the Executive Council, which included the director of Medical and Sanitary Services, also served ex officio as members of the Legislative Council. The Legislative Council did not control the executive, nor was it controlled by the electorate. Given its origin, the Legislative Council was bound to be dependent on the executive and unresponsive to policy demands made by outside groups. Until 1947 the government was highly centralized under the central secretariat headed by the chief secretary, who was the governor's deputy, leader of government in the Legislative Council, and general supervisor of the administration. All departments (labor, education, agriculture, and so on) were under the chief secretary and had their offices in Dar es Salaam.

The country was divided into provinces (at various times they numbered eight, nine, or eleven),[2] each under a pro-

2. For most of the period of British rule there were nine provinces, which were periodically renamed and the districts within them regrouped. Two years after independence, the nine provinces became seventeen regions.

vincial commissioner, who served as a central territorial administrative officer. Provinces were divided into several districts, each under a district commissioner, who acted as an agent of the central government. Down to this level, all officials were British. Indirect rule was implemented at the next lower level through the "native authorities" (chiefs or councils), which gave limited powers of local governance to Africans. Provincial and district commissioners supervised the African councils: they also made local regulations or required Africans to do so, exercised powers of magistrate in cases affecting Africans, supervised and controlled the functioning of African courts, and supervised the collection of house and poll taxes.

The central government gazetted African councils in each district after 1926. These authorities were required to levy local rates, maintain local order, and collect taxes. Through this system of indirect rule, the colonial administration wanted to establish the political organization of Africans in local affairs using African leaders and, so far as possible, African institutions.

Adopted on grounds of expediency, indirect rule was rationalized as the progressive adaptation of African institutions to modern conditions. This form of administration enabled government to be carried on, justice to be dispensed, and law to be enforced within the familiar context of the local environment and according to African law and justice (Cameron 1939). Chidzero, however, notes,

> there is no doubt that indirect rule tended to perpetuate tribalism and to arrest development. . . . The powers of the Provincial and District Commissioners were strong and overriding. Thus while it is true that the British administration . . . gave powers—executive, judicial and fiscal—in local matters to chiefs or councils, it is equally true that a strong paternalism reigned during this period. This paternalism, embodied in the institution of Native Commissioners, tended generally to reduce native authorities to mere agents of central Government. (Chidzero 1961:131)

At the same time indirect rule dissolved linkages between people of different ecologies and reconstituted each group as a social formation exclusive unto itself (Bryceson and Mbilinyi 1978:33).

Heussler misunderstands the aims of Britain and sees the maintenance of chieftainships as contradictory:

the continuation [of chiefs] in a context of European supervision and a developing economy was a curiously unnatural
and self-defeating thing in practice. They were not allowed
their old methods of collecting tribute, dispensing justice,
and giving rewards in an atmosphere of authoritarianism
mitigated only by clan and tribal custom; yet the new tasks
they were asked to perform were uninteresting to them, or
mystifying, and they and their traditional supporters did not
become educated to new roles enough to evolve local administration of a hybrid kind, as happened for example, in
Northern Nigeria. (Heussler 1971:57)

It is hardly likely that the British would have implemented
a self-defeating measure in 1926, after years of administrative experience in both East and West Africa. Brett (1973:67)
suggests that the very viability of the colonial system depended on the maintenance of traditional values because
they were the primary source of control for the regime. Traditional communities played an important role in the production and reproduction of cheap labor; African authorities were in part created to control and preserve the sources
of the work force. Evidence for this assertion can be found
in the annual report for 1927 of the Tanganyika Territory
Labour Department, which declared that "the native authorities as a whole have been distinctly beneficial to labour"
(Tanganyika Territory 1928b:8). The policy was consciously
based on the South African model; the same report notes
that the "Labour Commissioner took advantage of his return
from home leave to make an extended tour to renew ac-
quaintance with conditions in South Africa, and to examine
personally the position of the labour market in Rhodesia
and the Belgian Congo" (ibid.:9). The labor market in those
countries was more organized than in colonial Tanzania.
Schapera (1947) illustrates the colonial manipulation of indigenous South African structures when he notes that
Tswana chiefs used their influence or authority to send
men to work in the mines.

Colonial Taxation

Taxation was the symbol of subjugation because it monetized the economy, forced Africans to sell their labor power
and their produce, and made them comply with colonial
law (Iliffe 1979:133). The German colonial authorities estab-

lished a poll tax of three German East African rupees per adult (equivalent to four German marks or one shilling). Tax defaulters could be assigned to work for private employers. The British authorities maintained this poll tax until 1922, when they substituted a hut and poll tax on Africans at the average rate of six shillings (there was parity between the British and East African shilling); some districts paid more and others less, but there was no variation according to individual income. The British also substituted labor on public works as a penalty for tax defaulters. One effect of the hut and poll tax was to place an additional tax on plural wives, a measure that was so unpopular as to force repeal in 1938, when many districts reverted to the simple poll tax. Until 1935 these taxes were the country's most important source of revenue, contributing one-third of the total (Leubuscher 1944:133–138).

In 1947 the district tax rates varied from six to twelve shillings. The rate imposed reflected to some degree the cash resources of the population. The generally low taxable capacity of the population in many parts of the country directly affected the revenue of the local treasuries; the main source was the portion of local taxes returned by the central government in a revenue-sharing scheme. The low taxable capacity also limited the possibility of improving revenue by raising local rates, which was permitted after 1942 in some of the more developed districts.

The districts were meant to be self-sufficient and to finance their own local services. Provincial and district commissioners were conservative in their management of local treasuries, which provided for medical and sanitation services, education, agriculture, roads and bridges, water supply, forestry services, and administration (as much as half of service expenditure was on salaries). Before the end of World War II, the only other source of funds besides taxes was the Colonial Development Fund, which had less than a hundred thousand pounds to spend on the whole country (ibid.:154–168).

During the colonial period the basic rate of taxation on companies, including plantations, was low in comparison with most industrial countries and lower than the rate charged elsewhere in Africa (World Bank 1961:244). In other East African territories tax revenue on company profits was the most important source of revenue from taxation. The British government introduced direct taxation of non-African persons and enterprises much later than direct taxation of Africans, and no income tax was assessed before World War II (Leubuscher 1944, 140).

The Colonial Economy

Colonialism undermined the economic base of African society. European goods drove African cotton, salt, and iron producers out of business; cattle herds were destroyed by the rinderpest unleashed on Africa by invading armies from the north; and eventually the colonial economy drove domestic food production into a period of declining productivity.

From the time the Germans took control of the country in the 1880s, there was a chronic shortage of labor in both private and public enterprise. Wages were low and working conditions bad; Africans from the areas surrounding estates came out to work only if forced to do so. Compulsory labor was common (Iliffe 1979:153). Plantation owners employed recruiters to go into the poorest districts, where they used deception, bribery, or force to supply workers. Corporal punishment was widely used on the plantations, and even the German administration admitted that flogging was almost unrestricted.

Structural changes instituted under colonial rule included the imposition of taxes and the export of raw materials. Not only did the tax bring in money to finance the colonial administration, it also brought out workers to meet the chronic labor shortage. The development of an export economy depended on plantations; production was determined by the wants of European powers, not by domestic needs. Initially, European industry required rubber, cotton, and sisal; later, there were demands for tobacco, coffee, and tea. These items came to be called cash crops, in contrast to the food crops that Africans produced for local consumption. Plantations were sited according to the suitability of the climate and the proximity of transportation. Parts of the interior that had good rainfall and fertile soil were left undeveloped because the cost of transporting produce to the coast would have been prohibitive. Instead, these areas supplied a migrant labor force and, with as much as a third of the adult males away at any one time, subsistence agriculture became severely depressed.

When the plantations did not produce enough to satisfy European demands, the colonial administration encouraged Africans to cultivate cash crops on their farms. Cash crops began to replace food crops on the limited land that could be cultivated, given contemporary forces of production: mechanization was unknown, there were no draft animals, and the plough had never replaced the hoe in East African agriculture. Small-scale farming increased cash crop production and also enabled the colonial administration to extract a direct surplus from the peasant economy. Cooperative societies were made the only legal outlet for peasant produce, and Africans paid a cess on every bale they sold to the government marketing board, which held a monopoly on exportation. During World War II, one of these societies in Songea, an impoverished part of southern Tanzania, raised thirty thousand pounds in bonds for the British war effort.

This marketing system also allowed the colonial government to regulate the labor supply. During economic recessions, the marketing boards would relax quality controls on peasant produce and buy large quantities. The prospect of profitable farming would induce migrant workers to return to their villages. (This system, incidentally, provided a cheap form of unemployment insurance.) When the recession was over and laborers were again wanted, the marketing boards would become more selective and reject much of the peasants' crop. Farmers would once more be forced to migrate in search of work that would pay the cash needed for taxes.

The cultivation of cash crops required new farm techniques, and the colonial government employed agricultural extension workers to teach African peasants. Extension workers, perpetuating the prejudices of Victorian England, invariably sought out men for instruction, and cash cropping became a male enterprise. Food cultivation never benefited from comparable improvements, and productivity fell behind.

In East Africa, food production was typically a woman's responsibility, but the availability of labor influenced the

cultivation techniques adopted. In the districts that supplied migrant labor, which was always male, women could
no longer employ labor-intensive methods and they tended
to revert to earlier practices of shifting agriculture, in which
land was cropped for seven or eight years and then left fallow, while virgin land was prepared for new cultivation.
These less productive practices reduced food supplies and
eventually the women became malnourished. They found
the work of clearing primary forest time-consuming and
difficult and they began to overcrop their small, exhausted
plots. Migrant workers could send little money to make
good the loss of their assistance, because the colonialists,
claiming that rural families were self-sufficient, paid a
worker only a single man's wage. Indeed, it was the colonial policy to keep the "traditional" sector of the economy
intact to fulfill the functions of a de facto labor reserve,
much like the tribal homelands of South Africa.

The cumulative effect of colonial administrative, fiscal,
and economic policies was uneven development—the differentiation of regions that created wealth in some and poverty in others. The process in Tanzania was initiated by
German and accelerated by British rule. Internal differentiation was exacerbated by Britain's incorporation of Tanzania
into the East African Community.

The East African Context

The three East African nations of Kenya, Uganda, and Tanzania all felt the impact of colonialism. A white settler population dominated Kenya, a peasant cash crop economy
characterized Uganda, and a mixed economy of peasant
farms and European-owned plantations shaped Tanzania.
To a certain extent the interaction of the three countries,
which contributed to the development of the region as a
whole, played a role in colonial economic strategy. But Britain's primary concerns were its own manufacturing and
capital-exporting needs (Brett 1973:71). Seidman (1972:13)
states that colonial rule, in the space of fifty years, shaped
the economies of all three East African countries to export a
few raw materials and to import manufactured goods. Yet
colonial economic strategy was not applied uniformly
throughout East Africa. The policies adopted were almost

consistently to the disadvantage of Tanzania. The result is that while East Africa as a region is poor, Tanzania is the poorest of the three nations.

In 1961, under the chairmanship of British statesman Sir Jeremy Raisman, the East African Economic and Fiscal Commission enquired into the advantages and disadvantages, fairness or unfairness, of the economic and fiscal arrangements for each of the three countries. It considered in particular the customs union,[3] through which, as Brett (1973) shows, Tanzania was made to subsidize Kenyan settler agriculture. From 1922, when Tanzania was integrated into the union, to the end of the interwar period, Tanzania generally maintained an increasingly adverse balance of trade with Kenya and Uganda. In the late 1930s, the economic center of gravity shifted decisively in favor of Kenya, which became the primary distribution, manufacturing, temperate-climate food-producing area for the region as a whole. From 1933 to the end of the decade, some 25 percent of Tanzania's imports were distributed from Kenya.

This pattern of favoring the northern territories over Tanzania was maintained and accentuated until independence. Brett believes that while Britain provided Tanzania with as much in the way of general developmental resources as she did Kenya and Uganda (a point on which Cliffe [1972] does not agree), these resources were far outweighed by the direct and measurable losses that Tanzania suffered as a result of a common transport and customs policy, and by the indirect and incalculable losses of foregone economic opportunities that were the effect of dependence on northern services, producers, and suppliers. This pattern persisted until 1963, when the Kampala Agreement was negotiated to correct the East African trade imbalance, which was then estimated to be £5.4 million between Kenya and Tanzania and £1.5 million between Uganda and Tanzania (United Republic of Tanganyika and Zanzibar 1964).

Ehrlich believes that of the three, Uganda was best prepared for independence: "[In Uganda] real income per head

3. In 1917 the customs departments of Kenya and Uganda were unified and free trade was established between the countries. Tanzania joined in stages, adopting the same external tariffs in 1922, free exchange of domestic goods in 1927, and finally, in 1949, merging to form an East African customs agency (Lomas 1966).

of the African population was higher, though there were serious regional inequalities. . . . In Kenya, African incomes
were lower but the economy was more diversified. . . . Tanganyika's economic inheritance was least enviable. . . . By
any standards of measurement she remained one of the
poorest countries in tropical Africa" (1968:347).

3

POPULATION AND LABOR POWER

Capitalism penetrated Tanzania under the protection of colonial power and dispossessed Africans of their physical resources—the best agricultural land, mineral resources, and raw materials—and eventually of their human resources—their health, knowledge, and skills. Sometimes the process of dispossession was brutal and abrupt, in other cases it was subtle and gradual. Apologists for the regimes like to draw up balance sheets and credit them with the signs and symbols of progress. In these accounts, development equals so many miles of roads and railways, so many harbors, airports, plantations, and factories. If there are debits in health and nutrition, they are written off against progress ("the price one pays") or abated by evidence of population growth.

The theory that the benefits from that sort of development "trickle down" to the populace has now been disproved, but what can be said about population growth in the face of increasing misery? Malthusian demographers cling to a theory of demographic transition according to which the precapitalist pattern was one of high death rates balanced by high birth rates (Gwatkin and Brandel 1982; Omran 1971). With the industrial revolution a transitional pattern emerged of falling death rates and continued high birth rates. Only the advanced industrialized countries have attained the new, desired equilibrium of low death rates balanced by low birth rates (for a sympathetic reappraisal see Freedman 1979). According to transition theorists, the Third World is caught in the second stage: modern medicine has brought down death rates but persistent high birth rates are defeating the efforts of planners and economists to eradicate poverty. Economic development cannot keep pace with population growth. In this view, immiseration is not a new phenomenon but a holdover from an earlier period, just as high birth rates are left over from the precapitalist era. Family planning or, more properly, population control is invoked as the technological solution to the dilemma (for a critique see Teitelbaum 1975). A recent variant of transition theory is the wealth flows theory (Caldwell 1981). According to this variant, in precapitalist societies wealth flows from the younger to the older generation, making it rational for families to have many children.

There are two levels on which to refute the demographic transition theory—at the epistemological level on which empirical evidence is used to disprove theory and at the ontological level on which the empiricist perspective is rejected. First, empirically, the theory is an inaccurate representation of reality because it posits one precapitalist pattern when in fact several existed, some of which (for example, hunter-gatherers and pastoralists) did not have high birth rates. High birth rates are peculiar to settled agriculturalists, and even shifting agriculturalists had somewhat lower rates. Although Caldwell (1981) claims a historical perspective for his wealth flows variant, he collapses all precapitalist economic formations—communal, slave, and feudal—into one, which he calls the familial mode of production. The familial mode of production cannot account for divergent mechanisms of wealth distribution in the three main precapitalist economic formations. (One wonders what wealth there was among slaves and serfs to flow in any direction.) The transition theory is also inaccurate because it assumes one natality pattern for all social classes. For example, slaves and slave owners, serfs and feudal rulers, are assumed to have the same high birth rates and, according to Caldwell, for the same reasons. Caldwell cannot reconcile his wealth flows theory with empirical evidence of differing population patterns within and among precapitalist societies.

At the ontological level, demographic transition theory is inadequate because it is premised on a neoclassical interpretation of development that has been refuted by Marxists; because, confusing cause with effect, it fails to explain why exploited Third World peoples now living under capitalist systems find it necessary to bear many children; because it assumes that precapitalist societies persist unchanged; and because it fails to take migration into account and focuses almost solely on fertility (van de Walle 1977 represents these failures). The inadequacies of the theory can be traced to the origins of demography and its relation to capitalism: the creation of the discipline is usually credited to William Petty, a seventeenth-century British statistician who named the field political arithmetic and used his new methodology to disprove mercantilism and establish capitalist ideology.

The ontological critique demands an alternative view of demographic dynamics: the one adopted here sees population patterns as related to modes of production, particularly to the different labor needs of each economic formation. It emphasizes the cultural controls of reproduction available to precapitalist societies and takes the position that "overpopulation" under capitalism is a symptom of underdevelopment, rather than a cause of poverty.

Estimating Life and Death

The data on population change in Tanzania must be examined in detail to establish the impact of colonial rule. To discern movement, one must analyze each of the three components—births, deaths, and migration. The problems of reconstructing population dynamics, with no baseline data (the size of the precolonial population is unknown) and very imprecise colonial records, are great.

In Europe and North America, information on mortality and the causes of death comes basically from death registration. In most of the Third World death registration is rarely complete enough to give any accurate demographic indices. The only places where birth and death registration begins to approach adequacy are small offshore islands like Mauritius and some urban areas, which are very atypical of the generally rural populace.

It is necessary to look elsewhere for demographic data. There are two main sources of information: first, large-scale demographic surveys and population censuses in which questions on fertility and mortality have been asked, and second, small-scale medical surveys and hospital and clinical records. In general, the information from small medical surveys and hospital and clinical records is much more reliable than the data obtained in the larger surveys and censuses. Unfortunately, data from small surveys may be unrepresentative because the survey area is not typical of the country as a whole, while the hospital data may be biased because records are obtained only from people who have access to the hospitals and clinics. They are of little use in establishing general mortality levels in an African country and we have to fall back on large-scale demographic survey and census data.

Practically none of the demographic surveys and censuses that give infant and child mortality rates provide information on the clinical causes of death. Most African deaths are uncertified; the dead have never been seen by a qualified medical practitioner. Even if death certificates were written by rural health personnel, they would probably not give the cause of death in a reliable, standard classification because the World Health Organization international classification of diseases is a very difficult and complex system that can be used virtually only by qualified medical practitioners on deaths occurring in hospital.

The mortality rates of African adults are unknown. Estimations are made using mortality tables based on experiences in other countries, or else infant and child mortality rates known from surveys are extrapolated for the adult age groups.

In most African countries infant mortality in the 1970s was between 130 and 200 per thousand live births (United States Bureau of the Census 1978:28–137). In other words, of all children born alive, between 13 and 20 percent will die before they reach their first birthday. Mortality remains high in the second, third, and fourth years of life, and by the age of five some 25 to 30 percent of the children will have died; perhaps another 5 percent will die before reaching the age of fifteen. A higher infant mortality rate cannot be correct: a rate of 400, for example, implies that at least 60 percent of the children born will have died by the age of five. Death rates of this magnitude cannot be true at the national level, though they may obtain in isolated areas, because they are incompatible with known levels of population increase, which are between 2.5 and 3 percent per year. To achieve growth rates that we know to exist in Africa with an infant mortality rate of 400 per thousand, each and every woman would have to average twelve to fifteen live births for completed family size, whereas we know that infertility is extensive. It is quite possible that in many African countries approximately half of the total deaths that occur in any one year may be deaths of children under five, but this is not the same thing as saying that half of the children die before reaching the age of five (Blacker 1971). Though many African women have ten, twelve, or fifteen children, between 10 and 20 percent of women living to the age of fifty will never bear a live child. In East Africa the average figure for completed family size is about six or seven births.

Population Growth

There are two hypotheses about nineteenth-century demographic trends in Tanzania; they agree there was a period of population decline but disagree on the dates of that period. The first, associated with Coupland (1939) and Alpers (1967, 1975), holds that internecine warfare and the slave trade created a decline from 1850 to 1890, when population began to rise; the second, associated with Kuczynski (1949) and Kjekshus (1977), holds that there was slow or no growth until 1890, when a sharp decline began that was not reversed until 1925. There can be no doubt that the first hypothesis is wrong as regards an increase in population from 1890; all the evidence points in the opposite direction. As to whether the decline began earlier than 1890 and as to when the trend was reversed, the evidence is less clear. Table 1 summarizes the results of past censuses and counts.[1] It shows that the African population declined slightly between 1913 and 1921; Kjekshus's early German sources, however, show a precipitous decline prior to 1913. Between 1921 and 1928, population began to rise, almost doubling between 1928 and 1957. The estimated populations for 1913 and 1921 were both believed to be overestimates, while each census since 1928 has been judged by the next to have erred on the side of underenumeration.

Kuczynski (1949:399) believes that an increase of 22 percent between 1921 and 1931 cannot be supported by the evidence. Recovery from World War I was not completed be-

1. The counts of Africans referred to the resident or de jure population and attempted to exclude people temporarily present and include those temporarily absent. Overland migration statistics (that is, for Africans not entering the country at seaports) were virtually nonexistent.

Table 1
Summary of Censuses/Counts, Mainland Tanzania

Year	African Population	Non-African Population	Total	Remarks
1913	4,145,000	20,777[a]	4,165,777	Estimate: includes Rwanda and Burundi
1921	4,106,890	17,438[b]	4,124,328	African count; non-African census
1928	4,740,706	—	—	African count only
1931	5,022,640	41,020	5,063,660	African count; non-African census
1948	7,410,269	70,160	7,480,429	Census with sample
1952	—	95,494	—	General census
1957	8,665,336	123,130	8,788,466	Census with sample
1967	—	—	11,958,654	Census
1978	—	—	17,048,329	Census

SOURCE: Tanzania Bureau of Statistics 1971:1, 8, 14; n.d.:177.

NOTE: Kjekshus (1977:24) gives the following additional early information from German sources: 1902–1903, 4,622,000; 1906–1907, 4,009,500; 1913, 4,043,500; his figures exclude Rwanda and Burundi.

[a]This figure varies from 13,541 to 20,777 in different sources.

[b]This figure varies from 14,991 to 17,438 in different sources.

fore 1925, and administrative reports from all over the country testify to the hardships the population endured in the postwar years. From 1925 to 1931 there was an increase, but it could not have been more than 8 percent, according to Kuczynski.[2]

Blacker (1963) compared the results of the 1948 and 1957 censuses in order to estimate the growth rate of the population. He judged the crude birth rate to be 46 per thousand but believed the death rate to be most uncertain—perhaps 24 or 25 per thousand population in 1957. This calculation was based on United Nations models that are not applicable to Tanzania. When other tables were used the results were 35 deaths per thousand. Blacker found that the intercensal growth rate could not easily be reconciled with the estimated rate of natural increase. The difference between

2. For the original data of the 1931 census see Tanganyika 1932. Later data and reviews are contained in Brass and Coale 1968; East African Statistics Department 1949, 1950, 1951, 1952; Goldthorpe 1952, 1956; Gulliver 1960; Lorimer and Karp 1960; Tanganyika 1957; Taueber 1949; United Nations 1953.

the birth rate of 46 per thousand and the death rate of 24 to 25 per thousand was 2.1 or 2.2 per year, a rate of natural increase that is higher than the average rate of growth, which was 1.75 percent per year between 1948 and 1957. Emigration was not a likely explanation, according to Blacker, because immigration was known to be higher. He guessed that the error lay in the estimate of the crude death rate, which was too low.

Blacker's judgment that the Tanzanian birth rate is high raises the question of whether colonial disruption of societies caused a relaxation of cultural controls on fertility, resulting in an increase in the birth rate. A related but slightly different question can also be posed. Did capitalist penetration of the country change precolonial social relations of production and create new economic hardships, and was an increase in the birth rate the response of the population to the transformation? We shall return to those questions.

Henin and Egero (1972) compared the recorded population of 1948, 1957, and 1967 and found the following trends for mainland Tanzania. Population grew from 7.5 million in 1948 to 8.8 million in 1957 and to 12 million in 1967. The annual growth rate, that is, the increase resulting from a surplus of births over deaths, was 1.8 percent in 1948, 3.1 percent in 1957, and 2.5 percent in 1967. The ratio of males per 100 females, an important index of migration, was 93 in 1948 and 1957, and 95 in 1967. The 1957 estimate of the crude death rate was 24 to 25 per thousand and life expectancy was thirty-five to forty years. In 1967 the crude death rate was estimated to be between 21 and 23 per thousand, and life expectancy, while probably over forty years, was certainly not as high as forty-three and was likely about forty-one years. The crude birth rate as calculated by Henin and Egero from the 1967 census was 57 per thousand—a figure they considered too high; they believed that 47 was a more plausible estimate.

To situate these figures within the context of world trends for developed and underdeveloped countries, the following figures given by the United Nations (1971) may be helpful. For developing regions, between 1900 and 1950, the estimated average annual birth rate was 41 per thousand, the death rate 32 per thousand, and the rate of natural increase (births over deaths, not allowing for migration) 9.

In contrast, much lower rates prevailed in the developed regions: the birth rate was 26 per thousand, the death rate 18 per thousand, and the rate of natural increase 8. Since 1950, the birth rate has remained high in developing regions but the death rate has fallen—to 22 per thousand in 1950–1960 and 17 per thousand in 1960–1970. The rate of natural increase rose to 24 per thousand in 1960–1970. In the more developed regions, the death rate was halved to 9 per thousand in 1960–1970, while the birth rate fell gradually to 20 per thousand. The rate of natural increase, therefore, rose slightly to 11 per thousand in 1960–1970.

In comparison with other countries, Tanzania has higher crude birth and death rates and a comparable rate of natural increase. While Henin and Egero's data point to a decreasing trend in Tanzanian mortality, the speed of the trend is difficult to assess on the basis of two such vague estimates of death rates.

Henin and Egero thought that infant mortality had declined from 190 per thousand live births in 1957 to 160 per thousand in 1967, but regional variations are great. The percentage of children dying during their first year of life ranges from 20 to less than 10 percent, while those surviving to their fifth birthday range from 65 to 85 percent. Henin and Egero (1972:9) suggest that the differences do not describe the situation exactly but indicate the wide variations in educational, medical, and economic standards that exist between districts in the country.

Although long-term population trends are unknown, two characteristics of Tanzania's population appear generally to be accepted: that mortality rates are high and that they are declining. Since early estimates for death rates are unreliable, recent population growth is taken as evidence of declining mortality—and not of increased natality. The latter is curious in view of Kuczynski's conclusions more than thirty years ago: "The yearly natural increase in East Africa cannot possibly be anything like 1.5 percent if mortality is as high as it is generally believed to be, even if fertility should be very high. . . . This would presuppose among other things that all the data indicating low fertility among some important tribes are wrong" (1949:124). According to Pradervand (1970:11), the view that fertility is high in Africa came into currency only recently (since 1968); rather than assuming a change in the birth rate, demographers believe that their earlier views were incorrect because of very insufficient knowledge of real trends. However, even if mortality has declined, this does not explain the change in population size or what produced it. Nor does it necessarily imply improvement in health, let alone say anything at all about the impact of health services.[3] Population increases have many underlying causes, some of which—at least in the short term—are compatible with deteriorating health.

If complete vital and health statistics were available for the eighteenth, nineteenth, and twentieth centuries, it would be possible to understand the relation of changes in health status to population change, as well as to answer questions about how Tanzanians came to be as disease-ridden as they are today and whether they always suffered so. Nonetheless, the questions must be posed and an attempt made to answer them with available data and information from disciplines other than health statistics.

Labor Migration

Analyses at the national level, where urban and rural populations and all social classes are aggregated, obscure rather than reveal internal labor migration and such population changes as deteriorating health. National aggregates are particularly misleading where there are pronounced regional variations in climatic conditions and economic activity. Of course, the regional approach is justified only if data of comparable quality to that of the national aggregates are available. In the case of Tanzania, analysis of data at the district level is more fruitful than at the regional level.[4]

3. The commonly held view that increase in population was a result of medical care or public health measures is questionable, especially in view of the very limited population reached by medical services in Tanzania. In the colonial era, authorities estimated that 4 percent of the population had access to medical care. In addition, there are questions about the efficacy of that care.

4. The level of administration immediately below the central government in colonial Tanzania was the province. Some reports of the early population counts give analyses at the national and provincial levels only; however, because of the boundary changes that complicate comparisons over time, it is more fruitful to pursue an analysis at the next lower administrative level, that of the district, which—with few exceptions—has remained fairly constant since 1920. One exception is Songea: the Tanzanian government changed its administrative boundaries in 1963, transferring

Two districts—Kilosa and Songea—were selected for a comparative analysis.[5] Kilosa is located about 320 kilometers west of Dar es Salaam in what is today Morogoro Region and what was, under British administration, Eastern Province. Songea is located in the southeast along the border with Mozambique in what is today Ruvuma Region and what was, during most of the British era, Southern Province.

According to the Government of Tanzania's *Atlas of Tanzania* (1967), Songea and Kilosa are similar in terms of potential land use. Most of Kilosa is moderately fertile, but some parts have alluvial soils of considerable potential; in parts of Songea the soil lacks valuable nutrients but most of the district has soils of medium to high fertility with high potential. In terms of rainfall, both districts are relatively well watered by Tanzanian standards. The agricultural potentials of the two districts are similar and average for Tanzania. However, as will be seen, their populations have widely differing characteristics and different health status.

An important study by Hirst (1970) concludes that net migration is the dominant component of population change in Songea District; in Kilosa net migration and fertility are of equal importance in accounting for population change. In the absence of any census or survey data on migration at the district level, Hirst found a way to calculate net migration patterns. He considered the spatial variations of population change in detail at the district level with two components—fertility and net migration. He did not take mortality into account because data were lacking at the district level, but he suggested that because there was little regional variation in mortality, the absence of this component

---

the areas of Matengo and Unyanja from Songea to form Mbinga District. See Thomas and Thomas 1971 for estimates of the population transferred between districts as a result of the change. Both Matengo and Unyanja are more mountainous, are more densely populated, and have higher population growth rates than the rest of Songea.

5. Fieldwork in connection with my doctoral dissertation was carried out in Kilosa in 1973; unfortunately, I could not visit Songea because of government restrictions on travel in that area during the liberation war in Mozambique, which borders on Songea. Fieldwork in Kilosa was carried out with teams of agricultural extension workers, nutrition educators, and child health personnel based at the Ilonga Research and Training Institute, which was attached to the Ministry of Agriculture.

was not crucial. However, as the three components are interrelated, the lack of mortality data remains an important gap in Hirst's study and weakens his analysis of the other two components.

Since the territorial census areas enumerated in the 1957 census are not comparable to the chiefdoms enumerated in 1948, Hirst examined population trends within the framework of the fifty-eight districts and divisions of 1957, adjusting the 1948 figures as far as possible. It is important to recall that both censuses were inaccurate: the 1948 census was subject to an underenumeration of 1.9 to 3.6 percent and the 1957 census to 5.4 to 6.3 percent. (Though Hirst assumed that the errors were not spatially biased, this assumption is questionable because remote and inaccessible districts usually experience more underreporting than those easily reached by rail and road.) Hirst tried to minimize the problem of underenumeration by examining the relative differences of growth between districts, rather than growth in absolute terms.

Problems in the measurement of fertility depend in part on the accuracy of age distribution data. In the 1957 census, women married before the age of sixteen were considered adults and recorded in the sixteen to forty-five age group, rather than with children. Levels of infant and child mortality—unknown and presumably subject to wide variation between districts—also influence the child-woman ratio on which fertility is calculated. (Here again Hirst assumed no spatial bias in the errors and limitation of the data. It might be more reasonable to assume that certain characteristics are clustered—for example, high infant and child mortality and high fertility. In this instance the bias in Hirst's calculation tends to underestimate fertility rates in Songea, given the higher than national average mortality rate in that district.)

Given the lack of data on which to calculate net gain and loss in population resulting from migration at the district level, Hirst estimated the relative net migration patterns using six variables based on ethnic, age, and sex imbalances (thus an area of net immigration would be characterized by ethnic heterogeneity and a predominance of adult males [see Hirst 1969]). In this way, Hirst identified three major groups of districts in Tanzania: (1) the group in which net migration is the dominant component of population

change, (2) that in which the level of fertility is the dominant component, and (3) that in which net migration and
fertility are of equal importance in accounting for population change. Songea District falls in the first category and
Kilosa in the third.

Hirst expected districts characterized by emigration to
have a larger proportion in the younger age groups as compared with the national age distribution. Using Hirst's national data for Tanzania, one may calculate from the 1957
census the age distributions for Kilosa and Songea districts
shown in table 2. The fact that the sixteen to forty-five age
group in Kilosa is so much larger than the national average
attests to the high rate of labor migration. Table 2 shows a
larger proportion of young people in Songea than in Kilosa,
but not larger than the national average. The population under five years is smaller in Songea as compared with Tanzania as a whole, but the population six to fifteen years old is
substantially larger—21.3 percent as compared to 17.7.
Since Songea's mortality rate is higher than the national
average, which Hirst does not take into consideration, it
may be that both infant mortality and fertility are higher
than Hirst estimates.

Despite reservations about the reliability of his method
—particularly as regards the omission of mortality data—
we can accept the conclusion that the dominant component
of population change in Songea is emigration in the sixteen
to forty-five year age group and that Kilosa is a recipient of
migrants in that age group. These facts are of major importance to the study of the political economy of those districts.

Table 2
Age Distribution in Selected Districts, 1957

	Age Group (percentage)				Total Population
	Under 5	6 to 15	16 to 45	46 and over	
Kilosa	21.3	19.4	50.1	9.2	151,157
Songea[a]	22.8	21.3	44.1	14.8	196,324
Tanzania	23.8	17.7	44.1	11.5	8,665,336

SOURCE: For Kilosa and Songea, Tanganyika 1963. For Tanzania, Hirst
1970.

[a]Includes Mbinga District, which was part of Songea District until 1963.
The data for Mbinga (a high fertility area) are in the same direction as that
for Songea (a high migration area).

The data for population change in Kilosa and Songea districts are meaningful only in the context of economic development, labor demands, and social change. As Marx (1974:140) observed, population is an abstraction if one disregards the classes of which it is composed. The analysis of classes entails an examination of wage labor, capital investment, and so on. The fallacy of defining overpopulation in terms of high birth rates is that the relativity of population to employment is ignored; that relativity is created by capitalistic accumulation, which produces a redundant or surplus population of laborers (Marx 1967,1:630). Of course people are not only laborers, but capitalism often reduces men to this single dimension and assigns women the task of reproducing the labor force.

Women in Production and Reproduction

Women's fertility is too frequently the sole focus of demographic studies, which suffer from neglect of the equally important subjects of women's mortality and migratory behavior. All three aspects of population dynamics—fertility, mortality, and migration—interact with women's productive activities, which are often underestimated and undervalued. Women's health is in part determined by women's work or, put another way, women's survival is a function of women's economic production and social position (Anker, Buvinic, and Youssef 1982:21). This formulation corrects the widely held but false assumption that medical care and public health programs are the main determinants of mortality and that differences in men's and women's mortality are either unimportant or are determined by a combination of biological and genetic factors. More valuable in understanding the mechanics of population change than medical or fertility surveys are historical studies that discern changes in women's economic contribution, social position, and political participation.

Though the material on how colonialism affected Tanzanian women is still very scanty, there is a special case to be made for women in considering population and labor power because colonialism did not affect them in the same way as it affected men and because they were more vulnerable to its ill effects. There is no doubt, as Pala (1977:11) points out, that women and men shared a subordinate role in the colonial era, but the same social and economic conditions affected women and men differently.

The health and nutritional status of women (and consequently that of their children) can be correlated with the political and social power of women, within the context of overall national health standards. This sociopolitical power is derived from their participation in productive activities, that is, work that produces material commodities, as contrasted with domestic services.

Since African women contributed heavily to subsistence production, their authority in precolonial societies was great, especially relative to that of their Asian sisters, who were often secluded at home, where their domestic activities were considered nonproductive. In comparison with women in Asia and Latin America, African women enjoyed greater independence in making decisions that affected food production and processing. Most important, they had control over the products of their labor and they could act to ensure their own and their children's health and nutrition, within the limits of their community's standards of living.

Colonial rule radically changed the position of African women. As Mullings notes, colonialism, which imposed a social structure based on stratification by class and sex, resulted in "the differentiation of social and domestic labor, the introduction of large-scale production for exchange, and the transformation of productive resources into private property—processes that significantly altered the status of women" (1976:247). Capitalism, penetrating under colonial rule, affected rural women in three ways: it lowered their standard of living by exploiting rural areas; it imposed Victorian notions of women's inferiority and used them to deny women access to education and technical training; and it reduced the importance of women's work by substituting cash crops for food as the valued commodity.

The introduction of a cash economy had significant consequences for Tanzanian women. Most Africans do not share Western assumptions that household members will pool their incomes, that total family consumption correlates with total family income, that fathers are obliged to support their families, and that wives and children have a prior claim (before other relatives) on the incomes of married men (Shields 1976:9–10). Familial arrangements associated with polygamy continue to exist even where monogamy is the norm. In the polygamous marriage, wives formed separate households and bore the responsibility of supporting their children, including the daily provision of food and clothing. With the introduction of the cash economy, men retained most of the cash income of the family and began to take responsibility for major expenses like school fees.

Wherever capitalism penetrated, the subsistence sector lost its self-sufficiency; when sufficiently impoverished and dependent, this sector could no longer sustain its arrangements with the capitalist economy. As the breaking point in the articulation of precapitalist (often polygamous) arrangements and the capitalist economy was reached, women were forced to turn to the cash sector to meet their family's basic needs, and if men controlled that sector, women were forced into a dependent relationship.

Bernstein calls this break in the cycle of reproduction the "crucial moment" of capitalist penetration (1977:62): it is accomplished by the substitution of commodities for articles of necessary consumption previously produced locally or acquired through simple exchange, by the imposition of taxes necessitating sources of cash income, and by the use of forced labor. His conclusion is interesting: once capitalism has destroyed the conditions of social reproduction, agricultural communities cannot be both perpetuated and undermined as Meillassoux (1972:103) suggests. Bernstein rejects this contradiction as illogical and also criticizes as sociological functionalism the proposition that capital determines the degree and forms of preservation or destruction in rural areas. For him the question is "how the conditions of production and reproduction are determined by the operations of capital (in particular social formations and at the level of the world economy) and of the state" (1977:61).

The power of women in Tanzania was not everywhere the same, not only because the country was unevenly developed by capitalism in the colonial period, but also because the precapitalist modes of production upon which capitalism was imposed were diverse. Power, as a function of the social relations of production, varies with the mode of production. The principal precapitalist modes were the hunter-gatherer mode, which was most egalitarian; the pastoralist, which was usually male dominated; and the shifting or settled agriculturalist, in which women's power varied with the degree of state formation.

Among hunter-gatherers who relied mainly on foraging and fishing, the sexes were likely to be equal, while those who relied on hunting to assure subsistence were male dominated (Sanday 1981:171, 175; see also Draper 1975, Etienne and Leacock 1980:9–12). Pastoral societies tended to be male dominated, not only because men owned livestock both collectively and individually, but also because herders were hierarchically organized, placing women in subordinate roles (Sacks 1979). Within the agricultural mode of production, social relations were organized in a wide variety of ways throughout Africa.

Some anthropologists categorize groups by patterns of inheritance, a peculiarly capitalist view of what is the common denominator of a society. Agronomists choose the staple crop as the outstanding feature, a view that is more consonant with the Marxist emphasis upon the economic base as a social determinant. Some economists have concentrated on food-producing technologies. For example, Boserup relates agricultural production to the sexual division of labor through the mediating factor of the instruments of production, that is, the agricultural implements used. She identifies two broad groups, shifting cultivators who use the hoe and settled agriculturalists who use the plough:

> the first type is found in regions where shifting cultivation predominates and the major part of agricultural work is done by women. In such communities, we can expect to find a high incidence of polygamy, and bride wealth being paid by the future husband or his family. The women are hardworking and have only a limited right of support from their husbands, but they often enjoy considerable freedom of movement and some economic independence from the sale of their own crops. The second group is found where plough cultivation predominates and where women do less agricultural work than men. In such communities we may expect to find that only a tiny minority of marriages, if any, are polygamous; that a dowry is usually paid by the girl's family; that a wife is entirely dependent upon her husband for economic support; and that the husband has an obligation to support his wife and children at least as long as the marriage is in force. (Boserup 1970:50)

Boserup does not consider the relation between sex and class, although she mentions the importance of stratification in relation to plough agriculture. This omission makes her analysis less applicable to societies transformed by capitalism in the colonial period. Ideally, an analysis of women's power and authority ought to begin with differences among women of different classes, go on to consider differences in female versus male jurisdiction over time for a historical perspective, and finally make a cross-cultural comparison of women's participation in different societies. At each stage, one would like to consider all variables of the economic formation: the instruments of production (machinery and tools for the production of food, clothing, and other material necessities of life); the means of production (land, forests, water resources, raw materials, and mineral resources, as well as factories, transportation, and communication systems); the productive forces (women, children, and men, as well as the instruments of production they operate); the social relations of production; and, finally, reproduction, both of people and of the mode of production as a whole.

Comparative studies of regional differences in women's authority as a function of the mode of production have not been made in Tanzania. A few reports from single regions give details of women's work, and it is with this scant information that we must proceed.

For Kilosa District, Beidelman (1971) collected data on Ukaguru agriculture at the end of the British colonial period. Then as now, the agricultural cycle determined work loads; the arrival of the first rains signaled the beginning of the cycle and a rapid acceleration of labor demands. No strict sexual division of agricultural labor existed in Ukaguru. It was assumed that when men were available (that is, not working in some other part of the country), they would do the heavier work of clearing the land, but some widows and independent women did this work themselves. Both sexes hoed and harvested. Men had leisure in the dry season, but women had to prepare food, fetch water and firewood, and tend children the year round.

Beidelman suggests that in precolonial times women were held in high esteem in Ukaguru and participated in the political life of their matrilineal clans on an equal footing with men, but that their authority was considerably

Table 3
Employment of Men, Women, and Children in Selected Districts, 1952

District	Employer Classification	Adult Males	Adult Females	Children	Total
Kilosa	Domestic	478	8	42	528
	Agriculture	18,663	436	1,713	20,812
	Private industry	931	11	59	1,001
	Public service	2,208	6	3	2,217
	Total	22,280	461	1,817	24,558
Songea	Domestic	159	18	18	195
	Agriculture	177	—	6	183
	Private industry	1,558	252	309	2,119
	Public service	869	23	46	938
	Total	2,763	293	379	3,435
Tanzania Total	Domestic	17,996	955	1,479	20,430
	Agriculture	189,369	17,570	26,088	233,027
	Private industry	95,851	2,017	2,753	100,621
	Public service	88,091	924	504	89,519
	Total	391,307	21,466	30,824	443,597

Source: Tanganyika 1953.

eroded under British rule. Not only did women lose their political positions, since they were discouraged from holding office in the local administrative system, but they also lost influence in the general shift of power from matrilineages and other kin groups to local British courts. Rights in property and the control of subordinates became matters for courts to decide. In economic life women also fell behind, first, because the principles on which the cash economy operated were "independent or even opposed to those determining traditional rank within a lineage," and second, because a large or regular income could not be gained directly from agriculture or herding but had to be sought elsewhere, for example, in military service, wage work in town, or government or mission employment (ibid.:54, 23). These opportunities were open to men, not women, as is evident in table 3. In 1952, women accounted for less than 5 percent of the labor force in Tanzania; in Kilosa the figure was under 2 percent.[6]

6. Recent feminist scholarship has shown that women workers were often invisible to male bureaucrats responsible for data collection (see Beneria 1981); table 3 should therefore be interpreted with caution.

A very different picture emerges from Bukoba District, an area west of Lake Victoria. Before independence the people of this area were stratified in a feudal society ruled by royalty. They had small, nuclear families, were rarely polygamous after the advent of Christianity, and lived in individual huts in the midst of their individually held plots of land. According to the patrilineal system, only one son inherited, and land was never subdivided among heirs. The large class of landless laborers thus included the disinherited sons of wealthy families. The wealthiest farmers cultivated plantains (the staple crop), beans (an important part of the diet), coffee (the cash crop), and stock cattle (to provide manure for the fields); the poorest cultivated plantains alone. Farm sizes ranged from 0.3 to 4.8 acres according to one estimate (Reining 1970).

Peasant agriculture in Bukoba was based on a sexual division of labor, men being in charge of perennial crops (plantains and coffee) and women taking care of the annual crops (beans and eleusine, a cereal). Once established, perennial crops demand less labor, leaving men increased leisure time and opportunities for casual employment to supplement their income (Rald and Rald 1975:96). Storgaard (1973:113) believes that the introduction of coffee as a cash crop at the beginning of this century put severe strains on the former system, which could no longer meet subsistence needs, and forced some peasants to seek employment.

Colonial administrators were aware that many women rebelled against patriarchal control and ran away to towns, where prostitution was often their only source of income (Molohan 1959). Some later returned to Bukoba, used their savings to buy land and hire laborers, and joined cooperative societies as independent members. Bryceson and Mbilinyi (1978:30) noted that all such women were labeled prostitutes regardless of whether they actually sold their sexual services, because they acted like men, that is, they took control, made decisions, behaved aggressively, sold cash crops themselves, and so on. Independent female family heads, both rich and poor, believed they were materially much better off than married women as regards cash and food consumption, and that they were "free from oppression."

One of the best-studied districts is Kilimanjaro. An area of intensive missionary activity, it was one of the first to be settled by Europeans in the colonial era, when large tracts of land were alienated. Located in the northeast on the Kenyan border, Kilimanjaro has undergone radical change in this century. From an area of banana cultivation and some cattle herding, it has become since the 1920s a center of coffee production for export. The colonial administrators, entrepreneurs, and clergy who initiated these changes brought with them a sexist bias that contributed to the deterioration of women's authority in the area. Colonial agricultural officers taught men to grow coffee; government and mission schools generally enrolled boys rather than girls; and the church and the government strengthened male authority.

Customary law in Kilimanjaro does not recognize the woman as an independent member of society with her own rights to land and property (Swantz, Henricson, and Zalla 1975). In the precolonial period, land belonged to brothers and their descendants, and the available patrilineage land could be divided among the brothers' sons according to their number and need. With the introduction of coffee as a cash crop, families became interested in owning land and in transferring it to their sons. Additional land, needed when the number of sons was large, had to be purchased, often at a distance. When land became scarce, inheritance problems intensified and quarrels among siblings frequently occurred. The first wife's sons were entitled to more land than the other wives' sons, and in cases where another wife was more favored or the first wife was divorced, the division of land caused problems.

One study found that how men in Kilimanjaro decided to use their money from coffee production depended on the amount involved and their sense of responsibility: some kept it all and spent it on drink. Others used it to pay for school fees, occasional medical expenses, and money for building. More rarely they bought clothes for their wives and children and meat for the family. Only exceptional or better-off fathers also contributed to daily household expenses (for example, purchases of salt, sugar, kerosene, flour, and milk) or bought clothes for the youngest child. "At every group discussion except one mothers complained that fathers were not using the coffee money for the needs of the family. At Ruya the parish priest estimated that 60 percent of the women in his area have to support their children and themselves out of their own incomes from maize, beans and bananas without receiving any help from their husband" (Von Freyhold, Sawaki, and Zalla 1973:175).

As more and more transactions became monetized, women were increasingly disadvantaged. For example, when land became individualized, men were registered as heads of household, and when cooperatives marketed crops, men were registered as shareholders even though their wives contributed some or all of the labor that produced the crop.

A further consequence of the capitalist transformation of Kilimanjaro was the increasing class differentiation of the population. In the colonial era Christianity opened the way for some families to education, wealth, and power; while a few individuals now own fairly large coffee plantations, others are landless. Inequalities affect women's work loads, and poor peasant women labor under greater strains than their wealthier sisters. Wealthy households employ hired labor in the fields, make use of available transport and even tractors, and can get a loan to buy a cow. Because there are no more open spaces and because good quality grass is not now available, poor families no longer keep a few head of cattle to supplement their diet. Dairy production has become commercialized and the custom of sharing milk with neighbors either has been abandoned or has come to follow class lines (it is reciprocal among people of a relatively high socioeconomic level who can repay) (Swantz, Henricson, and Zalla 1975:36, 38, 63).

Before the colonial period in Kilimanjaro, each wife had a house and a plot of land outside it for subsistence production for herself and her family. She did all the work on her plot, including clearing bush and trees. After about 1920, much of the land that women had cultivated outside the homestead was used by their husbands for coffee production. More and more food was purchased rather than grown, creating insecurity in times of rising food prices. As the economic situation became more depressed, men began to seek wage labor and their wives took over coffee production in addition to their subsistence tasks. By the 1950s, even this arrangement was insufficient to provide for family needs, and many women were forced to engage in seasonal casual labor on nearby coffee plantations (Bryceson and Mbilinyi 1978:26).

The decreasing ability of peasant producers to meet their basic needs has a direct effect on maternal and child health. Crude birth rates in Kilimanjaro are among the highest in Tanzania. Rates of malnutrition and infection are high in Moshi, the principal town of Kilimanjaro, and child mortality rates are higher than the national average. Specifically, about 15 percent of the children under five years of age are malnourished and about 2 percent are severely malnourished. In all about two thousand children are in need of rehabilitation (Swantz, Henricson, and Zalla 1975:11).

Among the functions women performed in African society was the care of the very young, the very old, and the sick. Women prepared meals, nursed infants, and undertook general child care. Contradictory pulls developed in the colonial period, on the one hand reinforcing this caretaking function in subsistence areas, especially source areas for migrant male labor, and on the other hand undermining it by socializing health care in clinics and by devaluing traditional medicine and replacing it with Western medicine. In the first instance, rural society became the provider of social services that capitalists were not willing to provide for workers, nor were workers paid enough to be able to purchase such services. But in the second instance, women were replaced by government and mission services, which condemned traditional medicine as witchcraft and ignorant superstition. Thus demand for home care was rising at the very time when traditional medical knowledge, especially of herbal remedies, was declining.

The time available for women to perform caretaking functions rested upon the nature of their general work conditions. Women were also the traditional producers of food eaten in the home, so that the family's nutritional status depended in part on women's agricultural productivity. As capitalism penetrated the rural areas, women often had to supplement staple food production with cash earning, and whenever the family's cash earnings were controlled by the husband, the authority of women in the home or the husband's sense of responsibility determined whether sufficient earnings were allocated to family welfare.

The relation between nutrition and health is well established, but the close and direct relation between the agricultural cycle and the health of different age groups is rarely spelled out in detail. In countries like Tanzania where the woman is the principal agricultural producer, as well as the bearer and rearer of children, there is an especial need to describe the dynamics of agricultural production, maternal and child nutrition, and health status.

Scofield (1974) has a set of hypotheses about the chances of child survival according to agricultural cycles in countries where there are two main seasons—wet and dry—as there are in Tanzania. Scofield begins with the simple proposition that there is maximum demand for women's work in the fields in the wet season when crops are sown, and minimum demands in the dry season. Because food stores are lowest in the wet season, when supplies from the previous year's harvest are running out, peak agricultural labor demands and reduced availability of food coincide during the wet season. The short-term effects are reduction in body fat stores, weight loss, depletion of muscle tissue (especially if protein intakes are correspondingly reduced), and increased susceptibility to infection. Disease incidence is highly seasonal in Tanzania, and infections have a higher incidence in the wet season; lowered host resistance to disease coincides with a greater probability of contracting disease during the wet season.

If a woman is pregnant during this period, it is possible that fetal growth will be retarded and even full-term babies will be born small (Rosa and Turshen 1970). The mother may also become anemic and deficient in iron, in which case the baby may be born with iron-deficiency anemia.

Scofield also points out that there is a necessary reallocation of women's labor during the wet season, when agricultural demands peak. Cooking practices change, and there is a tendency to substitute quick, easy-to-prepare staples like cassava for the nutritionally superior but labor-intensive cereals like millet. Meals are prepared only once a day; if prepared in the morning and left simmering in the pot, they are likely to lose their vitamin content by evening. The intrafamilial distribution of food is also affected. When the single hot meal is served at night, for example, small children may already be asleep and may miss out or eat only cold leftovers the next day. Women may not have time to prepare special meals for weanlings who still have trouble digesting adult food. Food gathering may be inhibited so that some types of food, such as green leafy vegetables, are excluded from the diet. Housecleaning, essential in over-

crowded and unsanitary conditions, may be done less frequently. And fuel and water collection, normally a woman's task, may be made less regularly. Finally, women will
have less time to devote to their children, who will be left
in the care of older siblings or elderly grandparents and
may be bathed less often (Scofield 1974, 26–27).

The results are that in the wet season birth weight is
lower, breastfeeding is limited and may even cease, supple-
mentary child feeding is limited because food supplies are
low and women are busy, infections are more common, and
child care is limited (ibid.:28). If women command sufficient authority, tasks may be equitably shared with men,
avoiding the worst consequences of maternal and child
morbidity and mortality. If the community is egalitarian, no
one family will suffer food shortage more than any other,
and severe malnutrition may be mitigated. But where
women are powerless and communities stratified, death
rates will rise in the wet season.

Clearly, women's productive and reproductive activities
interact in complex ways; both were influenced by changes
in economic and social organization imposed by colonial
regimes. Morbidity and mortality rates reflect shifts in standards of living; those standards are affected by the ways in
which labor power is allocated and remunerated, and in
particular by the use of migrant labor; and fertility, or reproductive behavior, is shaped by the exigencies of work
life and labor demands, on the one hand, and by standards
of living, on the other. To examine women in relation to
fertility alone is to miss the interplay of production and reproduction and to risk misinterpretation of the dynamics of
population change.

4

LAND AND AGRICULTURE

Structured by social relations, land and agriculture form the basis of a society's food system. In precolonial Tanzania, as in much of sub-Saharan Africa, food systems depended principally on women's labor. Women's contribution, which extended from food production to the preparation of meals, determined the family's nutritional status and thereby its health. Colonialists fundamentally changed the precapitalist agricultural system in two ways: they imposed capitalist relations of production—for example, they introduced private land ownership, commercial agriculture, and wage labor—which affected women's productivity as well as their power; and they transformed the African ecology, which also affected productivity, created malnutrition, and produced a new disease environment. This process of capitalist penetration—documented in detail in the districts of Kilosa (a center of sisal plantations) and Songea (a labor supply area)—demonstrates the interrelationships between women, food, and health, as well as human agency in disease causation.

The questions of agricultural development taken up here are those of the food system, that is, of food production and distribution, processing and consumption, domestic and international markets, imports and exports. The questions are important because people's health status depends to a great extent on the availability of food for a balanced diet, and availability is mainly determined by government policy. Answers can be found in an examination of past and present agricultural policies only if one takes into account the transformation of social relations (that is, the creation of capitalist class structures in the colonial period) and the effect of political independence on those relations.

The modernization of agriculture is one aspect of Third

World development; another very important aspect is industrialization. The problems of Tanzania's failure to industrialize are addressed by Coulson (1982) and Rweyemamu (1974). They are taken up in this book only in relation to agricultural development.

The issues of land tenure, agricultural policy, and industrial development are part of an important, ongoing debate about the nature of underdevelopment, the origins of capitalism, class structure in developed and underdeveloped countries, and the ways in which classes and countries relate to shape the modern world (Brenner 1977; Fine 1978; Foster-Carter 1978). The outcome of this debate is critical to health policies, both because disease is rooted in modes of production and because health ultimately depends upon the development of forces of production adequate to ensure society's basic needs for food, clothing, and shelter. Without this development, socialist redistribution becomes an exercise in the management of poverty. For health planners, the crux of this debate turns on whether Third World countries are developing (that is, in an early stage of industrialization) or whether they are blocked in the transition to development. If, as I believe, the latter is the case, it is imperative to understand the nature of the blockage. An analysis of colonial land and agriculture policies furthers our understanding.

Land Tenure

Eric Wolf (1969:277) has written that land is not a commodity in nature; it becomes a commodity only when so defined by a cultural system intent on creating a new kind of economics: land is not created to be bought and sold, nor is it regarded as a commodity in societies where rights to land and the use of land are aspects of specific social relationships. In precolonial Tanzania, there was no individual ownership of land. Clans claimed land according to a wide variety of customs and inheritance laws, but no one person could accumulate fallow land (a sensible arrangement because without mechanization, the amount of land any one person could cultivate was limited).

There are few surveys of land tenure systems in Tanzania and none comparable to the one undertaken by White

(1959) in Zambia between 1956 and 1958;[1] the Zambian
study is described here, in the absence of Tanzanian data.
According to White (1959:173), there are four basic types of
land tenure in Africa:

1. Lineages as landholding units, with limitations upon
   the land rights obtainable by nonlineage members.
2. Feudal systems with landlords owning large tracts
   used by tenants, as in part of Uganda.
3. A descending hierarchy of estates in which chiefs exercise direct control over allocation, and an automatic
   right of reversion to the next higher estate holder
   when a piece of land ceases to be used. This system is
   typical of Botswana and Lesotho.
4. Individual land rights obtained by residence (normally
   in a village community) and not by allocation through
   a hierarchy of estates, hence no automatic reversions
   to higher levels.

White found the last to be the normal pattern in Zambia
and it is the one most frequently reported in Tanzanian
studies. White interpreted the system as a prototype of individual ownership rather than a new or revolutionary principle: since rights in land could be transferred, sale was a
simple development of land transfers within a cash economy. Though in former times, the "consideration" for
which land might be transferred was often goodwill, to
which there was, presumably, equal access, under the colonial cash economy, access to cash was not equally distributed among the sexes, races, and classes.

Among the Ngoni of Zambia rights over fallow land were
very strongly marked and inheritance of land might be a recent development due to increasing land scarcity, for most
individuals had acquired their land by clearing bushland
over which no prior rights had been claimed. White argued
that because the Ngoni responded slowly to the introduction of cash cropping and improved farming, the cash economy hardly affected their customary land rights (ibid.:177).
Gulliver (1955) made similar observations about the Ngoni
of Tanzania. But the cash economy did affect land rights by

1. For a partial account of precolonial customs in Tanzania see Dobson 1954.

increasing demands for land. White underestimated both the speed and intensity of capitalism, which affects precapitalist economic formations in the way infectious diseases decimate populations with no prior exposure.

Land was never sold in East African economies before the colonial period, and in matrilineages women had the right to inherit land. With the introduction of colonial laws to protect the private property of Europeans, and the alienation of some land by colonists, the concept of legal and exclusive ownership began to spread. Gradually African systems of allocation were eroded, with uneven results, depending on race, sex, and class.

Tanner (1960) studied three coastal villages in colonial Tanzania in an area of sisal plantations that offered opportunities for wage work. Maize, cassava, rice, and coconut palms were the major crops. Tanner characterizes land tenure as neither individual nor communal: cultivated land was the object of an amalgam of rights and obligations, not only in the land itself, but in the ownership and control of the harvest. Village elders no longer appeared to have control over land allocation. Individuals made arrangements to buy and sell land without any formal reference to village elders, and the payment varied from "gate money," paid to gain access to fallow land in less settled areas, to outright purchase in areas of land shortage. Standing crops such as maize and cassava were occasionally sold, but such sales gave no option on the permanent occupation of the land.

Land was obtained in several ways: through the mother's or the father's line (more commonly the latter); by marriage; by clearing new land; and by purchase. According to Tanner, the rights of women to land must be considered independently of their marital status, not only because the married family is very impermanent and does not form an agricultural unit, but also because many divorced or widowed men and women prefer not to remarry since marriage encumbers them with obligations they consider to be profitless under a cash economy. Tanner's data show that land is owned more frequently by men (61 percent of all plots in his sample) than by women (39 percent). Most men obtained possession by clearing land (32 percent) or by inheritance (21 percent). More women obtained possession by inheritance (18 percent) than by clearing land (17 percent) (ibid.:59).

Islamic influence is strong in this area. While the Muslim presence is not atypical of the country, it does represent a departure from earlier tradition, particularly with respect to the position of women. Unlike women in non-Muslim areas, some married women here did not cultivate because they considered that under Islamic law their husbands should provide for them. Nor did Islamic custom require women to assist their husbands in agricultural work. However, women are easily divorced under Islam, and most women preferred to cultivate separately for security. Women also cultivated when their husbands were unable to provide adequately for them and their children (ibid.:16).

In Tanner's study no women acquired land through purchase, presumably because they could not afford to do so. Without access to wage employment, it was extremely difficult for women to accumulate cash. Though a woman may cultivate a field by herself and own the harvest, she has an obligation to contribute to the maintenance of her family. If she is assisted in the field by her husband, she will own only part of the crop, although she will control the use of the harvest for the benefit of the household. Correspondingly, the husband may own the crop and have the right to sell it, although he will have little to say in its use within the household. Cash crops, however, are the outright property of the owner (who is usually male), although after their sale, he will still have to fulfill his family obligations with the proceeds (ibid.:14).

A divorced woman has no one who is obliged to work for her, and although she may live with one of her parents, she must maintain herself just as if she were living separately. Most of these women take over rice plots from their mothers or open small cassava fields in the coconut plantations of their relatives. A recent tendency for divorced women to remain unmarried has resulted in both sexes having the same rights to their own fields, as well as sufficient land for their needs where they live. Only a few women take up fallow land for the planting of perennial crops (for example, coconut palms), although many women do so for the cultivation of annual crops (maize, cassava) (ibid.:17). The ability to raise cash is clearly a deciding factor: land required for or already planted with coconuts is sold in all three villages, and women never purchase land.

Swantz (1975) found that in certain matrilineal societies

of the coast (for example, in Uzaramo and Ukwere), labor power was a person's main asset, and women were able to secure labor through the services of their sons-in-law when at least part of the bridewealth was paid by labor. In matrilocal groups, the son-in-law settled in the neighborhood of his wife's family. Though divorce was easily obtained, women continued to belong to their own clan and were not left without the right to a piece of land. According to Swantz, coastal women commonly own permanent crops (such as coconut palms) that they have developed on such land and thus have an independent income. Had the Islamic system allowed them greater freedom through education, women on the coast would today demonstrate considerable economic power. However, women's position was restricted within the Islamic family system.

Among the inland societies (for example, in Uchagga and Upare), the situation of women was slightly different, according to Swantz. As these societies adjusted to the cash economy, the units holding land rights were narrowed down to smaller and smaller family groups. This development had the effect, on the one hand, of limiting the potential of individuals to acquire land within the wider clan territory and, on the other hand, of defining land rights more clearly in relation to specific family members. Eventually this process led to the individualization of rights; at present, one individual in a family group holds the rights to any inherited piece of land and is obliged to pass it on according to the system common to the clan. This custom does not preclude the sale of land, however, which does now occur. Swantz argues that so long as land was held by a clan, it was understandable that passing land through a woman to her children and, potentially, through them to their father's clan, would have endangered the rights of the clan to its inheritance. This position has been invalidated, however, by the practice of selling land.

The need to accumulate land was a direct creation of the colonial system: the introduction of taxation together with a demand for cash crops gave rise to a need for more land than was formerly required for subsistence food production. When money from the sale of cash crops accrued to men, not families, and when wage labor was not open to women, women could not purchase land. When sales of land began to occur, it was men who had the money for purchases, and in this way the possession of land gradually

passed from women to men. The exclusion of women from
the cash economy did not occur in the traditional sector
alone, where customary law was subverted by new social
relations. African women and men were discriminated
against in colonial land policy.

Colonial Land and Agricultural Policies

A legal system of ordinances and regulations established
land policy in the British colonial period. The Land Ordinance of 1923 introduced the right-of-occupancy system;
under section 6, the governor could grant rights of occupancy to European settlers at a rent and for ninety-nine
years. The Land Regulation of 1926 and the Land (Pastoral
Purposes) Regulation of 1927 imposed development conditions on rights of occupancy. The Land Regulation of 1948
closed loopholes in the old law by specifying the development activities to be undertaken by occupants. Within this
legal framework, the plantation system was created. The labor supply system, which was a necessary concomitant,
was legalized by the Master and Native Servants Ordinance
of 1923.

Credit restrictions adopted in 1923 further limited African development (Rodney 1980:158). Land possession became a prerequisite for agricultural credit. The security demanded by the Land Bank against loans was a mortgage on
a freehold, or leasehold interest in land, or a mortgage on a
right of occupancy having not less than fifteen years to run.
This requirement effectively excluded Africans. The Land
Bank Ordinance of 1947 granted long-term loans (up to
thirty years) for the acquisition of interest or title to agricultural land; short-term loans (maximum five years) were for
buying seed and agricultural equipment and for meeting
the costs of cultivation, harvesting, processing, and marketing crops (Fimbo 1974:135).

Plantations had access to international capital markets
that African smallholders could not draw upon. William
Jones (1968:157) speculates that those markets were closed
to farm credit banks or even national governments seeking
funds for smallholders. The exclusion of farm credit banks
would effectively neutralize the African cooperative society, which was formed to give greater leverage to individual
farmers. The exclusion of national governments would
limit the ability of government land banks to fund African

farmers. In effect, only the plantations belonging to multinational corporations (for example, tea estates owned by Brooke Bond) would have access to these capital markets.

Colonial rule transformed the precapitalist land tenure systems in order to implement an agricultural policy responsive to metropolitan industrial and commercial interests. The effect was not merely to restructure production. Colonial agricultural policy impaired nutrition and thereby undermined the health of Africans.

In the period from 1884 to 1914, the Germans alienated some five hundred thousand hectares of land and created a plantation economy with sisal, coffee, cotton, tea, rubber, and cinchona (for quinine to treat malaria) as the main crops (Ruthenberg 1964; World Bank 1961). In the last decade of German rule, and especially after the Maji Maji rebellion in 1905–1906, the colonial administration increasingly supported the views that plantations alone could not achieve the desired level of production, that conditions were unsuitable for settling German farmers on family holdings, and that therefore African production should be encouraged. These views continued to represent colonial policy after 1919, when the country came under British administration. Africans were encouraged to produce cash crops, mainly coffee and cotton. To secure its control, the new government repatriated German settlers and sold their plantations; until the process was completed, few new land grants were made.[2]

> By the terms of the peace treaty all Germans, missionaries as well as settlers, were required to leave Tanganyika and surrender their property. Their estates, upon the quick recovery of which the immediate revival of Tanganyika's economic prosperity might well have depended, were left vacant. There was nothing in the treaty to suggest that the land formerly alienated to German settlers should be restored to tribal ownership. It was, therefore, with considerable annoyance that prospective buyers with capital to develop the former German sisal estates learned that no German land could be alienated until the Tanganyika Order in Council setting up the Mandate had been published [July 20, 1922]. Because of this Tanganyika was unable to benefit from the post-war boom. (Ingham 1958:9)

2. Only twelve thousand hectares were restored to African owner-

In the years 1922 to 1925, the administration established the legal framework for agricultural production, which expanded rapidly after 1925. Exports rose in value from U.K. £1.3 million in 1922 to £3.9 million in 1928. The sisal, coffee, rubber, and cotton plantations that had been owned by Germans passed into British, Asian, and Greek hands. (Under the terms of the League mandate, the government could not discriminate as it did in Kenya.) In the next two decades, however, the worldwide economic depression and the dislocation of World War II set back production. The overall emphasis of British policy in this period was less on agricultural development than on orderly administration, which was in accordance with the League mandate. The value of exports did not rise again until after 1946. Then it rose from £16.2 million in 1948 to £44.3 million in 1958 (World Bank 1961).

A Tanganyika Territory Legislative Council (1926) sessional paper on African labor and the production of economic crops summed up the priorities that governed agricultural policy, at least till World War II. The first priority was the supply of migrant labor to work on European estates; the second, African production of cash crops, especially cotton; and the final, the planting of food crops for domestic consumption. While acknowledging the problem of periodic famine and the vital need to increase the supply of locally grown foodstuffs, the government encouraged peasant cultivation of crops for sale or export, and cotton or other seed was distributed free of cost: the decision to make seed distribution conditional upon the cultivation of food crops in certain areas was left to the discretion of the administrative officer. But in no circumstances was food or cash crop cultivation to take precedence over wage employment. On this the Legislative Council's instructions were unequivocal: "No steps should be taken by Administrative Officers or the Agricultural Department to induce natives who have contracted the habit of working on farms in their neighbourhood to abandon that habit in order to grow their own crops for sale or export."

The agricultural officers assigned to various districts were concerned not with food but with cash crops. For example,

---

ship after World War I (see Ingham 1958:9). Germans were allowed back after 1925.

the officer assigned to Songea District in 1928 had been sent to Malawi for special training in teaching Africans to grow tobacco (Tanganyika Territory Department of Agriculture 1930). The one concession made to food cultivation was the insistence on root crops (for example, cassava and sweet potatoes) as provision against famine. The effect of this policy was the substitution of a staple containing little of nutritional value for the traditional millets, which were rich in proteins and vitamins.

Further support for the contention that cash crops took precedence over food crops comes from reports on agricultural research. The British inherited a research station at Amani from the Germans but did not put it into operation until 1928. In 1930/1931, they decided on a five-year research program: crop investigations were to focus on coffee, sisal, tea, cinchona, and pasture and browse plants. Not until 1939 were proposals drafted for a general scheme to improve African food crops and, because of World War II, not for another ten years were they implemented (Great Britain Colonial Office 1930/31, 1939, 1941–1944).

When Tanzania became a United Nations trust territory in 1946, a Labour government was in power in Britain, and British colonial policy changed.[3] Efforts were made toward economic development, though immediately after the war less importance was attached to African commercial farming than to plantations and large-scale farming. This was the period of the groundnut scheme and the extension of European rights of occupancy.

---

3. Brett (1973) believes this was not so much a change of policy as the implementation of policy created after World War I. He explains this consistency in terms of the initial stimulus to colonial development in the years immediately after World War I when the threat to political stability in Britain was at its height. He sees the same factors continuing to operate during the 1920s, culminating in the passage in 1929 of the Colonial Development Act, which he characterizes as "a much misunderstood and underestimated piece of legislation." The situation changed in the 1930s when the apparent potential for colonial trade and development was reduced; after the depression, with rising prosperity and a return to earlier optimism, the British attempted to rectify the limitation of the 1929 legislation by adopting the Colonial Development and Welfare Act in 1940. Aid efforts in the 1940s and 1950s were based on that act. Flint (1983) has an altogether different argument, which centers on the failure of British attempts to plan decolonization; his evidence supports my contention that policy did change.

The groundnut scheme launched by the British government's Overseas Food Corporation in 1947 is the development project most often cited to illustrate the shortcomings of colonial agricultural policy. Briefly, the plan was to develop 107 units, each of 30,000 acres, of which 80 units were to be in Tanzania, 17 units in Zambia, and 10 in Kenya. Groundnuts were to be the unique crop planted on the 3,210,000 acres, only half of which would be under cultivation at any one time. Annual production was expected to attain 600,000 tons within five years. (By comparison, the production of groundnuts in the whole of Africa was 4,000,000 tons in 1960 [Jalée 1974:33].) The scheme was designed to meet the needs for fats and animal feed, not of Africa, but of Britain. Its promoters in colonial Tanzania did not consult the peasants of the Kongwa area, who knew that it was subject to drought and that the soils were unusually hard, which is why it was uninhabited. Instead low population density was a reason for siting the 80 units at Kongwa, since no peasants would be displaced. (According to Iliffe [1979:441], displacement was politically unthinkable.) Frankel (1953) says that Africans were regarded as obstacles and the plan called for almost total reliance on mechanization: belief in the power of the machine was part of the tenet that capital could do anything. The scheme foundered on all counts: drought, hard soils, and bush— the woodland or *miombo* that encroaches on uncultivated land.[4]

In the early 1950s agricultural policy was implemented through three departments. The Department of Agriculture was responsible for organizing local markets, providing famine and flood relief, improving production through the supply of better seeds, introducing new crops, popularizing better methods of land use, guiding Africans on irrigation and land reclamation, running nurseries, controlling agricultural credit, and carrying out agricultural research and education. The Veterinary Department handled cattle markets, slaughterhouses, meat inspection, the leather industry, animal health (including the control of tsetse fly), animal breeding, and animal husbandry. The Department of Water Development and Irrigation had responsibility for provid-

4. For a brief account of the elaborate medical and public health services planned for the groundnut scheme see Winteler 1949.

ing drinking water for people and animals through the construction of wells and small dams (some with irrigation projects). Upon completion the management of these water projects was transferred to African local government. The projects were financed mainly by government credits that had to be repaid with interest by local government from tax revenues (Ruthenberg 1964:31).

The measures introduced by the agricultural department may be grouped in three categories: (1) anti-erosion measures, for example, compulsory tie-ridging (an indigenous method), terracing, contour cultivation, destocking of cattle herds, and control of grazing; (2) improved methods of cultivation and of animal husbandry, for example, destruction of old cotton plants, mulching of coffee, cattle dipping, stall feeding, and bush clearance; and (3) famine prevention, for example, compulsory production of some drought-resistant root crop like cassava.

The policies, often drafted under pressure for more rapid change and in the absence of sufficient staff, at best arrested the spontaneous development of productive forces and at worst destroyed African relations of production (von Freyhold 1979:4). The government tended to adopt blanket formulas and apply them nationwide, often without prior experimentation. To combat soil erosion, for example, agricultural officers required Africans to reduce cattle herds by fixed percentages and, in mountainous areas, enforced contour or tie-ridges and bench terracing. The results of the land usage scheme in the Uluguru mountains were negative: rice yields were frequently better on untreated land than on terraces, and bench terracing led to the exposure of subsoil (Cliffe 1972:19). Colonial policies were made compulsory because the colonialists regarded the African peasant as inherently conservative, instead of healthily skeptical. In the face of growing resistance, force was used to ensure that the regulations were obeyed. Traditional agricultural practices were often misunderstood. For example, colonial authorities opposed the use of fire because it led to soil erosion; they overlooked the fact that it cleared areas of harmful insects, rodents, and diseases such as rusts harbored in the soil (Gerlach 1965:248). And in the absence of mechanical and chemical aids, fire shortened the work of felling trees, while ashes fertilized the soil.

Ruthenberg summarized the economic development efforts of the early 1950s:

It may almost be considered a rule for small agricultural schemes in Tanganyika that in the beginning some successes are achieved, whereupon optimistic reports are written (at least one was concerned with showing the United Nations that successful work was being done in developing the country); then, however, obstacles arise and the project is abandoned. The personnel change. After a few years hardly anybody knows that there had been a scheme which had failed. (1964:59)

Not until the late 1950s was a strategy for African agricultural development worked out. It relied mainly on the persistence of extension officers in an expanded agricultural service to persuade peasants to improve existing farms; on closely supervised projects—for example, irrigation, ranching, and plantation schemes; and on organized sales through cooperatives and marketing boards.

The balance sheet, as the country approached independence, would list in the negative column, in addition to the failure of the groundnut scheme, the failure to mechanize smallholder farming, to make profitable the mechanized Tanganyika Agricultural Corporation farms, to achieve agricultural improvement by compulsion, to persuade people of the benefits of erosion-control measures, and to improve animal husbandry, especially methods of grazing. On the positive side, the following successes could be counted: the increase in market production by peasants, associated with increased extension personnel and increased funds for the agricultural department; the expansion of production through the encouragement and support of cash crops, which resulted in increased income; and the introduction of simple and profitable innovations by agricultural extension workers once the use of compulsion was abandoned.[5]

This account of colonial agricultural policy in Tanzania differs somewhat from that of Brett (1973), who, in contrasting it with settler agriculture in Kenya, found policy in Tanzania to favor African agriculture. In fact, that is what the government believed it was doing. The East Africa

5. For a more positive assessment see Fuggles-Couchman 1964; the author was an assistant commissioner for agriculture in colonial Tanzania.

Royal Commission, established by Britain in 1953 to examine measures required to improve living standards in East
Africa, noted that a "consistent policy of considering African interests to come first has been pursued since the beginning of the British Mandate" (1956:22). From another perspective, it can be seen that this policy was not pursued for
the majority of the African population of Tanzania. Primary
emphasis was on cash crops for export—whether produced
by Europeans or Africans—at the expense of food production for domestic consumption. Government agricultural
extension programs actually affected only a small number
of Africans. If we exclude the people of Usukuma, a large
area to the southeast of Lake Victoria, who grew cotton (an
essential raw material for Britain's textile industry),[6] we
find that official encouragement of African peasant production was confined to a few small, densely populated areas,
with two to three hundred thousand people in each, that is,
Bukoba (west of Lake Victoria), Kilimanjaro and the Usambara mountains in the northeast, and the Southern Highlands. According to Tanganyika's *General Census* of 1957,
the combined population of these four areas was just over
one million (Tanganyika 1963). The population of Usukuma also numbers a little over a million, while the total
African population approached nine million. Thus three-
quarters of the African population was not included in
this program.

In most areas, agriculture was untouched and in many,
this lack of any investment by government or private enterprise left Africans without the means of raising cash for
taxes and other needs, forcing them to migrate in search of
work. Most migrant labor was drawn from four provinces—
Western, Central, Southern, and Southern Highlands—with
a combined population in 1957 of 2.7 million.[7] According

6. For a critical study of the agricultural development of Usukuma, see
De Wilde 1967, 2:ch. 6.
7. In 1957, the only year for which such figures exist, the areas that
supplied migrant workers had, for the most part, quite small populations,
while the areas that benefited from government agricultural programs
were, on the whole, quite large. The following sources of labor are taken
from Gulliver (1955:i), census figures are from Tanganyika (1963): Southern Highlands (Uwanda 9,477, Ulambia 15,803, Umambwe 25,115,
Unyamwanga 34,706, Unyiha 54,384, Usafwa 63,027, Ukinga 65,467,
Upangwa 70,721, and Ubena 195,802); Southern Province (Unyasa 65,514,

to Gulliver, "It is clear that the tribes and areas which regularly supply large numbers of migrant workers are those whose current resources are poor—almost too poor in fact to satisfy even the low standard of living of their peoples" (1955:i).

A Lack of Markets

Agriculture is the basis of important market relationships that affect development as they spread through the economy (Beckford 1973:143). For example, they spread forward to create industry because primary products require some form of processing before they are exported. They also spread backward into the local economy because commercial agricultural farms must purchase some supplies locally, and their demand creates income and employment opportunities.

Plantation economies distort this picture of agricultural development and market expansion in several ways. Plantation enterprises are frequently foreign-owned and vertically integrated, that is, the same overseas firm owns commercial farms, processing plants, and transportation (for example, banana boats). Vertically integrated plantations are relatively self-sufficient (William Jones 1968:154), and they cross national boundaries to establish linkages within the structure of the parent company and not within individual national economies (Beckford 1973:147). Vertical integration has a negative impact on market relationships because it dissipates the spread of development and minimizes transactions among national industries.

African agriculture might have survived the lack of government investment in the labor supply areas and developed into a productive sector if a new marketing structure had been created to replace the old trading networks destroyed by colonial conquest. There are two types of market

---

Ungoni 68,223, Ungindo 88,397, Umakua 123,316, Umwera 138,210, Uyao 144,198, Umakonde 33,897); Western Province (Ufipa 86,462, Uha 289,792, Unyamwezi 363,258); and Central Province (Uturu 195,709, Ugogo 299,417). Areas that benefited from government programs were Lake Province (Buhaya 325,539, Usukuma 1,093,539); Northern Province (Uchagga 318,167); Southern Highlands (Unyakyusa 219,678); and Tanga Province (Usambara 193,802).

to be considered—internal and external. Internal markets are local ones, the African equivalent of Western shopping centers; external markets are world markets for cash crops (Bauer and Yamey 1968). The two are related in that the capital gained from the sale of cash crops in external markets and the marketing structure developed for their sale are necessary inputs to local market development.

The East African situation is often contrasted with that of West Africa, where markets are said to be an indigenous institution, predating the colonial period (Hodder 1965). Historians taking this position maintain that markets and trade diffused into East Africa from elsewhere. Alpers (1969), for example, maintains that regional trade networks developed in the coastal hinterlands of Tanzania only in the early nineteenth century. But evidence to support a nationalist history has come to light. Before 1800 the people of Upare in northeastern Tanzania had market systems that catered to both the members of their own society and foreigners (Kimambo 1969:25). Various forms of economic exchange were held in internal rotating markets or in border markets fixed specifically for exchange with neighboring peoples.

Gray and Birmingham suggest that there was a market-oriented commerce in East Africa but that it disintegrated under European contact in the nineteenth century: "The pre-colonial economic tragedy of East and Central Africa principally consists of the dissipation and disruption of those industrial and specialised skills under the impact of violence and the slave trade so that eventually they were judged by colonial governments to be irrelevant and incapable of exploiting the opportunities which improved communications were to bring to twentieth century Africa" (1970:12). Kjekshus (1977:112, 125) confirms the existence of indigenous markets in the precolonial era and the negative influence on them of overseas trade introduced in the nineteenth century.

The colonialists, however, proceeded on the assumption that Arab and Asian traders introduced markets to the East African coast and that with German rule, the creation of plantations, and the building of railways, trade began to spread inland. And chroniclers of the colonial period take the position that colonial administration facilitated market development where no markets had existed (Good 1971). Import firms were mainly European, while the smaller wholesalers and retailers were Asian and Arab. Permanent shops were established at various centers where there were European farmers, administrative officers, or missionaries (Hawkins 1965:20). But whether or not indigenous markets existed (and I think they did), the question of the effect of colonial administration on later African market development remains.

The East Africa Royal Commission found that colonial government policies were restrictive and tended to discourage African participation in the market economy. It criticized the system of state trading by government-fostered and partly government-sponsored institutions: "We have come to the conclusion that a continuance of this state-marketing system is having a deleterious effect on the proper exercise of the commercial system of distribution and that it is now a retarding factor in the economic development of East Africa. We also consider that it is a hindrance to efficient African participation in the commerce and economy of the territories as a whole" (East Africa Royal Commission 1956:65). The commission also criticized the system of licensing and administrative control to which the distributive trade was subjected for not achieving the intended effect of assisting Africans. Other policies faulted for not obtaining the desired objective were credit restrictions adopted ostensibly to protect Africans from indebtedness; quality regulations to protect the public against adulteration; differential pricing of export crops between domestic and overseas markets to restrain the rise in the money cost of living; and restrictions on the use of marketing facilities in order to rationalize them. In general the commission found the marketing mechanism to be elaborate, complex, and expensive, and disadvantageous to the African.

One result was that inter-African contacts established in the precolonial era were broken; in the future intercourse would be controlled by the state. A second result was that no modern system of food distribution developed in the place of old trading networks. The importance of local markets to the health of Africans is most obvious when natural disasters occur: markets afford growers an opportunity to make good shortfalls in their own food production. Food shortages may be localized and temporary, but if communications are poor and local markets lacking, famine may result. Of course the purchase of food is only one way to supplement deficient diets, and the existence of markets may be a necessary but not sufficient condition of adequate food consumption. Nutrition experts also stress the need to increase food production and improve food distribution and storage (Mzingi 1969).

The East Africa Royal Commission noted that the goal of colonial policy was to prevent food shortages; in order to achieve security in the food supply, district and regional self-sufficiency were encouraged. At various times and in various districts, African producers were discouraged from marketing food surpluses beyond the limits of particular regions, or even particular districts, lest a food shortage occur at some later date. "But the effects of the system of district self-sufficiency are not in doubt," the report concludes. "It perpetuates the vicious circle in which all subsistence economy moves, owing to the absence of those wider markets which alone can ensure that a crop failure in one area can be overcome by attracting supplies from further afield" (East Africa Royal Commission 1956:66).

One can see the purpose of restrictive government policy as Hawkins (1965:31) does: by preventing growers from selling their crops for cash at harvest time, the government sought to protect them from running short of food later in the year and having to buy foodstuffs at much higher prices. Hawkins's criticism is that this restriction is paternalistic, perpetuates subsistence agriculture, and denies Africans the opportunity to learn how a market economy operates.

The long-term effect was to arrest capital development. As Bernstein (1977:65) points out, colonial regulations often dictated very precisely the type of production process to be employed and tied producers to the use of particular cultivation techniques that usually involved a greater expenditure of labor time. With marketing strictly controlled, this process led to a cycle of indebtedness, instead of to savings and productive investment.

Communications Networks

The question of distribution was especially critical in colonial Tanzania because of the sparse and scattered population in some of the food-deficient areas, and because of the country's poor system of communications (Hawkins 1965: 31). The development of the communications network was

slow and never extensive. Only 10,000 kilometers were
added to the road network between 1938 and 1960; the percentage of main roads remained constant at under 20 percent. The railways gained 700 kilometers between 1938 and
1953; at independence the network was 3,300 kilometers
(Stephens 1968:82).

Many of the roads and railways were constructed by the
Germans before 1918, and Hailey (1938) argues that the
roads were based on a wartime system that had little regard
for correct alignment and grading, which are important for
motorized vehicles. British resources after World War I
were used mainly in road improvement. Hailey stated,
"Given, however, the large area of the territory, and the
character of the existing railway communications, which
were designed for strategic rather than commercial purposes, the mileage of main roads is clearly still inadequate.
The greater part of both the main and district roads is un-
surfaced, and the district roads are for the most part unsuited for traffic in wet weather" (1938:1554). From 1938 to
1960 there was about a 36 percent increase in the total kilometers of all roads and a 28 percent increase in railways.

Luttrell (1972:126) disagrees with Hailey about the purpose for which the system was designed. Luttrell argues
that the country's transport network was externally oriented via terminal links with the ports of Mtwara, Tanga,
and Dar es Salaam to European and empire markets. In
other words, the system was created by the German and
British colonial regimes to service the export sector. As a
result, regions possessing a high potential in the production
of those agricultural commodities or industrial ores that
have no substantial external market were not developed
and, given high transport costs and weak internal markets,
remain relatively difficult to develop. Kilosa District, for example, benefited from the central railway line that traversed
the district and from a main north/south road. In Songea,
the main road extended only as far as the district capital
and there was no railway connection. The lack of adequate
communications probably prolonged head porterage, the
use of men to transport goods, in Songea and constituted a
further drain on labor resources.

The transport network was only one element of the inadequate infrastructure upon which local production had to
depend: marketplaces, storage depots, and other facilities

were also lacking. Storage, for example, is an important factor in market supplies throughout the year and for reserve in times of famine. The Great Britain Colonial Office (1950:3–6) stated that storage was so deficient in Tanganyika that it was normal to ship maize to Kenya after the harvest and to ship Kenyan maize to Tanganyika at the end of the season; the report also noted that African methods of storage appeared to be superior to government techniques. The government invested little in the creation of storage facilities before the 1950s.

The process of decapitalization—in which Tanzania became a source for metropolitan capital accumulation and development—generated unproductiveness. Where subsistence agriculture was maintained (without improvements) alongside the cultivation of cash crops for the metropolitan market, the peasants endured increasing poverty. Their immiseration took the form of declining productivity and increasing dependence on a monetized market for food supplies, which led to malnutrition and ill health. Colonial agricultural policy was premised on a system of land tenure alien to the customs Africans had evolved over centuries. The policy of private ownership would have been less destructive had Africans been allowed to adapt to it, but through the administrative apparatus of indirect rule and the financial structures that restricted credit, all but the elites were barred from participation. African women suffered more than men from this exclusion because the new system passed landholdings from women's to men's control and because most other avenues of development were closed to women.

The availability of money to develop the infrastructure was ultimately determined by colonial fiscal policy, which was concerned to ensure self-sufficiency and balanced budgets (Brett 1973:141). Overall colonial policy was reflected in the conservative management of money at the district level, where investment depended on local treasuries. The immediate effect of this arrangement was to handicap market development, which discouraged African food producers; in the long run, because the poorer districts collected less tax and eventually had less money for capital expenditures, the system exacerbated regional inequalities.

5

DIFFERENTIATION AND INEQUALITY

Precolonial Tanzania was not a homogeneous society in terms of either culture or the way people supported themselves. The diversity of precapitalist economies astonishes the eye accustomed to the homogeneity of North America. Colonialism imposed on these varied societies a universal rule of law, which produced a conformity that was rigid and not as progressive as the unity dictated by capitalism.

Paradoxically, colonialism also distinguished people in a new way by segregating them in groups called tribes, and capitalism differentiated societies economically to a degree not previously experienced. Regions became polarized, and within regions, social classes expressed the new disparities.

The resultant inequality had profound implications for the health, nutrition, and population distribution of Africans; some of these implications are probably still not understood. Food was more widely available, but the variety was restricted. Some land became more productive in the colonial era; but the fruits of their productive labor did not redound to the majority of Africans or raise their standards of living. Some land became less productive, and the standard of living of Africans in these areas fell. Population was more concentrated in some areas and more sparsely distributed in others. These differences were neither random nor geographical accidents but the result of human agency.

The importance of the evidence for involution and the process of differentiation and growing inequality in the country is that it demonstrates the pattern of structural underdevelopment, that is, a pattern of social and legal institutions responsible for regional disparities in a way not accounted for by the conventional model of a dual economy.

The Myth of Dual Economies

In its report on measures required to improve living standards in East Africa under the heading "the dual economy and its implications," the East Africa Royal Commission defined economic development as the evolution "from an almost complete dependence upon subsistence activities to activities which are concerned with the earning of money either by wage labour or by producing goods for sale in the market" (1956:46). In other words, the commission equated development with capitalism. The commission thought that the persistence of subsistence economies, in which the development of modern commercial markets was necessarily inhibited, was the principal reason for the basic poverty of East Africa. Obscured from their view by the ideological blinders they wore was the economic impact of capitalist penetration on the countryside. Using norms derived from classical liberal economics, the commission calculated that poverty would disappear with development:

> The growth of income and the raising of living standards, which the division of labour through exchange has made possible in money economies, is a process of expansion and differentiation both in space and in time, brought about by the widening of markets and by the inauguration of activities which may span considerable periods of time. The raising of income and living standards is nothing but the expansion of the exchange economy, the division of labour as between persons and regions and the spacing of activity over time, from activity for the present to activity directed to the future. (Ibid.)

The commission accepted the dual model, as did many contemporary economists (Fei and Ranis 1964; Lewis 1954, 1955). The concept of dualism was first outlined by J. H. Boeke, a Dutch sociologist writing about Indonesia in 1942, who divided the colonial economies into a modern, capitalist, export sector (the enclave) and a traditional, subsistence sector (the hinterland) (Frank 1971). The concept was extended from economic to social structures by Jacques Lambert (n.d.) in an analysis of Brazil, with the effect of justifying the attribution of inferior characteristics, such as lower intellectual capacity, to Africans. Dualism was adopted by some Marxists with an important modification: the two sectors were seen not as separate but as dynamically interrelated (Brett 1973; Seidman 1972; Szentes 1971). Frank (1969) initiated a debate on dualism by attacking Latin American communists for accepting this concept and for basing their political strategy upon it. The Latin American communist parties believed in the desirability of extending capitalist penetration of the feudal countryside and of completing the bourgeois democratic revolution as a necessary prerequisite to socialism. Frank's position was that there exists no dual society in the world today, that all non-socialist societies are integral parts of the imperialist system. Frank rejected the position that socialist revolution is tied to a certain level of development of the productive forces, pointing to successful revolutions in nonindustrialized countries. There is no question of delaying socialist revolution until capitalism asserts hegemony.

Seidman, in an early work, *Comparative Development Strategies in East Africa* (1972), applied the neoclassical economic model of duality to East Africa. She admitted of a dynamic relation between the two sectors insofar as the hinterland is a source of labor power for the enclave. In all other respects she accepted the neoclassical description of the enclave as the sector shaped by colonial rule to export a few raw materials and to import manufactured goods, and of the hinterland as the sector that perpetuates the ancient subsistence agrarian economy. Excerpts from Seidman's book appeared in the *East African Journal* in April, May, and June 1970. In February 1972, the *Journal* printed a stinging reply by Mafeje, who attacked Seidman's picture of the unchanging and unresponsive peasant as a colonial myth, pointing out that Africans responded to European penetration by selling their labor power—an indication of adaptation:

> Although dualistic theories of economic growth are, ostensibly, an objective description of the colonial legacy in Africa and elsewhere, in reality they are permeated with colonialist assumptions. First, the idea that the colonial world, despite the pervasive and disruptive penetration by the colonialists, could be realistically divided into urban (European) and "Native" areas is colonial. Second, the tendency to discount cheap "native labour" as an important factor in the development of "European areas" in spite of ceaseless efforts at the beginning by colonial authorities to force African labour out of the traditional economy, is colonial. Third, the belief that

only Europeans and European-like individuals have a propensity for development and economic rationality and that the "natives" are basically "subsistence men", is colonial.

Mafeje (1973) later carried this analysis further, giving reasons for rejecting all theories of dual economies. He examined the economies of southern, central, and eastern Africa and showed how their precapitalist economic formations were destroyed in the period of colonial rule: capitalist domination was complete, and village autonomy and the traditional mode of production were "an inexcusable mythology." Capitalist hegemony has not depended on the emergence of a proletariat, which Mafeje argued had been delayed by mitigating factors—tenuous ties to land, dependence on kin, labor migration. Underdevelopment and dependency were actively maintained through the separation of production relations from capital and market relations. If this separation were not maintained, "the system would collapse or move in a different direction" (ibid.:46). Bernstein (1977:64) believed that peasants retained limited control of the organization of the production process but that commodity relations ultimately determined peasant production and reproduction; commodity relations, which tied the producers more closely to particular kinds of production, included economic and political measures such as cultivation regulations, compulsory land-improvement schemes, and credit and extension services.

The existence of colonial development projects, as well as schemes to improve the health and welfare of Africans, can be explained in terms of capital accumulation. In some instances, development assistance such as peasant production of tobacco in Songea was really to the advantage of the colonial government: not only did peasant agriculture absorb unemployed workers during recessions, it was also a direct source of capital. In other instances, welfare schemes were a necessity created by the colonial labor migration system; they had to be undertaken to prevent productivity from falling so low that it would threaten the reproduction of labor power. But the investments were minimal, as Wolpe (1972:440) points out, because soil conservation measures, irrigation schemes, fencing, mechanization, and agricultural training required heavy capital outlays. Large-scale investment in the labor supply areas would make cheap labor costly because the accumulation advantages to capitalism deriving from migrant labor would be lost or reduced if the surplus were used in the rural areas.

The World Bank recognized that the comparatively high ratios of capital formation that characterized Tanzania in the colonial period were partly due to "the fact that much of the basic demand for food is satisfied in the subsistence sector and that, as a consequence, a higher proportion of monetary income can be devoted to capital formation than in an economy where monetary income covers the bulk of consumption needs" (1961:25). What the bank ignored in its first report on Tanzania was precisely the failure of the subsistence sector to produce enough food and the increasing necessity for a cash income to purchase basic commodities. The result was what Bernstein calls the "simple reproduction squeeze"—a reduction in levels of consumption or an intensification of commodity production, or both simultaneously. Its purpose, Bernstein writes, was to intensify household labor in order "to maintain or increase the supply of commodities without capital incurring any costs of management and supervision of the production process" (1977:64–65).

When the East Africa Royal Commission blamed African economies for inhibiting the development of modern commercial markets and thereby perpetuating basic poverty, it indicted the victims of the colonial suppression of indigenous capitalism, rather like the doctor blaming the sick for their illnesses. Capitalist penetration of the Third World, under the protection of the colonial state, failed to carry with it capitalist economic development.

Uneven Development

Dos Santos (1970) maintains that inequality in underdeveloped countries is the internal reproduction in acute form of the unequal character of capitalist development at the international level. Capitalist development is unequal or uneven because some parts of the system are developed at the expense of other parts. As in metropolitan-peripheral relations, within underdeveloped countries resources are transferred from the most backward and dependent sectors

to the most advanced and dominant ones; this transfer explains the inequality, deepens it, and transforms it into a
necessary structural element of the world economy.[1]

By tracing agricultural policy in Tanzania through the
German and British administrations in chapter 4, we followed the evolution of the process that dos Santos describes. Changes in the agricultural sector from the early
nineteenth century developed in response to both long-distance caravan trade and the plantation economy of Zanzibar
(Iliffe 1971). By the time of the German conquest, surpluses
were produced in many parts of the country. Despite severe
losses incurred in the resistance to German colonization,
African agriculture constituted a rival to the European plantation industry introduced at the turn of the twentieth century: there was a constant struggle between European farmers, who sought to reduce the African to a proletarian, and
Africans, who wanted to retain the maximum amount of
economic independence (ibid.:13). But the struggle was not
only about labor, it was also about land.

Land is the key resource in agriculture: although Europeans alienated only 1 percent of the land in colonial Tanzania, it was frequently the land with higher grade soil.
This area should not be compared with the total land area,
or even with the 27 percent said by the World Bank to be
suitable for cultivation, but with the 8 percent actually cultivated by Africans (World Bank 1961:82, 461). Berry and
Berry (1969:6) give an even lower estimate of 5 percent for
land cultivated in 1969 (mostly in small holdings, with
only about 0.7 percent in large-scale agriculture). Thus the
proportion of arable land alienated was quite high.

The introduction of property rights may have had a
greater initial impact on internal class structures than on
land ownership per se because, though theoretically communal patterns of ownership were maintained in areas under indirect rule, and property rights applied to Europeans
rather than Africans, in practice the introduction of property rights created tensions that increased with pressure on
available land, while indirect rule empowered a new class
of Africans who controlled land allocation and distribution.

---

1. For a review of the literature on the subject of unequal development
see Special Issue Editorial Collective 1978 and for the views of radical geographers see Santos, O'Keefe, and Peet 1977.

Post (1972:228) suggests that land-use rights were more important in the African context than property rights: because ownership was mediated through the communal group, whether or not the products of the individual's use of the land became his or her private property was the crucial point. With the introduction of cash crops, which increased the demand for acreage, the importance of land-use rights grew, and control over the products became critically important to women. Bernstein (1977:61) makes the more general point that the colonial state was instrumental in organizing the conditions of exploitation of both land and labor. But he does not go on to relate internal class dynamics to the external forces that acted on various regions in the colonial period.

The process of differentation that occurred in Tanzania under colonial rule created great disparities. By 1940 regional inequalities were relatively fixed and rigid. The country was divided into three types of economic region: (1) those that specialized in export production (for example, towns, sisal plantations, and main cash crop areas); (2) surrounding regions that supplied export producers with food and other services (for example, Uzaramo, Uluguru, and Rufiji, which supplied food to Dar es Salaam, and Kondoa, which supplied cattle for the Tanga and Korogwe markets); (3) peripheral regions that either supplied migrant labor or stagnated in near-isolation from the territorial economy. The whole country was focused on export production. Dependence on external economic forces and the growth within the country of regional inequalities are evidence of the emergent pattern of structural underdevelopment (Iliffe 1971:42). Unbalanced development characterized the areas specializing in export production, while stagnation or involution was experienced in the peripheral areas. One form of involution was depopulation.

> Parts of Tabora and Kigoma regions, for example seem to have entered a vicious circle of labour migration and the expansion of the tsetse fly, the absence of men reducing the labour available to clear the bush and thereby allowing the fly to advance and make the area totally uninhabitable. This combination seems to have entirely depopulated the Ugogo/ Ukimbu border by the 1930s, and it may have been one of the most important of all factors in regional underdevelopment—the evidence at present is too scanty to per-

mit a conclusion. In other areas, the reverse process happened: a rapidly growing population, which because of an unsuitable environment or inadequate transport could not produce a cash crop, could reach a point where land shortage and the exhaustion of the soil produced a gradual involution of agriculture in the form of reduced yields and periodic famines. (ibid.:32)

Data from Kilosa and Songea districts substantiate some of Iliffe's points. Table 4 indicates declining productivity for food crops, particularly as regards yields per acre of maize and millet, which I take to be evidence of reduced soil fertility. If the population growth in this period is taken into consideration, then the figures indicate even more strongly the decreasing ability of the peasantry to meet its needs for basic foodstuffs. The trend to increased production of starchy staples such as cassava in Songea would have contributed to a growing malnutrition.

Figures on cash crop production (table 5) support the view that colonial agricultural policy emphasized production for export over domestic consumption. The steady growth of acreage devoted to sisal production in Kilosa and the improved productivity of that land stand out from all the other data: these acres were privately owned plantations managed by Europeans and Asians. Cotton was produced by African peasants until the postwar period, when

Table 4

Food Crop Production in Kilosa and Songea Districts for Selected Years
(yields per acre in pounds; three-year averages)

	Kilosa			Songea[a]		
Crop	1936– 1938	1946– 1948	Percent Increase or Decrease	1936– 1938	1946– 1948	Percent Increase or Decrease
Maize	1,145	561	− 51	900	574	− 36
Millets, sorghum	1,111	511	− 54	800	510	− 36
Beans, pulses, peas	600	482	− 20	400	436	+ 9
Groundnuts	769	1,120	+ 46	534	400	− 25
Cassava	—	—	—	1,334	2,000	+ 50

SOURCE: Compiled from data in Tanganyika Territory, Blue Books (Dar es Salaam: Government Printer), for years mentioned.

NOTE: Figures are for local consumption and export.

[a]Includes Mbinga District.

Table 5
Cash Crop Production in Kilosa and Songea Districts for Selected Years
(three-year averages)

	Kilosa District		Songea District[a]
	Sisal	Cotton	Tobacco
Acres under cultivation			
1926–28	5,700	27,333	500
1931–33	9,148	24,433	500
1936–38	15,500	21,666[b]	1,100
1946–48	45,533	23,143[c]	3,333
Gross quantity of produce (tons)			
1926–28	1,566	2,155[d]	293
1931–33	3,033	2,516[e]	36
1936–38	5,833	1,174[f]	234
1946–48	13,956	300[g]	400

SOURCE: Compiled from data in Tanganyika Territory, Blue Books, for years mentioned.

[a]Includes Mbinga District.

[b]1938 includes 10,000 acres farmed by Africans and 6,000 acres farmed by Europeans.

[c]1946 includes 49,425 African and 1,006 European acres; 1947 includes 3,600 African and 5,400 European acres.

[d]1926/27 includes 400 tons raw and 680 tons ginned cotton.

[e]1932/33 includes cotton seed.

[f]All lint except that 1938 includes 720 tons lint produced by Africans and 300 tons cotton produced by Europeans.

[g]1946 includes 214 tons lint produced by Africans and 118 tons lint produced by Europeans; 1947 includes 122 tons lint produced by Africans and 57 tons lint produced by Europeans.

there was an attempt to curtail African production in favor of European cultivation.

These tables establish low levels of agricultural production in Songea, a necessary condition of labor migration according to Wolpe's (1972:437) findings in South Africa. High output farming would tend to render the population immobile because its labor demands are high as are its economic returns. On the other hand, if output is allowed to drop too low, then the population of the reserves would depend more on subsistence wages, which if not increased would threaten the reproduction of migrant workers.

In the 1930s peasants were encouraged to cultivate tobacco in Songea, but the government did not make a serious effort to support this industry. In 1936 the Ngoni-Matengo Cooperative Marketing Union was created, but

general policy stayed in the hands of the government-con-
trolled Songea District Native Tobacco Board, which received a cess from the marketing union of thirty-four shillings per ninety-kilogram bale. The cess paid for European
supervision and housing, as well as other expenses not directly concerned with marketing (Great Britain Colonial
Office 1949). Production fell after 1943, when prices fell. In
any event, Songea was never the major colonial effort in tobacco production. The European plantations in Iringa District were: in 1958 they produced 2.7 million pounds of
cured leaf (World Bank 1961:381).

Beyond encouraging peasants in a few areas able to produce agricultural commodities desired by an external market, the colonial government did little to develop African
commercial agriculture and virtually nothing to expand
food production. Except for areas like the Uluguru mountains, where fruit and vegetables were cultivated to supply
the Dar es Salaam market, the colonialists provided few in-
centives for the production of foods that could correct dietary imbalances. Compulsory cultivation of root crops offered protection against starvation, but few crops with a
protein or vitamin content that could ward off malnutrition
were produced in quantity for sale. The emphasis placed
on cash crops to the detriment of food production probably
reduced the variety as well as amount of food customarily
available to peasant cultivators. The lack of markets was a
disincentive to the production of surpluses, and the restriction of domestic sales in times of scarcity denied growers
access to purchasable commodities that might supplement
their inadequate reserves. Apparently no such restriction
was placed on overseas export: Kreysler (1973), in a critical
summary of colonial nutrition policy, quotes one instance
of maize exports to Australia during a period of famine.
The result was the degradation of subsistence agriculture
with negative effects on agricultural productivity, which increased as the soil became exhausted. In the long term,
there was a deleterious effect on nutrition and on health. In
view of the magnitude of malnutrition known to colonial
authorities, neither the agricultural nor the medical measures taken were adequate to correct the situation.

6

KILOSA: A
PLANTATION ECONOMY

Plantations and labor reserves are inextricably linked: the latter are creations of the former, not only because plantations employ relatively large numbers of unskilled workers, but also because plantation agriculture—through inefficient use of such resources as land and the tendency to encourage food imports—depresses the indigenous economy (Beckford 1973:140, 144). Myint ascribed the neglect and impoverishment of subsistence agriculture to a deliberate colonial policy, which helped planters maintain low wages on their estates (cited in Brett 1973:191).

Colonial administrations sought metropolitan investment in plantations. They favored the plantation system because it brought newly conquered regions under centralized control, pacified the population, was self-sufficient in economically isolated areas, and created its own infrastructure—communications, public utilities and services, and internal security—relieving the government of these burdens (William Jones 1968:158).

The plantation structure was the leading expatriate sector in Tanzania and sisal was the most important crop it produced (Brett 1973:232, 289). Sisal is a cactus plant that measures ten meters in height at maturity and looks like the top of a giant pineapple. The leaves yield a fiber used as rope or twine. Sisal cultivation was introduced by German colonists first on the southern and northeastern coasts where commodities could be exported by sea, and then, after the construction of the central railroad in the early 1900s, in Kilosa.

While rural in character today, having only the two towns of Kilosa and Kimamba, Kilosa District has never been isolated. The central railway line links it to the capital, Dar es Salaam, and to Mwanza on Lake Victoria. In the nineteenth century, long-distance caravans regularly passed through on their way from the coast to the interior, and Mamboya, located in the northern half of the district, was an important provisioning station for them. Since 1877 Mamboya has been a mission center.

People of the Mamboya area, which was known as Uka-guru, have had contacts with foreigners since the early part of the last century. There are no records of the quality of those contacts or of slave raiding in the area. We do know that in 1884 Karl Peters, a German explorer, met in Mamboya with twelve chiefs, assembled by their leader Saidi Chimola. The purpose of the conference was to negotiate certain "treaties," according to which the Africans handed over large tracts of land "for all time." Thus in Kilosa the Germans were able to establish control without a fight.

The people of Ukaguru were farmers who cultivated maize and millet. They lived in a sort of symbiosis with pastoralists who herded cattle near what is now the Dodoma regional border. Under German rule, the center of economic activity shifted from Mamboya to Mpwapwa, which is to the west of the present district of Kilosa.

The southern half of Kilosa was known as Usagara. Beidelman (1967) believed the early inhabitants of the area came in clan divisions, independently of one another, each clan with its own head. Oral history indicates that leadership above the clan level came into being around 1880 in response to an African challenge from the south, but it may have been a reaction to European encroachment. From that time, chiefs began to rule more than one clan, evidence of consolidation of power.

The people of Usagara engaged in agriculture. According to Chipindulla's (1968) oral history, the main crop was rice, maize or millet being planted where rice could not be grown; but Kjekshus (1977:36) says rice was secondary to sorghum, maize, yams, beans, groundnuts, sesame, and sugarcane. Each family worked its farm plot—shamba in Swahili—of little more than an acre, with most farm work being performed by women and children. Men engaged in other work such as laboring on Arab or Asian cotton farms, for which they were paid in kind, usually in cotton cloth. Surplus food was bartered or exchanged rather than offered for sale since there was no need of money; the clan heads did not levy tax, though they sometimes exacted fines in the form of farm or house-building labor.

The German conquest and administration of Kilosa in the 1890s profoundly changed the political economy of the district and the life of its inhabitants. The Germans converted Kilosa town into a military station, levied a tax of crop dues (later changed to three East African rupees), and introduced the compulsory cultivation of cotton on two-acre plots at Kibanda Hodi, twenty-two kilometers east of Kilosa town along the present railway line. Corporal punishment awaited anyone who failed to comply with the new regulations. Popular resentment was great and culminated with participation in the Maji Maji War of 1905–1906. The people of Usagara besieged the military fort at Kilosa town for three or four days until German reinforcements came from Mpwapwa and defeated the rebels. Sporadic guerrilla fighting is said to have gone on for six or eight weeks, the rebels hiding in the mountains of Ukaguru. (The mountain residents apparently did not participate, although they are known to have revolted in 1893 [Kjekshus 1977:36].) Unknown numbers of rebels died in battle and in the public hangings of captured prisoners that followed. Even more people are thought to have perished in the famine caused by the German policy of destroying all crops and food reserves. One witness gave the following account:

> I was born during the famine of "Homa Homa", which happened after and as a result of the war of "Homa Homa"—Maji Maji as you call it.[1] It was out of sheer luck that I survived. Many children died during that famine. We are told by our elders that people were reluctant to bear more children, for they could not feed them. Only the noble families could afford to have children. Some of the children were abandoned by their parents. A wealthy man could attract and marry many wives. Parents were glad to have the number of mouths to feed reduced by making their daugh-

---

1. *Homa Homa* means "to spear the enemy"; in Kilosa people called the war Homa Homa instead of Maji Maji. This interview was conducted as part of the Maji Maji Research Project, which was carried out by the History Department of the University of Dar es Salaam during 1968–1969. The Maji Maji papers include essays as well as interviews; the collection is housed in the University Library, Dar es Salaam.

ters get married quickly. There was very little dowry. (Maji
Maji Collected Research Project Papers 2/68/2/3/7)

After Maji Maji, the Germans introduced plantation cultivation of sisal and cotton in Kilosa District. A Stuttgart mil-
lionaire opened a huge cotton plantation near Kilosa town
and employed many Europeans thought by the local people
to be ex-convicts; he spent vast sums to mechanize the
farms but succeeded only in ploughing up infertile subsoil.
In 1910 curly-leaf disease destroyed the crop and the experiment ended in 1914, a failure (Iliffe 1979:145). Sisal fared
better despite large investments in decortication machinery
(required to process the leaves), the high cost of transport,
and labor-intensive operations. With its long gestation period, sisal was able to ride out fluctuations in world market prices.

The economy was severely disrupted during World War
I. With the British blockading the port, German troops were
entirely dependent on local food supplies, which they
seized without regard to African needs (Kjekshus 1977:
152). As the defeated Germans withdrew, British and South
African troops resorted to similar practices for provisions.
The effects were felt for five or six years after the war. By
1925 the British were reviving the plantations and alienating more land.

But within five years the worldwide economic depression
intervened, disorganizing the plantation economy. The sisal
planters formed an employers' organization, the Tanganyika Sisal Growers Association, in December 1930; the association controlled wages and working conditions on plantations for nearly thirty years. Wages were paid under a
system that gave full pay only after the assigned work was
completed, which might take thirty to fifty days. Migrant laborers worked under this system on contracts that ranged
from six months to two years (Coulson 1982:45–46). In
1944 the planters organized an agency to recruit workers,
the Sisal Labour Bureau (Silabu) (Iliffe 1979:345).

In World War II, the ability of the growers association to
force plantation labor to work for reduced wages—given
wartime labor shortages which should have driven up wage
rates—can be accounted for only by the threat of military
conscription. According to Iliffe (1979:354), a sisal worker's
real wage was lower after the war than it had been before

the depression and was possibly at an all-time low. The planters did not face organized resistance until the late 1950s; before trade unions existed, workers expressed their dissatisfaction by deserting the estates, by calling in government officers to mediate disputes, and by downing tools. Iliffe characterizes the strikes of this period as anonymous and often riotous, in recognition of weaknesses resulting from lack of leadership—itself a result of individual vulnerability stemming from lack of solidarity—and the ignorance, inexperience, and fears of migrant workers (ibid.: 309–310). The workers were divided, not only by the tribal labels tacked on them by colonialists, but also by the rigid hierarchy of plantation organization.

Skill was the primary divider of the work force. Skilled supervisory personnel, however, were never African, though they might be Arab or Asian, and unskilled African laborers earned dramatically lower salaries (Coulson 1982:46). On sisal plantations migrant workers cut, bundled, and stacked leaves or performed the worst-paid work of clearing, planting, and hoeing. Between these two strata were two others: administrative and service workers who were literate (for example, clerks and medical auxiliaries), and foremen who tended to settle rather than migrate (Iliffe 1979:309). The consequences of this hierarchy according to Beckford (1973:148) were twofold. First, low wages lowered demand for products, which in turn limited the size of markets and precluded production of consumer goods; in contrast, plantation owners and managers engaged in conspicuous consumption of luxury imports and invested in nonproductive assets. Second, the rigid class lines and weak community cohesion of plantation societies restricted social mobility, adversely affecting labor adaptability, and impeded the development of large-scale units of collective action.

The first trade union of sisal workers was formed in Eastern Province in 1956 and was followed the next year by other provincial unions. The Tanganyika Sisal Plantation Workers Union won recognition in 1958. Three years of industrial conflict ensued as strikes multiplied. Planters opposing unionization prohibited meetings and fired workers who joined the nationalist movement. Other owners tried to co-opt union drives by establishing the Central Joint Council for the Sisal Industry with equal representation of work-

ers and employers (Iliffe 1979:540). Labor unrest on the sisal plantations of Kilosa was not reported by the provincial
commissioner until 1958, when he stated that "the feature
of the year was the struggle of Trade Unions for recognition
and their emergence as powerful organizations. A campaign
was mounted by the Tanganyika Sisal and Plantation Workers Union against the traditional and largely nominated estate council of elders and widespread strikes throughout
the industry, particularly in Kilosa and Morogoro Districts,
were called towards the end of the year" (Tanganyika Territory 1959:39).

Health Effects of Plantations

There are good grounds for believing that with the introduction of taxes, plantations, and cash crops, standards of
health and nutrition fell. Plantations expose workers to parasitic and infectious diseases: where irrigation is used, for
example, as on the sugar estates of Kilosa District, the incidence of schistosomiasis (a snail-borne parasitic condition)
increases, and where housing conditions are crowded or
unsanitary, diarrheal diseases are common. Plantation work
also introduces new diseases, such as byssinosis (brown
lung) in sisal processors, and new risk of accidents from
unguarded machinery or poorly maintained equipment.

Plantation economies do not produce food for domestic
consumption and therefore rely on high-priced imports,
which are often paid for with scarce foreign exchange, or,
in periods of war or depression, they rely on domestic produce. High-priced imports do not meet workers' needs for a
cheap, balanced diet, and as a result laborers must spend a
high proportion of their meager wages on starchy staples.
Domestic produce, when not ordered on a regular basis,
may not be plentiful enough to supply subsistence and
plantation needs.

Various official annual reports paint a picture of slow
economic growth in Kilosa District under British rule. Agricultural output of cash crops increased steadily; for example, raw cotton marketed by Africans rose from 1,488 tons
in 1934 to 2,994 tons in 1937 (Tanganyika Territory
1938a:12). But there were frequent failures of food crops,
which caused localized shortages. The failures were due to
overworking the limited land available to Africans in an

area of large European holdings. The limitations were compounded by the influx of Africans from other parts of the country seeking work on sisal plantations to earn cash needed for taxes and other essentials. Some laborers never returned to their homes and settled on land near the estates. In Kilosa District they were accepted as having a status and rights equal to those of the indigenous peoples after residing there for a length of time (Molohan 1959). The colonial report of 1941 noted land scarcity when an agricultural officer tried to get cultivators in the Masanze-Tingida-Rudewa area to allow their overworked land to lie fallow (Tanganyika Territory 1942:11). Pressure on arable acreage was also increased by the planters' tendency to apply the short-term solution of opening up new land to two long-term problems, namely, soil exhaustion and reduced yields; both were caused by the failure to use fertilizers on their estates. This failure was evidence of environmental carelessness, by the standards of the time, and the desire to keep costs down.

Gradually, courts, roads, schools, and health facilities were built, though the quality of services was inferior. But the health of the population was poor: smallpox was still endemic in 1939, outbreaks of dysentery and cerebrospinal meningitis were periodically reported, and widespread hunger required frequent famine-relief measures. In 1940, in the course of recruitment for the East African Military Labour Service and the Kenya and Uganda Railway and Harbours, there was occasion to measure the health status of the population. The provincial commissioner reported:

> A disquieting factor has been the physical condition of the so-called able-bodied section of the community as shown by the large number of recruits rejected on medical grounds. Malnutrition, coupled with disease, moves in a vicious circle. . . . Many of these people have insufficient energy to do a full day's work owing to the poorness of their diet and are, consequently, unable to grow sufficient food to pay their taxes and to feed themselves sufficiently well to overcome the effects of malnutrition. (Tanganyika Territory 1941:12)

There is no more detailed information on health status in the colonial period than the remarks of government officials in annual reports. The lack of data reflects colonial neglect rather than the absence of ill health. Ill paid as plantation workers were, migrant laborers were often better off than

Africans in the stagnant subsistence economy (see Waterman's 1975 summary of the debate about unionized wage workers constituting a privileged and conservative aristocracy). To appreciate the health effects of plantations, it is necessary to look beyond the labor force to other inhabitants of the district. Evidence of widespread and increasingly chronic malnutrition comes from oral histories gathered in a part of the district. Mkunduge (1973), who recorded oral histories, found accounts of frequent famine in Gairo, an area in the northwestern corner of Kilosa District. Some of the oral accounts concord with written district records. According to Mkunduge, the people of Gairo attributed the food shortages to a variety of conditions such as drought and flood, pests and vermin, miscalculation in food storage, and maladjustment to changing availability of food (see table 6). The Gairo chronology corresponds very closely to Rigby's (1969:21) chronology of famines, droughts, and heavy rains in Ugogo, which is due west of Gairo.

The consequences of food shortage need not, of course, be famine. The outcome depends in part on the redistributive mechanisms of the society. Wisner (1973) maintains that peasants have a very large repertoire of effective responses to drought and that government measures are usually out of step with indigenous responses. The example of colonial government restrictions on sales of foodstuffs in Kilosa District supports Wisner's claim. It is important to look, therefore, at those mechanisms that have operated in the past in Gairo in response to famine and food shortages:

1. *Exchanges.* One person could obtain food from another, either as a gift or in exchange for livestock (or more recently, money). The sale of animals for grain is a two-way adjustment, a practical form of food insurance. Animals accumulated in good years that would otherwise die in drought years are exchanged for grain reserves. Exchanges, however, have sometimes caused critical food shortages in Gairo (what Mkunduge [1973:74–75] calls miscalculation in food storage and maladjustment to changing availability of food). The colonial government tried to restrict the movement of food across district boundaries by setting up road blocks.

2. *Food substitutes.* In times of crop failure of staple foods, a wide range of grasses, seeds, roots, bamboo, and so on is consumed (ibid.:76).

3. *Farm dispersal.* The practice of scattering farm holdings throughout the area and even in surrounding districts means that in any given year there is sufficient microvariation in climatic conditions for a farmer to obtain some food from one of these plots (ibid.:82).

4. *Wage labor.* Large numbers of peasants seek employment on sisal and other plantations in the district (the local populace does not customarily work on these estates). On the other hand, this practice increases the estate demands on local food supplies and, when wage workers cannot grow their own food, further reduces food stores in areas like Gairo.

5. *Migration.* Individuals, families, villages, or even whole clans will temporarily leave their homes in times of prolonged drought and return when rain comes and farms can once again be cultivated.

Two points about Mkunduge's summary of famines in Gairo Division are of interest. First, although people invoked natural causes, the famines correspond very closely with historically specific struggles. The dates of almost every reported famine correspond to important events in colonial history. Second, in a 110-year period, more than half of which passed under a colonialism that is supposed to have brought development, good harvests were reported in only fifteen years.

One fatal famine is remembered from the precolonial era. It occurred in 1860/1861, a period when Arab presence was already established and Europeans, who traveled in large caravans which purchased important quantities of local foodstuffs, were exploring the area. The "greatest remembered famine" occurred in 1893/1894, a time of open warfare with German invaders (Kjekshus 1977:189). People attributed the next famine, in 1918/1919, directly to German and Allied armies' requisitioning of food reserves. That famine was experienced throughout the country.

From 1928/1929 to 1934/1935, the period of worldwide economic depression, there is an unbroken record of famine and food shortage. Plantation wages were cut and many

Table 6
Summary of Famines in Gairo Division, 1860–1970

1860/61	Severe famine caused by drought; many deaths
1893/94	Greatest remembered famine, caused by locust invasion. Thousands of deaths; smallpox epidemic
1918/19	Famine caused by drought and requisitioning of food reserves by German and Allied armies. Many deaths; hepatitis [influenza?] epidemic
1928/29	Famine caused by drought and locust invasion
1929/30	Famine caused by floods; fifteen deaths due to starvation reported
1930/31	Localized food shortages caused by uneven distribution of rains
1931/32	Localized food shortages caused by floods and vermin
1932/33	Famine caused by drought and locust invasion
1934/35	Famine caused by locust invasion and unseasonal rains
1938/39	Localized food shortages caused by irregular rains
1939/40	Food shortages caused by vermin; epidemic of dysentery, many deaths
1940/41	Localized food shortages caused by failure of rains when crops were ripening; severe food shortage in Mpwapwa District resulted in influx of people with goats to exchange for food
1941/42	Severe famine caused by drought followed by floods
1942/43	Very severe famine caused by poor rains
1945/46	Severe famine caused by inadequate short rains and poor distribution of rainfall
1947/48	Poor harvest caused by vermin and army worm invasion
1948/49	Food shortages caused by drought
1952/53	Famine caused by severe drought
1953/54	Localized food shortages caused by drought. Situation exacerbated by influx of migrants from Dodoma Region
1954/55	Food shortage caused by invasion of Sudan dioch or Bishop's birds; surplus food exported to Kenya to supply British government troops suppressing Mau Mau rebellion
1955/56	Localized food shortages caused by floods
1957/58	Very localized food shortages caused by severe drought
1960/61	Famine caused by army worm invasion
1962/63	Food shortage caused by floods
1965/66	Localized food shortages caused by floods
1967/68	Localized food shortages caused by floods
1968/69	Localized food shortages caused by drought
1969/70	Localized food shortages caused by drought

Source: Based on Mkunduge 1973:8, 66–71.

workers were laid off. Yet the colonial administration continued to collect taxes and drain resources, while all development activities were suspended. From 1938/1939, the beginning of World War II, successive yearly food shortages culminated in a series of famines in 1941/1942, 1942/1943, and 1945/1946. The very severe famine of 1943 spread

throughout the country. According to Iliffe, "the war gener-
alised, intensified, and prolonged the famine. Government
promoted the export of grain and cattle for military consumption and encouraged the production of drought prone
maize rather than resistant millet. Shipping was not available to import food. . . . Transport and administration were
run down." (1979:351).

Food distribution is mentioned in official annual reports
in connection with the famines of 1929/1930, 1941/1942,
and 1942/1943. For example, the commisioner for Eastern Province (of which Kilosa District was part) reported
in 1943:

> Food shortages continued in Kilosa; in western and northern
> areas, 241 tons of foodstuffs and 35 tons of seed were distrib-
> uted. The Native treasury handled all without government
> assistance. Relief was, whenever possible, sold at cost prices
> and no advances or free issues were made. The famine
> reached its height in February and was generally over by the
> end of April though, owing to the drought, some misgivings
> were felt as to the future of crops in the western areas. For-
> tunately, no further relief was necessary though food was
> still definitely short in the northern and western areas.
> (Tanganyika Territory 1944:22)

From 1947/1948, the record of famine and food shortage
continues unabated to independence, evidence of chronic
malnutrition. The increasing frequency of famine and food
shortage cannot be attributed either to poor memory of earlier times or to changes in natural factors.[2] What it reveals
is the growing vulnerability of the population (O'Keefe,
Westgate, and Wisner 1976:595). One would like to know
about farmers' indebtedness, whether it increased in this
period, and its contribution to farmers' vulnerability to the
vagaries of weather and the environment. The introduction
of maize monoculture in the 1940s altered the ecology as
well as the availability of labor. Both changes affected food
supplies and population size.

2. The Disaster Research Unit at Bradford University in England analyzed reports of natural disasters throughout the world between 1925 and
1975 and found a rise in the occurrence of large-scale disasters, an increased loss of life per disaster with the greatest increase observed in underdeveloped countries, and no major geological or climatological changes
(O'Keefe, Westgate, and Wisner 1976:565). I thank Richard Franke and Barbara Chasin for this reference.

The Paradox of Population Growth

It is difficult to draw any definite conclusion about mortality trends in the absence of deaths rates comparable over time. Henin and Egero (1972:52) estimated a death rate of 25 per thousand for Kilosa District in 1967, when the national average was 23. There is evidence of population growth, but it may not indicate a decline in mortality because Kilosa was a center for migrant labor. Hirst's (1970) study qualified Kilosa as a district of high fertility as well as high immigration, so that a high birth rate, rather than declining mortality, may have contributed to population growth.

Henin and Egero (1972) estimated population growth after World War II as being between 2.3 (1948) and 2.4 (1967); in absolute numbers, this rate represented an increase from 124,000 (1948) to 153,000 (1957) and 194,000 (1967). The continuous drop in the male/female ratio from 126 (1948) to 118 (1957) and 107 (1967) is the result of changes in the sisal industry and a subsequent falling off of male labor migration.

At the level of administrative units within the district, Thomas and Thomas (1971) compared the results of the 1957 and 1967 censuses. They documented population growth in Kilosa District and gave a more detailed picture of population changes than did Henin and Egero. The highest percentage of population change, 150 percent, occurred in Gairo. Some of this increase might be due to an influx of people following the shift of the administrative center from Mamboya to Gairo after independence; some may represent an influx of settlers from impoverished and drought-stricken areas to the north and west. The change may also be due to an increase in births and a decline in mortality.

Judging by information from the Gairo oral histories, deaths from starvation have been declining in Gairo since World War II, which suggests that a decline in mortality may account for some part of the population growth. Famine (rather than food shortage) is reported only in 1952/1953 and 1960/1961. The reduction in famine deaths is presumably related to the famine-relief measures undertaken by the colonial government. It may be, therefore, that improved communications and a famine-relief policy, re-

sulting in a more constant and certain food supply, were responsible for population increase in Gairo. But the decline
in deaths from starvation does not imply improvement in
health status or even a decline in morbidity. Despite relief
measures, it is clear from the Gairo study that food shortages continued to occur. Nutritional status was generally
marginal and, because of the synergistic action of malnutrition and infection, health status was also poor. The significance of a marginal nutritional status for health is not always obvious, even in statistics that show death by cause.
Careful investigations, however, such as that carried out by
the WHO Regional Office for the Americas, reveal the major
underlying role of malnutrition in infant and child mortality and morbidity (Puffer and Serrano 1973). Malnutrition
increases susceptibility to infectious disease and also influ-
ences the course and outcome of illness. (This point is discussed in detail in chapter 8.)

Population growth is a complex phenomenon linked to
changes in the mode of production—in this case from subsistence agriculture to plantation economy. The population
of Kilosa District has been increasing at least since World
War II. Immigration, which accounted for much of the increase in the interwar period when the migrant labor force
was organized to work on sisal plantations, is responsible
for a diminishing proportion since a permanent work force
was substituted. A drop in mortality was achieved by the
control of peaks in the death rate due to starvation and has
probably contributed to population growth. On the other
hand, as we shall see later, population growth is compatible
with deteriorating health and nutrition.

7

SONGEA: A
LABOR RESERVE

L abor reserves perform a specific function in plantation economies: they reproduce the labor force in
order to supply the proletariat required by the colonial power. In the words of Samir Amin, "In the region that I have called 'Africa of the labor reserves' capital
at the centre needed to have a large proletariat immediately
available. . . . They forced the 'traditional' societies to be
the supplier of temporary or permanent migrants on a vast
scale, thus providing a cheap proletariat for the European
mines and farms." (1981:39).

A plentiful supply of cheap labor is a prerequisite of
plantation economies—not relatively cheap in the relation
of costs to productivity, but absolutely cheap because
wages are low and skills are few (William Jones 1968:155).
The mobilization of unskilled labor gives plantations an
economic advantage similar to the one derived by the first
factories in the era of competitive capitalism, when women
and children were employed at low wages for long hours.

Labor reserves can be implanted where the economic order is rudimentary and the population illiterate and ignorant of modern agricultural techniques (ibid.:158). If workers are trained and other occupations open to them, their
wage demands will rise beyond what plantations pay and
the pool of unskilled labor will be drained. Workers migrate because they need cash to pay taxes and brideprice, a
requirement that cannot be met by remaining at home. In
East Africa plantations depended on the failure of colonial authorities to develop the districts designated as labor reserves: an extension of cash crops there would have
reduced the supply of labor or increased its price to a
level that only the most efficient planters could have paid
(Brett 1973:290).

Songea, situated in southeastern Tanzania along the international border with Mozambique, is one of several districts that colonialists turned into a de facto labor reserve. Despite high agricultural potential, commercial production was never developed and the district remained isolated: there was no regional communications network, no railway, and only one main road connecting it with the coast.

The political economy of the district changed radically twice in the nineteenth century, first in the 1860s when the Ngoni occupied the region, and then in the 1890s when the Germans annexed it. An agricultural people believed to be the original inhabitants of Undendeuli, the area around Songea town, were conquered and turned into serfs by the Ngoni, who settled in the region in 1862 and founded two independent but friendly chiefdoms—Njelu and Mshope (Gallagher 1974). These Songea Ngoni were part of a group that originally fled from Natal in the path of the advancing Zulu nation pushed north by Europeans (Gulliver 1956).

Unlike the indigenous agriculturalists, who appear to have been aggregations of scattered clans, the Ngoni had a strong military organization, which they had adopted in their northward migration. The organization was based on a system of age regiments. At the head was the *nkosi* or chief; below him were the *manduna* or subchiefs and below them the *madoda* or lieutenants. All men living under one chief were said to be of the same *kabila*; a *kabila* was divided into clans and the clans into families, each consisting of one man, his wives, and his children. According to Spies (1943), the strongest bond was between clan members, whose relations were based on mutual respect and help; next came blood brotherhood, which was really an extension of the clan relation to foreigners. A third type of relationship was the *mtanga*, which bound all people born in one year (agemates) to help each other (Large 1938).

During their migration, the Ngoni had raided along their route, meeting little resistance from the decentralized groups of the southeast. (That the Ngoni military techniques were very quickly imitated by the peoples living north of Lake Nyasa—in Usangu, Uhehe, and Ubena—indicates the need for political centralization.) The Ngoni had absorbed members of the raided groups, illustrating the point made earlier that tribal identity is not a fixed or hereditary characteristic (see chapter 2). They continued to raid their neighbors after they settled in Songea. While some captives may have been sold as slaves to Omani or Swahili traders, more likely many were taken into Ngoni households, where they worked in the fields and entered military service. They could become Ngoni and, if they were able and successful in raids, they could rise to be subordinate leaders and counselors. Female captives were married off and the bridewealth (customarily paid in cattle by husbands) became the property of the Ngoni homestead. In this way the Ngoni, who numbered perhaps a thousand people when they crossed the Zambezi River in 1835 (a date remembered for the eclipse of the sun), grew in strength so that by 1905, when they rebelled against German rule, it was estimated that they could put eight to ten thousand men in the field with little delay (Gulliver 1956).

German colonial rule came to Songea at the end of the nineteenth century. Initially there was little resistance to the changes that colonial rule entailed. Taxation was introduced, there was some forced labor, raiding was curtailed, and certain rituals connected with witchcraft were stopped (Turuka 1968). After 1901, however, German economic policy in the colony changed. According to Iliffe (1967: 559–560) a new governor, Graf G. A. von Götzen, adopted a scheme originally devised for the German colony of Togo to secure raw materials for German industry. The plan was to induce Africans to grow cotton as a *Volkskultur*, a peasant crop. This scheme is widely thought to have touched off the Maji Maji War of 1905–1906.

Götzen's advisers insisted that African farmers would never understand the economic advantages of the plan and that official compulsion would be necessary. The government decided to use the forced communal labor of neighborhood units to grow cotton and to withhold payment until the cotton had been sold, when one-third of the proceeds would go to African producers, one-third to the government's non-European agents, and one-third to district funds. The scheme began in Dar es Salaam district in 1903, eventually extending all over the southern coast and inland to Kilosa and Songea. By 1905, there were said to be five thousand acres under cotton in Kilwa district alone (ibid.:560).

In July and August 1905, as the time to pick the year's cotton was approaching, the peasants rebelled, signaling the start of the Maji Maji War. The Ngoni figured prominently in the war, attacking the fort at Songea, burning to the ground the Benedictine mission at Peramiho, and killing non-European government agents and a European missionary. Because of their military reputation, the Ngoni were especially feared by the Germans, who reacted with savage reprisals that continued for a year after the rebellion had been crushed. Some one hundred leaders were publicly hanged between January and April 1906, effectively destroying the social as well as military organization of the Ngoni.

Mapunda and Mpangara (1969) report estimates of five thousand deaths in the famine that resulted from the German policy, which lasted two years, of destroying crops and food reserves. Thousands of people migrated west of Songea to Unyanja and Matengo, areas that were not involved in the war and hence were a source of food supplies. The Germans forced fifteen hundred war captives to work on plantations elsewhere in the country, thus inaugurating the pattern of Ngoni labor migration. An added touch of cruelty was the prohibition on cultivation the following year; a missionary was told by German authorities, "The people should know what it means to stage a rebellion" (Kozak 1968:104). In this way, many areas were depopulated and formerly cultivated fields abandoned. Apparently few of the thousands who fled ever returned to Songea.

Fears that Maji Maji might be repeated dominated German administration, and under the new governor, A. Freiherr von Rechenberg, African peasants were freed from most compulsory cultivation. Rechenberg's reconstruction program was defensive and minimal, concentrating on the preservation of peace and order at the least possible expense. By 1914, German policy vigorously encouraged European agriculture and settler political control. Iliffe (1967:575) speculates that the change in policy was a reaction to the violence of African resistance. Then World War I broke out, creating new havoc.

It is difficult to quantify the impact of German rule on Songea. An 1894 German report quoted by Kjekshus (1977: 40) stated that one-third of the countryside was under cultivation and that the region around Songea was thickly populated; the nkosi of Mshope was thought to rule 50,000 to 60,000 people in the north, and the nkosi of Njelu an equal

number in the south. In 1902/1903, German officials estimated that 166,000 people lived in Songea District: five
years later one observer thought that no more than 20,000
were left (ibid.:150). The precipitous decline in population
after 1905 was the result of the combined impact of German
colonization, the brutal suppression of Maji Maji, and emigration from the area to escape death from starvation.

Ecological Consequences of Population Decline

The depopulation of Songea was to have important and un-
foreseen consequences. The Ngoni were originally cattle
herders, having come from a pastoral society in the south.
The cultivated fields of Undendeuli complemented the
grasslands on which Ngoni herds grazed. Cultivation and
grazing kept the bush at bay and the tsetse fly, carrier of
sleeping sickness, confined to the wild areas that formed
frontiers between nations (Ford 1971:136). The exodus of
population was followed by an ecological transformation.
The land reverted to thorn trees and bush, creating a favorable habitat for the fly. A 1913 German map of tsetse belts
shows the southeastern corner of Songea District occupied
by flies (Kjekshus 1977:164). By 1937, the belt covered a
third of the district. The westward spread continued in
the 1940s.

The first decimation of Ngoni stock took place in the
1890s, when rinderpest wiped out most herds (ibid.: 62).
The second occurred after the Maji Maji War, when the
Germans acted to deprive the population of all food resources. A third may have happened during World War I,
when the German and British armies commandeered cattle
to feed their troops. Another major decline was registered
after 1933, when numbers fell from 25,000 (the 1931–1933
three-year average) to 12,750 (the 1936–1938 average). By
1946–1948, there were fewer than 9,500 head, according to
official colonial sources (Tanganyika Territory 1947–1949).
The decline after 1933 was laid to tsetse; a second epidemic
of rinderpest caused the further reduction in the 1940s
(Tanganyika Territory 1954:10).

According to Ford (1971:198), the massive resettlement
experiments that the British undertook in the interwar
years, in which people were concentrated in fly-free areas,
accomplished the opposite of what was intended. Instead of

halting the spread of the fly, the projects abandoned huge tracts of fertile land to tsetse, confining the population to small, soon exhausted farms. In reclamation experiments undertaken in Songea in the 1950s, Bursell (1955:591) discovered traces of former civilization, evidence of the emigrants' abandonment of land to the fly. Extensive glades, representing old village sites, were scattered through the woodlands; the remains of domestic utensils found in them are evidence of former occupation. Large parts of Songea infested by flies are now uninhabited.

The repeated destruction of cattle herds led to the dismantling of Ngoni pastoral society. Money replaced cattle as the payment for marriage. The nutritional consequences of the decline in milk and meat consumption must have been considerable and were probably unevenly distributed in this hierarchically organized society. Able men joined the migrant labor force, while those who remained behind to rebuild Ngoni society found their productive energies sapped by the chronic malnutrition characteristic of immiseration.

The people of Undendeuli continued to practice agriculture with diminishing returns. British agricultural officers, after suppressing peasant opposition, successfully introduced tobacco as a cash crop in the 1930s. No new food crops were introduced because only products commanding a relatively high price on the world market could offset the practically prohibitive cost of transport from Songea to the coast. No attempt was made to create regional markets. There was no railway and only one main road, which was impassable in the rainy season. It was profitable to process high-grade tobacco leaf only, and quality control resulted in the rejection of part of peasant production (Tanganyika Territory 1942:47). Low-priced foodstuffs such as wheat flour that came from farther than two hundred kilometers away could not be marketed at the port of Mtwara (Songea is more than six hundred kilometers from the port). The provincial commissioner in 1940 saw "the whole of the economic welfare of the district dependent upon the [tobacco] industry" (Tanganyika Territory 1941:42).

Despite this attempt at economic development, the district remained poor, a source of cheap labor for the rest of the country. In their annual reports provincial commissioners stated that "economically, Songea has been badly hit"

(Tanganyika Territory 1931c); "activity has been much hampered by the poverty of the Native Authorities" (1932a). Taxes were reduced from seven shillings in 1930 to five shillings in 1933, but in 1942, despite continuing poverty, they were raised to six shillings to help finance World War II. Venereal disease was rife, smallpox was endemic, and yaws, leprosy, and sleeping sickness were common. Yet in 1940 it was reported that "there was no expansion of the medical services during the year" (Tanganyika Territory 1941:44). In 1945, the district was described by the provincial commissioner as "backward."

Labor Recruitment

The focus of British administration in Songea, as reflected in various official annual reports, seemed to be first, concern with administering a "difficult" district, and second, preoccupation with organizing the district's labor force. The district was said to be difficult to administer because of the rivalries that developed between the Njelu and Mshope chiefdoms. The British colonial administration, in accordance with the principles of indirect rule, tried to reconstruct the hierarchical organization of the Ngoni, which had been destroyed by the Germans after Maji Maji (see Wyatt 1944). But, for reasons that will be given later, succession to titled positions within the nation was no longer orderly. The labor question was a constant preoccupation throughout the period of German and British colonial rule and the subject of numerous official British reports (Orde-Browne 1946; Tanganyika Territory 1928b, 1931b, 1938b). Given the dependence on manual labor of African agricultural systems (and the failure of colonial authorities to introduce mechanization), the employment of adult males in colonial government service or private enterprise is of direct importance to the nutrition and health of the communities from which they were recruited.

The British administration attempted to organize the labor market. Minimum conditions were laid down by the government for contracts, board, lodging, and so on, but government officials rarely visited the plantations to supervise the arrangements. Camps were created where workers could rest on their journeys, which were usually accomplished on foot (the distance from Songea to Kilosa, where more than 40 percent of Ngoni found work, was about five hundred kilometers).[1] Wage rates were fixed. The Labour Department watched supply and demand carefully, especially in connection with public works. For example, in 1930 the government reported that it employed sixty thousand porters, for a total of 330,853 man-days (Tanganyika Territory 1931b:15).

The demand for labor almost constantly exceeded supply. The provincial commissioner's annual report for 1937 noted, "In 1936 the number of contracted labourers recruited in Songea amounted to over 2,100 and it was feared that the new service of labour transport by motor lorry would in 1937 denude the district of a high proportion of its male population. . . . it is estimated that, as usual, some further 2,500 native residents went to work independently. Therefore some 4,000 (i.e. 15 per cent) of the Songea male population will be absent from their homes for at least one year, and many probably much longer" (Tanganyika Territory 1938a:57). By 1943 the percentage had increased: in Songea 23 percent of all taxpayers were known to be absent either in military service or plantation employment (Tanganyika Territory 1944:62).

World War II exacerbated the labor shortage. According to a study by Orde-Browne, the war occasioned an increased call for labor in almost every direction:

> The East African industries were all producing useful supplies while certain of them such as sisal and pyrethrum were in urgent demand. In other directions new requirements appeared; the derelict rubber estates were exploited, and considerable additional labour was required for such purposes as the construction of reception camps for Italian civilian internees, Polish refugees, etc. All these together with the presence of large bodies of troops represented an additional strain on the food supply of the country, the maintenance of which thus became additionally important, and most unfortunately the years 1942 and 1943 saw widespread drought and consequent famine. The great additional burden thus placed on the labour resources of the country will be evident; consequently the requirements of the essential industries became steadily more pressing until resort to conscription for civil employment could no longer be avoided. (Orde-Browne 1946:41)

---

1. For an account of the facilities eventually provided see Hurst 1959.

British administration of Tanzania was more closely controlled under United Nations trusteeship than it had been under the League of Nations mandate. The UN regularly sent missions to trust territories to review conditions. The report of the United Nations Trusteeship Council Mission that visited Tanzania in 1954 was more than usually critical in its assessment of British policy and said about labor conditions:

> The labour force in Tanganyika, and especially the unskilled labour force, is essentially an African force. It is relatively small in size, but it is important for two particular reasons: firstly because the non-African plantation and mining economy, in particular, as well as the public works and similar activities of the Government, are organized on the basis of a supply of comparatively cheap labour, and secondly, because that supply is largely contingent on the generally low subsistence level of large parts of the African population and the precarious nature of their food supply. . . .
>
> The main source of labour is the African peasant family; when the rains are normal and the harvests generally good, there is usually a shortage of labour coming forward for wage-earning employment, but when, as in 1953, the rains fail in many parts of the Territory, the supply of labour improves from the employers' point of view and surpluses may occur. (United Nations Trusteeship Council 1955:99)

Following a general sociological study of the Songea area carried out over ten months in 1952/1953, P. H. Gulliver, a government sociologist, undertook a comprehensive study of labor migration in 1953. Fourteen sample areas were chosen. In nine areas, over a period of seven to ten days in each, a detailed family survey was made, including the completion of questionnaires for each adult male regarding his migratory labor history; the questionnaire was completed whether he was at home or away at work. In five areas, quick community surveys were made by arranging with local headmen to meet the men on a given day and to obtain details about them and their families in an open meeting. The detailed family survey plus three of the community studies yielded statistical information on fourteen hundred men, women, and children—just over 4 percent of the total population at home and abroad. (The other two community studies were less successful and provided only general information.) Ngoni laborers were also interviewed on the sisal plantations to which they migrated. The Ngoni represented an important segment of the migrant work force of Tanzania, constituting 10 percent of all long-distance migrants.

Between 1943 and 1953, the percentage of men away from Songea District at any one time rose from 23 percent to 33 percent. Gulliver summarized the effects of labor migration on the rural economy of Songea:

> (1) By labour migration men are able to earn and bring home money and goods that under present conditions in Ungoni they are unable, or feel they are unable, to obtain there. Thus there has been an immediate effect of raising or at least maintaining the standard of living at home;
>
> (2) the recourse to labour migration as a source of income saps the effort and will of the Ngoni to work more diligently at home in developing the resources of their own fields and country. There is therefore a depressing effect on the general tribal economy, and this is the most serious disadvantage of the system. It is a serious and pernicious effect. There is also a distinct loss to Native Authority revenue due to the constant absence of so many men who thus do not pay their tax at home.
>
> (3) The individual peasant-family economy is little affected by the ordinary short-term absence of the husband-father, nor do wives and children encounter any grave disabilities. In the short view the family gains from the money and goods brought back by the returning migrant; but,
>
> (4) the deserted wives and children of long-term absentees do often (though not always) suffer poverty and severe difficulties; and there has also been a fall in moral standards of marital and sexual relations which does not stop at the deserted wives but colours general Ngoni attitudes; this latter point should not be overemphasized.
>
> (5) Neither tribal nor family authority have been especially undermined by the temporary absences of young men, but both have been more adversely affected by the general conditions of change in modern Africa.
>
> (6) The Ngoni migrant learns little whilst he is away and he brings almost nothing back in the way of new ideas and values, new techniques or standards, or a renewed spirit. He is content to be back home in the old life. (Gulliver 1955:15)

Gulliver, like Watson (1958) in his study of the Mambwe who lived on the Zambian border, sought to show that tribal life persisted despite labor migration and may even

have profited from it. The idea that standards of living rose
runs counter to other colonial anthropological studies: Read
(1956), Richards (1939), and Wilson and Wilson (1945)
have demonstrated that labor migration impoverished rural
life in central Africa.[2] Perhaps because Gulliver did not
also study land tenure, he assumed on the basis of population density figures that land was plentiful in Songea and
that the people were easily able to continue farming. He
may not have realized that labor shortages had forced a re-
gression from more sophisticated agricultural techniques. A
later intensive survey of a small part of Songea revealed a
peculiar pattern of land-use rights that complicated the returned migrants' access to land and that tended to restrain
the wives of migrants from shifting off exhausted land.

Effects of Labor Migration in Songea

In 1956, Dr. J. R. K. Robson, then district medical officer for
Songea, noticed a high incidence of malnutrition in the
children living near Maposeni, a village 35 kilometers
northwest of Songea town. Robson perceived the social and
agricultural aspects of the problem and decided to place it
before the Songea District Team, which was composed of
government officers representing various disciplines. Over
the next two years, the medical, agricultural, and veterinary
deparments coordinated their activity in order to assess and
alleviate the acute nutritional problems of about a hundred
families living in an area of 27.5 square kilometers around
Maposeni, which was once the seat of the Njelu kingdom.

The team carried out a family survey (Robson et al. 1962).
From parish records of baptized children they determined
with certainty the year of birth of all but twelve persons.
They also carried out a dietary survey. Because accurate
diet patterns cannot be determined by retrospective inquiry, the team used results to give only a very general picture, not scientific data. The survey did reveal that cassava
was the staple food and at certain times of the year practically the only food eaten.

The clinical survey consisted of an examination of children under the age of fifteen years. In all, 141 children were
living in the area and 99 were examined for certain known

2. I thank Ron Frankenberg for these references.

signs of malnutrition. A very high proportion of children had signs of marked protein deficiency (the highest incidence occurred in the one to four age group), a fairly high percentage showed signs of vitamin A deficiency, and a small percentage exhibited symptoms of riboflavin (part of the vitamin B complex) deficiency.

Malaria, a disease associated with malnutrition, was prevalent in the area. Malarial parasites cause nutritional anemia (Layrisse, Roche, and Baker 1976:65); by destroying red blood cells, malaria may tip the nutritional balance in people on a borderline diet. The incidence of hookworms (which continually drain blood from the intestinal wall, requiring protein to replace lost blood) was not ascertained in this study, but another study cited by Robson et al. in a similar area in Songea revealed that 92 percent of school children were infected with hookworm. Schistosomiasis, a parasitic disease associated with pellagra (a vitamin deficiency) (Barakat 1976:128), was extremely common as the parasite inhabits snails, which were present in the area's many perennial streams and stagnant pools.

The main cash crops of the survey area were sesame and groundnuts; only 5 percent of the people grew tobacco. The team thought the whole area had been cultivated at some time during the past fifty years and the land was worked out, with signs of soil erosion. Yet these people were once experienced in husbandry and keen conservationists. The labor migration system changed the political economy of this formerly prosperous land.

With the exception of rice, and of millet during the first year, crops were ridged, that is, mounds of earth were raised between the rows of last year's crops. Formerly, the farmers created ridges to hold weeds, which they used as green manure, but that labor-intensive practice died out and the soil was left untreated. Plants were no longer thinned after germination. Crops such as beans, pulses, groundnuts, sesame, sunflower, and cassava were placed in between maize and millet plants. The 1958 survey revealed that three to ten crops were grown together. The senior field officer took this finding to mean that the people had little confidence in the soil, were convinced that it would not stand having crops planted closely together, and perhaps were afraid of a particular crop failing if planted on its own. These conclusions are an instance of colonialist prejudice since intercropping, a widespread practice in Africa, is known to protect against the insect damage to which monocultures are prone, especially in the absence of chemical controls.

The Maposeni people practiced crop rotation, using what is called a medium fallow system (the resting period varies between seven and ten years). This system was probably a retreat from longer fallow periods, lasting up to thirty years. After clearing the bush by burning it, trees were cut down and left to rot out by insect damage; stumps were never completely removed from farm plots. In the first year millet was broadcast or interplanted with sesame; in the second and third years, maize or sorghum was planted with beans, groundnuts, sesame, and sunflower; by the fourth year little more than cassava could be planted, and in the fifth and sixth years only cassava was grown. Very rarely was maize planted after the fourth year as the land appeared to be completely worn out. Groundnuts may, however, have been interplanted until the fifth year. Cassava, which can be left in the ground for several years, was added until the sixth year; it was then left until about the eighth year, by which time it was all harvested.

The agricultural cycle began in October/November, when the bush was burned. Cultivation usually began in December, at the outset of the rainy season, when the rains had softened the unusually hard ground. Crops were harvested in April and May. The hungry months were December, January, and February, when only cassava was eaten. In March the early planted maize and some beans were eaten, but food was seldom sufficient before April. Groundnuts, a source of protein, became ready in August and some were consumed, but often they were sold for cash to pay taxes.

Many of the Maposeni men migrated to Kilosa and the northeastern coastal area around Tanga to work on sisal plantations; others worked in Songea town or at the nearby Benedictine mission in Peramiho, "for whom they provide a convenient source of casual semi-skilled or unskilled labour" (Robson et al. 1962:68). The absence of many male adults was a particular hardship in Songea. For the families of labor migrants the burden of cultivation fell completely on the wives, with the consequence that farm plots were small. The absence of male workers may also have led to overcropping since the clearing of land was time-consuming, hard physical work that required teams of laborers. Migration also aggravated the high dependency ratio:[3] proportionately there were fewer adults to work and support young dependents. In Songea District as a whole, the proportion of the population under fifteen years of age in 1967 was 43 percent (this figure is typically 30 percent in North America and 25 percent in Western Europe).

Despite low population density in Songea and the plentiful land that this normally implies, land scarcity existed and accounted for some nutritional difficulties. Robson et al. (1962:67) reported an atypical pattern of land-use rights: the chief claimed suzerainty over the whole region, retaining a small domain over which he had direct authority and dividing the rest among his subchiefs. The subchiefs also kept sufficient land for their personal use and divided the remainder among their lieutenants. In return for the land, a lieutenant was expected to supply warriors or laborers whom he produced from among his own relatives and from those strangers and captives to whom he had given permission to cultivate on his land. The authors note that, while this organization seemed fixed, in fact it was still evolving at the time of European conquest. German rule brought further changes. The chief moved to Ndirima, three miles from Maposeni, accompanied by his lieutenants and "serfs" who were allocated tracts of land. Lieutenants controlled fairly large land areas. This "ownership" affected strangers, as it meant that they must obtain the lieutenant's permission to settle in his area and get the chief's approval of the proposed settlement. The aim of the formal interview with the chief was to find out why the stranger had moved from his old home and whether he would be likely to be a troublesome or useful neighbor. If the request was approved, the lieutenant would show the foreigner where to build his house and grow his food, and when the time came to shift, the lieutenant would allocate another place to cultivate (ibid.:68–69).

---

3. A dependency ratio is the population under fifteen years plus those sixty-five years and over divided by the population from fifteen to sixty-four years old. In Songea this ratio was 91 in 1967, while in Kilosa it was 81 (in North America it is about 61 and in Western Europe about 58).

According to Large (1938), a Ngoni man could live and cultivate only in his own family area, since the chief had power to require his people to live in particular places. This power was based on military necessity. If land was not in the vicinity of other land occupied already, a man could take it up without permission. If land was near other occupied land, he first had to consult the community in case any members had planned expansion in that direction. A woman's access to land was mediated by the man she married. Women had no individual claim other than as wives, and no direct access except through their husbands.

A cultivator had exclusive rights over occupied land until it was abandoned (ibid.). If his intention was to leave it fallow and to cultivate it in due course, his rights could be maintained only if a relative resided on the spot (that is, to guard the rights). If duly maintained, the rights were good against everybody—even a chief could not deprive a man of his land except on compensation and if for the good of the community. A man could give his land away or could abandon his rights to any other man who eventually took up the land. Land was never sold, but improvements (for example, mango and banana plantings) could be purchased.

This feudal system was severely distorted by first German and then British rule. The Germans not only massacred Ngoni leaders in 1906 but also systematically substituted German appointees for the Ngoni lieutenants, giving foreigners the right to allocate land and control its distribution. These foreigners maintained an economic ascendancy by hoarding land. The British, by restoring the old Ngoni aristocracy to power and establishing indirect rule, facilitated the consolidation of autocratic control. But the old structure now worked to the extreme disadvantage of the commoners. Raids had once provided the rank and file with opportunities to demonstrate their leadership ability and to rise in the hierarchy, but the colonial powers had suppressed raiding and there was no longer any way to move upward. The former system of personal allegiance (as contrasted with allegiance to land) now also worked to the commoners' disadvantage: the power to allocate land was in the hands of the aristocracy, who thus had a virtual stranglehold over the common people. It is not surprising, therefore, that the formerly friendly chiefdoms of Njelu and

Mshope became rivals or that there were fights over succession to titled positions.[4]

The demand of the colonial plantation economy for migrant labor created social problems as well as political disruption and economic dislocation in the labor supply areas. Long periods of separation of husband and wife, father and children, harmed family life. The physical vulnerability of women and children, who are known to be more susceptible to malnutrition and disease than men, can be heightened by social hardships, and women and children left behind by migrant workers may run an increased risk of ill health. These social problems were recognized by the colonial government:

> Clearly, home and family life cannot be generally maintained under prolonged separation. The wife is deprived of normal economic and social support, assistance and protection; she is not able usually continuously to obtain enough money herself for adequate clothing and other necessities for herself and her children; she is deprived of the normal sex relations of marriage. The children themselves suffer from the absence of paternal guidance and help. Adultery amongst such wives is a good deal more prevalent than amongst other women—for whom, in fact, in Ungoni, this offense is not particularly widespread. With or without adultery, such women are perhaps the most numerous category of divorcees. If the deserted wife is past her youth she may find it difficult to re-marry and may have to eke out a burdensome life as the poor, dependent relative of her husband's or her own kin. If she does re-marry, she is compelled under Ngoni law to leave her children behind at their father's home. (Gulliver 1956:38)

The colonial labor migration system, coupled with the autocratic control that developed under indirect rule, thus had serious consequences for nutrition and health. Land was worked out, showing signs of overcropping and erosion, and fallow periods were shortened. Advanced agricultural practices such as green manuring and thinning of plants were abandoned for lack of necessary time and labor. Groundnuts, a potential source of protein, were sold to pay

4. It is possible that there was an element of religious rivalry in this struggle. The Mshope Ngoni chiefdom, which was almost wholly Muslim, contained the former serf population of (mainly) Ndendeuli; the Njelu chiefdom was mostly Roman Catholic (see Gulliver 1955: iii; Komba 1968).

taxes. Wives of migrant laborers were able to cultivate only small farms, and the exhausted soil produced little more than cassava after the first four years. The women could not move off the land without losing the family's claim to it, unless they could spare someone to guarantee the claim through physical occupation. Men were not available for the time-consuming, hard physical work of bush and tree clearance to prepare new land for cultivation and, if they returned from their migrations, they had to apply to a lieutenant for permission to shift to new land.

Immiseration and Population Growth

Even if estimates of 166,000 inhabitants in Songea in the early twentieth century (Kjekshus 1977:150) are exaggerated and the devastation following the peasant rebellion is overstated, the historical evidence indicates that colonial rule reduced a once-flourishing district to extreme poverty from which the people have yet to recover. The reports of nineteenth-century travelers, who commented on thickly populated settlements, on extensive well-tended fields with straight ridges, on numerous goats and herds of cattle (ibid.: 40), contrast vividly with accounts of underpopulation, apathy, and ill health, of very poor, small fields, and of few cattle at the end of the British colonial period (Robson et al. 1962). The population growth shown by postwar census data in no way contradicts governmental accounts of malnutrition and general misery.

Henin and Egero (1972:46) estimated demographic changes in Songea. The population is supposed to have increased over 60 percent, from 94,500 in 1948 to 151,400 in 1967, but the breakdown of these figures in terms of the three components of population change makes that percentage highly unreliable. (In addition, the census figures for 1948 and 1957 are thought to be inaccurate.)[5] The ratio of males per 100 females was 80 in 1948, demonstrating clearly the labor migration pattern (the national average was 93 that year). Gulliver (1955:2) thought that migration had peaked in 1952; the ratio was 84 in 1957 and 89 in 1967. His view is confirmed by total labor migration

5. The population figures for 1948 and 1957 have been adjusted for the 1967 administrative boundaries of Songea District.

statistics for the territory (Hurst 1959:84, table 1). The 1967 figure may also be influenced by a change in migration patterns, which became less sex selective after permanent work forces of settled families were substituted on plantations.

The annual growth rates in Songea are highly irregular, ranging from 1.1 percent in 1948 to 3.8 in 1957 and 2.5 in 1967; only the 1967 figure matches the national average (Henin and Egero 1972:46). But elsewhere Henin and Egero (1972:52) give a rate of 1.8 percent for 1967, a figure that is supposedly corrected for migration. The conclusion is that the 1957 figure is wrong, and that population grew slowly in Songea. This view is reinforced by Henin and Egero's birth rate of 45 per thousand, which is below the national average of 47, and death rate of 27, which is above the national average of between 21 and 23 in 1967 and also above the higher estimate of 24 to 25 in 1957 (ibid.).

There is some evidence from anthropological studies that the present birth rate may represent an increase over precolonial norms. The Ngoni were raiders who incorporated subjects and captured peoples; their fertility may usually have been low and they may have relied upon raiding to increase their numbers (see Cordell 1983). Descended in large part from the Swazi, the Ngoni maintained Swazi military organization. Swazi married late. Their young men were organized into military regiments: members of a senior regiment married at roughly twenty-five to thirty-five years of age and a new regiment was inaugurated (Kuper 1965:121). In a study of a related group of Ngoni in Zambia, Barnes stated that "warfare, not domesticity, was the right and proper occupation of young men, and the age at which men married for the first time was probably about thirty. Informants all stressed that in the old days [pre-1898] first marriage took place at later ages for both men *and women* than it does now" (1951:11; emphasis added). Redmond (1972: 132, 239) confirms the practice of late age at marriage among the Songea Ngoni and states that the last age-set was formed in 1905, a date that corresponds with the German suppression of the Ngoni following the Maji Maji War. It is likely that the loss of this cultural control of fertility was a consequence of the social disorganization of Ngoni life following German reprisals.

The demographic importance of late age at first marriage,

if accompanied by a taboo on premarital intercourse, is that women are removed from the childbearing population during their most fecund years (eighteen to twenty-five). Late age at marriage also lengthens the interval between generations so that fewer children are born and the overall birth rate is lowered. (Young [1978:32] points out a curious demographic law: when the average age of marriage is high, a relatively large proportion of the population never marry at all. Perhaps this law obtained in Songea.) If Ngoni began to marry at younger ages after 1910, both fertility rates and birth rates would have risen. The increase in male migration, which rose from 15 percent in the 1930s to 33 percent in the 1950s, would have tended to depress the birth rate unless taboos on adultery were ignored (and according to Gulliver they were). Migration also represented the penetration of capitalism into Ngoni life and may have acted as a stimulus to population growth.

One could argue that the birth rate increased in response to the radical change in social relations of production following capitalist penetration under colonial rule. Interesting parallels can be drawn between Songea in the early twentieth century and rural England in the last half of the eighteenth, when population increased markedly. Migration to employment on the sisal plantations can be seen as proletarianization, the process of turning peasants into wage laborers, and as an expansion of demand for labor in the capitalist sector. In England both phenomena accompanied the agricultural and industrial revolutions. Lazonick's interpretation of the change in England may apply as well to Songea:

> Feudal customs which discouraged [early] marriage were disregarded, the direct tie of the mass of the people to their means of production was broken, an impersonal and uncertain labor market replaced more personal and stable employer-employee contractual relations, and the economic positions of women and children were drastically altered. The new class of proletarianized wage-laborers as well as other classes in capitalist society undoubtedly responded to particular economic incentives which the society presented. Earlier marriages and larger families were specific results of the transition from the feudal mode of production to the capitalist mode of production in England. (Lazonick 1974:25)

In Songea, earlier marriage took place among the Ngoni after 1906, the suppression of raiding broke the direct tie to the means of production, an impersonal and uncertain migratory labor market replaced personal allegiance, and the economic position of women and children left behind by migrant laborers was altered significantly.

Young (1978:38), however, who reviewed the detailed demographic studies of the transition from feudalism to capitalism in seventeenth-century England and showed the very close correlations between the rise of rural industrialization and the fall in the birth rate, also quite rightly warned of falling into the trap of economic determinism. She concluded that increasing poverty, not increasing employment opportunities, led to increased fertility. Poor families tend to produce many children in situations where capitalism creates material insecurity because children can be put to work even at very young ages. The increasing poverty of Songea may thus account for rising birth rates.

Meillassoux (1972) made a similar point in an analysis of the structure of African precapitalist societies in the colonial era; he suggested that population growth was a logical response to capitalist exploitation. Meillassoux argued that migrations between the capitalist and the rural sectors are undertaken when people are compelled to earn cash to pay taxes. That this is true of the Ngoni is confirmed by Gulliver, who gave it as the reason for labor migration: "Without question the overwhelming reason why Ngoni leave their homes and their country to seek work abroad is economic. Men cannot, or feel they cannot, earn sufficient money at home to satisfy their basic cash needs and their minimum standard of living; alternatively, men feel that it is easier to earn sufficient abroad than at home" (1955:16).

Demographic expansion was also the logical solution to the social security problems created by colonial pressure. Meillassoux (1972:105) maintained that when the capitalist system does not provide pensions, sick leave, and unemployment compensation, workers have to turn elsewhere to meet these vital needs. In the colonial period, no provision was made for these social benefits in Tanzania; in fact, in 1943 dock workers went on strike in Dar es Salaam over demands for sick pay, old-age pensions, and annual leave, as well as higher wages (Iliffe 1969:149).

Meillassoux argued that preserving village relations, continuing the familial community, and maintaining the traditional mode of production were essential for the survival of
wage earners. The failure of colonial rulers to perceive this
necessity, in his view, led to

> such contradictory conclusions as that underdeveloped
> countries are "dual economies". . . . The "dual" theory is in-
> tended to conceal the exploitation of the rural community,
> integrated . . . as an organic component of capitalist produc-
> tion to feed the temporarily unproductive workers of the
> capitalist sector and supply them with the resources neces-
> sary to their survival. Because of this process of absorption
> within the capitalist economy, the agricultural communities,
> maintained as reserves of cheap labour, are being both un-
> dermined and perpetuated at the same time, undergoing a
> prolongated crisis and not a smooth transition to capitalism.
> (Meillassoux 1972:103)

Meillassoux is wrong to suggest that the connection was
not recognized by colonial rulers, who always saw their
problem first and foremost as a problem of labor shortages.
It was only their academic apologists who came up with
the dual sectors and the backward sloping supply curve of
labor to show that driving people out of the poor sector was
not only necessary (backward sloping supply curve) but
also good for them (dualism).[6]

Dualism concealed both the exploitation of rural communities and the ways in which the system of labor reserves
actively impoverished the peasantry. Population growth
was a defensive response to pauperization, the threat of being destitute; it was not, as Malthusians would have it, the
cause of misery. The migratory labor system contributed to
the destitution of rural peoples; migration did not represent
positive opportunities for economic betterment, as Gulliver
would have us believe.

It is well established that colonial rule created the need
for its own labor force. In Kenya, Zimbabwe, and South

6. Some European complaints of labor shortages were disguised refusals
to pay subsistence wages; for a discussion of the issues see Wrigley 1965.
However, when Europeans raised the wages of Africans, they received less
labor rather than more; thus the curve shows that as demand increases,
quantity of labor decreases. I thank Fred Bienefeld for these insights.

Africa a legal system of reserves was instituted. In Tanzania, possibly because of Britain's late entry and the country's status as a League of Nations mandate, a de facto system was maintained in districts such as Songea. The changes that colonial rule brought to African societies, such as organized labor recruitment and the imposition of taxes, were designed to encourage Africans to leave those districts.

When tax alone no longer sufficed as an incentive to the African worker, Europeans found other inducements to maintain the labor supply. The introduction of cash items that were not formerly part of the African budget but that became necessities increased the need for cash. Arrighi (1970:212) demonstrated in the case of the Zimbabwean peasantry how items of discretionary consumption tended in time to become necessities: for instance, new goods came to be desired and items that formerly were produced by African craftsworkers and obtained by barter came to be supplanted by European manufactures that had to be purchased with cash. In his study of Songean peasants in Tanzania Gulliver recognized this manipulation of the need for cash ("A garden hoe . . . is now bought from a trading store or mission rather than from a local blacksmith"), but he maintained that "demand has not been much affected by the industrial products of the modern world except in clothing" (1955:18). It is known, however, that cash payments replaced cattle as brideprice, and a study of Tanzanian household budgets made in the colonial era mentions one fact that contradicts Gulliver's conclusion about demand: the ratio of registered bicycles to population in Songea in 1952 was 1:150, a high figure for so poor a district (E. O. Wright 1955:80).

In Zimbabwe, Arrighi (1970:212) noted, the spread of missionary education became one of the most powerful factors altering the nature of African participation in the money economy: education (even that limited to religious texts) changed tastes and wants, and expenditure on education lost its discretionary nature, as wage employment increasingly became the source of subsistence; eventually education became one of the major expenditures in African family budgets. This was also the case in Songea, where the Benedictine mission was very active in primary education and where primary school enrollment was relatively high.[7]

Labor migration and the pauperization it engendered were of direct consequence to health in rural areas: higher than average death rates in Songea and widespread child malnutrition are direct evidence. The effect of the labor migration system in areas like Songea that supplied labor power was to depress the economy and disorganize social life, to decrease food supplies and disrupt traditional patterns of mutual assistance, to debilitate the population left behind and diminish their chances of improving their standard of living. This system contributed to the economic, social, and political underdevelopment of Tanzania in the colonial period. Colonial rule, in response to the demand of the metropolitan capitalist economy, created structural distortions, of which the labor migration system is only one example, with direct, negative implications for nutrition and health.

7. The extent to which foreign religions also contributed to the breakdown of Ngoni life is in dispute. Gulliver (1955:iii) believed that they contributed greatly; but some Tanzanians do not accept the erasure of old religions as fact (see Komba 1968).

8

COLONIAL MEDICINE

The German medical response to health conditions in Tanzania was that of an invader: given the years of armed struggle with a population that resisted conquest, it was logical to build military hospitals in fortified towns where the wounded could be treated. The British medical response was that of a colonial power settling in for a long period of rule: medical services were more diversified, serving planters and civil servants as well as the military and police forces and, eventually, a part of the African population. What the regimes shared was a common nosology and belief in the superiority of Western medicine over African practice.

In the nosology of clinical medicine, diseases are classified according to mode of transmission (for example, contaminated water), location in a human organ (gastrointestinal, heart, or lung diseases), or disease agent (viral, bacterial, and so on). These categories are narrow and exclusive, encouraging specialization not only among physicians but also among medical researchers so that data are collected for each disease entity separately. Data processed in this way have little relevance to daily lives caught in the social transformations of colonialism and capitalism. They reveal little of Africans' experiences and nothing of human agency in disease causation.

Colonialism and Disease

Malaria, sleeping sickness, bilharzia, yellow fever, leprosy, yaws, and syphilis are thought to be indigenous to Africa (Hackett 1971).[1] Because infectious diseases produce long-

---

1. Evidence for this distribution of disease comes from paleopathological records. Most of the known organic and microbial disorders of humans and animals are extremely ancient, but the comparative prevalence

lasting immunity and do not become endemic in small groups living in relative isolation, Africans were immune to many indigenous infections. But the 1880s and 1890s in Tanzania were decades of social dislocation, the cumulative effects of the slave trade, rebellions, foreign exploration, and wars of conquest. People moved around on a scale and at a rate never before experienced in East Africa. Epidemics spread rapidly in these unsettled circumstances. Some occurred because European explorers introduced new diseases (many of them, like measles, thought of as childhood diseases in Europe), which severely attacked Africans of all ages, who, unlike adult Europeans, had no natural immunity. Other epidemics flared because travelers circulated indigenous pathogens that had been dormant for centuries, or because the conquerors so disturbed the existing order that endemic diseases broke the boundaries Africans had created to contain them. After the proclamation of *Pax Germanica*, epidemics occurred most commonly because colonialists imposed conditions that broke the "ecological backbone" of the East African economy and with it, the population's resistance to disease. New chronic conditions like malnutrition appeared as a consequence of the imposition of the capitalist mode of production.

Rinderpest, a disease of wild game and domestic cattle, illustrates vividly this interaction between colonialism and disease. It is not indigenous to Africa and was imported with diseased cattle from Asia. It did not penetrate south of the Sahara till 1864, when it spread to the area now known as Mali. In 1865 it assumed epidemic proportions in West Africa. The first recorded outbreak in East Africa was in 1889 in Somalia, after diseased cattle were brought from India and Aden to provision of the Italian army on its first campaign in Eritrea. The British campaigns against the Sudan in 1884–1885 spread the infection to cattle of the Nile valley as far south as Khartoum. The disease touched Lake Tanganyika toward the end of 1890. It was extremely

---

and severity of various diseases changed greatly in the course of history (Dubos 1959:172–173). There is no consensus on syphilis. I find convincing Hudson's (1965) argument that yaws was present in equatorial Africa in paleolithic times and that it changed to syphilis in cooler and drier areas. For a general discussion of the controversy on the origins of syphilis, see Crosby 1972:122–164.

virulent and mortality rates reached 95 percent (Mettan 1937).

The rinderpest epidemic of 1890–1891 nearly exterminated cattle herds throughout East Africa. The loss of cattle, the basis of pastoral economies and an important source of protein for many semipastoral groups, precipitated an exodus and created a famine in which endemic disease became epidemic. Thorn trees replaced grassland, and bush crept over formerly cultivated fields, creating an environment favorable to the tsetse fly. This ecological change has proved difficult to reverse; the British made several misguided attempts before and after World War II (Ford 1971).

The tsetse fly carries a parasite, the corkscrew-shaped trypanosome, which burrows into the brain and causes sleeping sickness. This popular name for trypanosomiasis is derived from the behavior of victims, who lapse into sleep during the daytime but become restless at night. The syndrome was brilliantly described in Joseph Conrad's novel *Heart of Darkness*:

> Black shapes crouched, lay, sat between the trees leaning against the trunks, clinging to the earth, half coming out, half effaced within the dim light, in all the attitudes of pain, abandonment, and despair.

The trypanosome appears to be indigenous to Africa, but an epidemic erupted in East Africa only in the tumultuous circumstances of the late nineteenth century. During the first decade of the twentieth century, the tsetse fly began to depopulate parts of Uganda, and the country as a whole lost a tenth or more of its people. In Tanzania, the fly made irrevocable the loss of cattle to rinderpest and spelled the end of herding for some peoples.

Ford (1971) maintains that Africans knew trypanosomiasis attacked cattle; they called the disease *nagana* and contained it in the unclaimed barriers of wilderness that fronted the territory of each group. In part it was the substitution of international boundaries for these frontier zones that destroyed the ecological equilibrium Africans had evolved over the centuries. In more than a third of Tanzania's districts today, the disease remains a serious impediment to economic development.

The loss of livelihood, the basis of all social organization, is surely the main precursor of disease since it spells the breakdown of both individual and communal defenses. The failure of epidemiological explanations, which concentrate on individual defenses, is illustrated by the epidemic of jiggers (sand fleas) that attacked Tanzania immediately after the rinderpest holocaust.

The jigger was introduced to West Africa in 1872 in sand ballast carried by a British ship returning from Brazil. The flea was carried up the Congo River to the site of present-day Kinshasa, where it became established and traveled from there along the steamship route to Stanley Falls. In 1891 it entered Tanzania at Ujiji and from there passed to Bukoba on Lake Victoria. In the same year, Emin Pasha, a German adventurer, made an expedition to Lake Victoria with hundreds of men, some of whom stayed in the lake region and became infected by jiggers. They were apparently the source of the epidemic that followed in Tanzania. Jiggers bore beneath the skin and lay their eggs; if not cut out, the eggs hatch and more jiggers work their way under the skin, creating large sores that easily become infected. Gangrenous sores may lead to death; survivors are not only incapacitated and unable to work, but also severely debilitated and vulnerable to other diseases. As a result of this epidemic crops were left unharvested, adding to food shortages created by the loss of cattle to rinderpest. A smallpox epidemic in 1891 also took an unusually heavy toll among adults as well as children.

Because Tanzanians had no indigenous medical defenses against jiggers, a relatively minor ailment assumed lethal dimensions. Moreover, the nursing services that families offered their kin broke down under the famine conditions that forced people to migrate. This breakdown must have affected the recovery rate. Among the gangs of porters who served in expeditions led by Stanley, Emin Pasha, and others, such services simply did not exist.

The medical history of the country written for the British government and published after independence (Clyde 1962) assumes that the state of health in Tanzania was always precarious, at least until the arrival of Europeans at the end of the nineteenth century. But there are few hard data to support either this assumption or the contention that the present situation, while a slight improvement over that existing after World War I, represents in many respects a

deterioration of the situation existing before the arrival
of Europeans.

A worldwide pandemic of influenza followed World War
I and in 1918/1919 claimed an estimated fifty to eighty
thousand Tanzanian lives (Ferguson 1980:324). In 1920, after the British had taken over the administration of
Tanzania, the colonial medical department found that the
population suffered a heavy burden of infection. Helmin-
thic diseases, malaria, relapsing fever, and venereal diseases (the last following in the wake of the slave trade and
World War I) were widespread; dysenteries, leprosy, schistosomiasis, tropical ulcer, yaws, and many other diseases
were common; anthrax, sleeping sickness, smallpox, tuberculosis, and sometimes bubonic plague occurred in places
(George Maclean 1950).

Colonial medical records contain little descriptive material on disease or reliable statistics.[2] In the absence of data,
it is not possible to prove conclusively that morbidity rates
have increased since the country came under British rule.
Existing statistics are not comparable, are often inaccurate,
and even when accurate may be misleading (Clyde 1967:
19–24). First of all, as the network of facilities spreads and
reporting improves, the number of cases goes up. Second,
the reports refer only to patients treated at health facilities,
a population that is not a representative sample. Third, the
translation of symptoms into an accurate disease category
(for example, fever = malaria) depends on the diagnostic
ability of the examining health workers and on the labora-
tory and other facilities available. Both of these have presumably improved since the beginning of British rule.
Finally, statistics indicate the presence of disease
but not the outcome if other than death: they say nothing
about the medical history of an individual and the interaction of diseases; they reveal little about the impact on re-

2. Sources of bibliographic information are Feierman 1979; Langlands
1965, Patterson 1978. Information on specific conditions can be found in
the following references: on mental health see Aall-Jilek 1965, Oliensis
1967, Orley 1970, and Smartt 1956; on cholera see Davies 1959; on tuberculosis see Gelfand 1961 and Wilcocks 1932; on cerebrospinal meningitis
see Lapeysonnie 1963 and Waddy 1962; on trypanosomiasis see McKelvey
1973; and on leprosy see Rogers 1954. Additional references are given in
the text.

latives of sick persons and even less about the effect on communities.[3]

Aggregated at the national level, existing statistics give little idea of the changing distribution of disease within the country; and, with little uniformity in reporting systems, they give no clues to changes over time. The few statistics given in various annual reports by colonial departments cannot be analyzed to show any coherent trends in the pattern of disease in Tanzania since 1921 (the year of the first British census). A historical approach to the epidemiology of disease might fill some of these gaps, but it cannot elucidate the interaction between disease and economic, social, and political factors.

There is no way of estimating the total number of deaths that may be attributed directly or indirectly to the European acquisition of East Africa, for even more than the introduction of new diseases, the disruption of the economy, the basis of the country's food supply, affected health in Tanzania. With the decline of food production under colonialism, malnutrition became a common condition, though it was not recognized as a syndrome until World War II (Trowell, Davies, and Dean 1954). Unlike famine, which is readily observable, malnutrition is an insidious process not easily defined clinically. Because it can be identified only by a trained eye, it is not noted as a cause of death as frequently as, say, infections, which are more distinct in their etiology and manifestation. Interacting synergistically with infection, malnutrition weakens the body's resistance to disease, which then takes a more severe course. Individual resistance to infection is determined by a number of factors, but a significant variable is the adequacy of immune response; available evidence suggests that malnutrition can depress resistance by impairing cellular immune response and antibody synthesis (World Health Organization 1972:24).

The interaction of nutrition and infection varies widely. The incidence of some diseases—tetanus of the newborn, smallpox, and most of the vector-borne infections—is not

3. Massive social dislocation can occur among small groups living in relative isolation when a large part of the community falls ill or dies and the sick cannot be looked after. See Siskind 1973:208.

dependent on nutritional status, although nutrition does affect case fatality rates. But the incidence and outcome of most of the communicable diseases of childhood, diarrheal diseases, and respiratory infections are very much conditioned by nutritional status. Measles, a minor childhood illness in affluent societies, is a lethal disease in Africa; in hospitalized cases in western and central Africa it is associated with mortality rates of 10 to 15 percent. Millar (1970:4) believes the highest mortality is the result of severe malnutrition occurring at the age measles most frequently strikes.

Famine has few long-term effects on survivors, whereas malnutrition lowers vitality and sometimes causes permanent damage to the liver and kidneys. Mothers and children are more vulnerable than adult men, and a pregnant woman whose iron stores are depleted will not be able to meet the needs of the baby she is carrying (Layrisse, Roche, and Baker 1976:59–60). In contrast, during a famine the reproductive organs usually cease to function and the condition does not affect the next generation; while many deaths occur, the survivors regain their former vitality and resistance to disease with the next harvest.

This does not mean that famine is preferable to malnutrition; the point is that the consequences to the health of a population are very different. The British colonial government instituted programs of famine relief that were paid for out of taxes and required villagers to earn the food they received by working on public projects. The programs probably reduced the number of deaths from starvation but did nothing to increase food production (see Bryceson 1980). The amount of food distributed was not enough to ward off malnutrition; the result was a larger population living at lower levels of health than before.

According to Clyde's official colonial medical history of Tanzania, before Britain and Germany agreed to the division of East Africa in 1886, "Africans were held fast in the bondage of chronic disease, went in constant fear of attack and enslavement by neighbor or stranger, and were dominated in thought and deed by witchcraft, whilst eking out a marginal subsistence from cultivation at the mercy of alternate flood and drought" (1962:1). Today, many Tanzanians believe this is a more accurate description of the situation after European intervention than in precolonial times.

Development of Colonial Medical Services

Western medicine was introduced into Tanzania in the second half of the nineteenth century by Christian missionaries. There were missionary physicians in East Africa from the time of Dr. David Livingstone (c. 1835), mainly to protect the health of the European population. But it was not until after the colonial partition of Africa in the 1880s— that is, when the missionaries were no longer dependent upon Africans for their safety, food, and shelter, but could rely on European governments to protect them (Temu 1972:8–9)—that the medical mission became a social institution of the Christian community, useful for the converts it attracted.[4] This interest in the conversion of Africans inevitably biased missionary medical work toward curative treatment, both because mass preventive health work would have made less impression on individual candidates for conversion and because the healing tradition was deeply embedded in Christian thought. Not until the 1950s did missions begin to play even a modest part in immunization and health education campaigns.

The first government medical services in Tanzania were installed by the Germans, originally to serve the army garrisons stationed there and only later to care for European settlers. Emphasis was naturally placed on surgery, since war casualties required that type of medical care. The first physicians sent to Tanzania from Germany were surgeons and held officer rank in the German army. Between 1891 and 1918 the Germans built some twelve general hospitals, the largest of which was a seventy-five bed hospital at Tabora. At the outbreak of war in 1914, the German army in East Africa marshaled sixty-three physicians, including those from missions, railways, and ships (Taute 1939).

4. See Ranger 1981 for a detailed history of the Universities Mission to Central Africa in southeast Tanzania; these missionaries believed in the power of Western medicine "to penetrate heathen and even Moslem societies which were resistant to evangelization" (ibid.:262). Beidelman has written that the medical services of the Church Mission Society at Berega in Kilosa District "provide a means of contact with non-Christians. A prayer service is held every morning before medical work begins, and all patients should take part, if only passively. The members of the clinic try to associate medical skill with Christianity: sometimes this line of proselytization succeeds" (1971:120).

Thus the initial direction of both missionary and German government medical services was toward curative treatment and hospital care. This emphasis was consistent with the policy that the British government pursued when in 1903 it established medical services in Uganda and Kenya, where, Beck noted, "the medical administrators were requested, first, to preserve the health of the European community; second, to keep the African and Asiatic labor force in good working condition; and third, to prevent the spread of tropical epidemics" (1970:200). Separate facilities were maintained for African, Asian, and European patients or, in hospitals where this was not feasible, racial segregation was practiced with separate wards for each race. The British pursued the same policies in Tanzania, at least until the local authority dispensary system was introduced in 1926, marking the first attempt by the government to attend to the health problems of the rural African population. The orientation of this system, too, was toward curative medicine.

This orientation differed from the practice in the French colonies of West Africa where, from 1915, the French pioneered rural morbidity surveys and eventually created a mobile preventive health service. In British African colonies the idea of field medicine was not accepted till the 1920s, and practical initiation was delayed by budget cuts made during the economic crisis of the 1930s. In Nigeria, for example, until 1946 the only public health measure was the sleeping sickness service, which functioned to control trypanosomiasis (Waddy 1958). Total government expenditures on medical services were negligible before World War II, averaging U.K. £180,000 between 1921 and 1938 (Great Britain Colonial Office 1931, 1932; Tanganyika Territory 1922, 1926, 1937b, 1939a). They did not rise significantly until the 1950s: in 1955/1956 expenditures were U.K. £1.67 million and in 1961/1962 U.K. £2.2 million (United Kingdom Colonial Office 1956, 1962).

Under British colonial rule, there were four types of medical care: government, missionary, industrial, and private. Government medical services were organized on the same basis as other government services in a three-tiered arrangement of central, provincial, and district administration. At the top of the central tier was the chief medical officer (called the director of Medical and Sanitary Services before the creation of the Ministry of Health); his staff at headquarters in Dar es Salaam included (by 1960) three principal medical officers, the principal matron, and the chief health inspector. Apart from certain specialist services (for example, pathology, pharmacy, and psychiatry), most personal and environmental services that had been provided directly by the central government were delegated after 1936 to provincial medical officers and to the superintendent of Dar es Salaam hospitals (virtually another province). The provincial medical officers held senior medical officer rank and were responsible to the chief medical officer. With some individual variations, their duties included administration of the provincial health services, clinical work in the provincial or district hospitals, medical oversight for the provincial town, and other specialized jobs (such as control of sleeping sickness or tuberculosis). The central tier received most of the health budget—64 percent in 1961—for recurrent costs (as opposed to capital investments) (Titmuss 1964:68).

Each district was assigned a medical officer whose headquarters was usually at the hospital under his supervision. He was responsible for local dispensaries and, after 1958, health centers, but he usually performed few supervisory functions. In theory this system referred patients in need of more sophisticated care from a rural dispensary to the district hospital, then to the provincial hospital, and eventually to the full range of specialist services available only in Dar es Salaam. In practice this referral rarely happened, supposedly because the network of communications in rural areas was too poor (the same excuse was given for the lack of supervision by district medical officers of rural dispensaries) (ibid.:40–41). As we shall see, this is at best only a partial explanation.

In addition to government services, twenty-one voluntary agencies, most of them missions, offered medical care through 48 hospitals, 64 large dispensaries, and 175 small dispensaries at the time of independence. Few of these facilities had any formal links with government services or with each other, making coordination virtually nonexistent and planning almost impossible. Grants-in-aid for staff, training, and hospital beds were paid by the central government to some 60 percent of these services; especially large sums were allocated after World War II. By 1961 these subsidies accounted for 14 percent of the government health budget (ibid.:68). The grants represented an important part of the total income of the voluntary hospitals and with patient fees possibly accounted for half of their funds.

Some employers on sisal plantations, in mines, or in factories offered medical services. Resources varied from a dispensary on the premises to a medical officer employed to examine recruits, treat injuries, and so on. Their total contribution was very small—in 1961, 3.5 percent of health expenditures (ibid.).

Medical care provided by the private sector was concentrated in five urban areas—Dar es Salaam, Tanga, Arusha, Moshi, and Mwanza—with a combined population, in 1961, of two hundred thousand. Serving these towns were 130 Western-trained physicians in private practice, or 72 percent of all physicians in private practice and 33 percent of all physicians in Tanzania. The ratio was one physician in private practice per fifteen hundred persons in those urban areas, whereas in 1960 for the whole country the ratio was one physician in private practice or government service per twenty-two thousand people (ibid.:69). Estimates of expenditure in the private sector on either modern or traditional medical services are difficult to make and at the time of independence no estimate could be arrived at.

The central government undertook most of the public health work (as distinguished from curative treatment of sick individuals). From the beginning of British colonial rule, public health services, then called the sanitation branch, were wholly separated from personal medical services. At the provincial level, the provincial medical officer was responsible for overseeing environmental health services, a task he (there were no women medical officers) was expected to perform with only one or two health inspectors on his staff. Because no fully qualified health inspector was posted at the district level, this responsibility fell on the town's assistant health inspector, whose duties included food and milk control and general sanitation. In the rural areas environmental health services were almost nonexistent. Vaccination campaigns were supposed to be carried out by the health inspectorate. Special units, administered centrally, were concerned with malaria, trypanosomiasis, health education, nutrition, and port health. Maternal and child care also fell under public health services; in 1961 the central government was responsible for 71 antenatal clinics and 69 child health clinics, local authority for 204 and 195 respectively, and voluntary agencies for 137 and 190 (Titmuss 1964:37).

In the period between the two world wars, antibiotics were not yet available and only some immunizations were in use. Yet scientists had made important progress in understanding the role of environmental factors in the etiology of disease and in applying that knowledge. In 1938 R. R. Scott, the director of medical services for colonial Tanzania wrote: "the reduction of preventable diseases and improvement of the people's health must go hand in hand with the treatment of individual sufferers and the improvement of economic conditions, education in the broadest sense, housing, food and water supplies and ordinary sanitation" (Tanganyika Territory Medical Department 1938:5). In particular, the role of nutrition in disease was recognized, though only partially understood, and the extent of malnutrition in the colony was acknowledged. A preliminary survey of nutrition concluded that "improvement in nutrition will result in better health and generally greater resistance to disease, in improved physique and therefore capacity for work and greater output" (Tanganyika Territory 1937a:8)

After World War II, with the introduction of new chemicals like DDT, the availability of penicillin and other antibiotics, and the development of new immunizations, mass disease control campaigns could have been mounted more effectively and less expensively than before. It is curious therefore that the Tanganyika Territory Legislative Council (1949), reviewing medical policy in 1949, decided to continue to concentrate resources on curative services. While acknowledging the more lasting beneficial effects of preventive and social medicine, the council rationalized its decision on the grounds that curative medicine was demanded by the people.[5]

Finally, at the time Britain was introducing the National Health Service at home, the director of colonial medical services in Tanzania recommended that all patients except the indigent should be charged for hospital treatment,

5. Gish 1975:17–20 has a contrary interpretation: in his view the author of the 1949 policy document, Dr. E. Pridie, had sound principles and saw the need for preventive work.

whether in-patient or out-patient, and that similar charges be levied by local authorities at rural medical stations under their control (ibid.). In the event, the central government and most local authorities continued to offer free services to African patients who were seen by medical assistants. (Normally European patients were seen by a medical officer, who was a physician, and were charged for services.)

Suppression of Traditional Medicine

Western medicine in Tanzania was superimposed on an existing health care system. Every society has some sort of medical institution or system to care for its sick (Saunders 1954:7). Tanzanians, like most other Africans, had known both traditional doctors and traditional pharmacists. There were many kinds of traditional doctors, each specializing in a particular activity. Omari (1972) lists wisemen, seers, diviners, rainmakers, curers, healers, and circumcisers, among others. Traditional medicine was an integral part of the social organization and had a holistic or unitarian character that has been lost in Western society (Ackernecht 1946:467). Powles (1973) describes this function as part of the nontechnical or "helping-to-cope" side of medicine, as distinguished from the technical mastery of disease.

The Christian missionaries opposed traditional medicine; all traditional practitioners were indiscriminately labeled "witchdoctors" to be eliminated because they symbolized "sub-Christian fears and hatreds" (Oliver 1952:211). The practice of traditional medicine was often confused with religious rituals and beliefs, and the art of the practitioners was disregarded.

Missionary objections were supported by Western physicians who deplored the standards of local practitioners: these physicians occasionally came across evidence of traditional treatment in their daily practice, which confirmed their prejudices about their supposed rivals (Una Maclean 1974:14). Their reluctance to admit the benefits of traditional medicine was also linked to imperial ideology: such an admission would run counter to the belief that Victorian civilization was the acme of human achievement.

The government, for its own reasons, also rejected traditional medicine; in the early 1920s it passed a witchcraft ordinance that provided for the prosecution of Africans it identified as sorcerers and witchdoctors. This measure was initially a response to the African witchcraft eradication movements that began in the 1920s, which centered around a prophet who was believed to have the power to abolish witchcraft and thus to diffuse social tension and fear (Ranger 1969:181). The ordinance could not be enforced universally and traditional medicine continued to be practiced, especially in rural areas, but without benefit of social progress. Without being able to teach new generations of healers openly, and lacking new knowledge to improve their techniques, traditional practitioners eventually came close to fulfilling the colonizers' prophecies.

The eventual impact of the rejection of traditional medicine was to deny a part of the African populace a potential source of medical care. No attempt was made by missions, the European medical profession, or the government to include traditional healers in organized medical services or to improve their skills by sharing new medical knowledge and technology.[6] Colonial medical facilities were sadly understaffed, but traditional practitioners were never looked upon as a source of help. Omari (1972) quotes one estimate of 30,800 traditional doctors in 1972, but the true number is unknown.

The rejection of traditional medicine by the medical corps deprived a growing number of Africans—converted to Christianity and educated by missionaries to look upon certain traditions as ignorant superstitions—of a store of traditional medical knowledge, especially of herbal remedies and other medicines, which was also a source of self-reliance. While not all equally efficacious, some of these remedies were found to be useful by European investigators (Mathias 1965).[7] Unfortunately, this insistence on sifting

6. In contrast, Mao Tsetung, within a year of liberation, directed the First National Health Conference in the People's Republic of China: "Unite all medical workers, young and old, of the traditional and western schools, and organise a solid united front to strive for the development of the people's health work" (cited in Horn 1969:76).

7. Improvisation during World War I by German army physicians prompted the discovery among East African drugs of substitutes for castor oil and digitalis and of a root used by traditional doctors as a remedy for diarrhea, as well as plant sources for alcohol for disinfectants and a good benzine substitute. Hippopotamus and elephant fat, and a mixture of wax and groundnut oil, were used for ointment bases (Taute 1939).

the "scientifically valuable from the dross of irrelevance" (Una Maclean 1974:155) also served to exclude traditional medicine from the mainstream. Just as traditional doctors were debarred from organized medicine, traditional pharmacists were never brought into modern laboratories, although their herbs and medicaments were. Western scientists focused exclusively on the pharmacologically active substances of these materials, diverting attention from the underlying methods and concepts that constitute the enduring value and continuing power of African medicine (ibid.). Expensive imported chemicals and other pharmaceuticals were gradually introduced to replace freely available and natural indigenous preparations.

There are underlying political and economic reasons for the rejection of traditional medicine by the colonial rulers of Tanzania. The missionaries rejected a set of beliefs that was in direct competition with the faith they wished to propagate. The European medical profession rejected the potential threat to their monopoly of another sort of magic—for example, injections that sometimes worked "miraculous" cures—which was also their source of revenue. The government's rejection was more complicated. The system of indirect rule depended on the development and maintenance of ethnic groups and their customs; in principle, therefore, certain indigenous institutions were to be preserved. Peasant agriculture and the indigenous judicial system were to be interfered with as little as possible, and the authority of chiefs was to be strengthened. Traditional medicine fell in the category of customs, rites, and institutions to be preserved; its rejection, therefore, was a departure from principle and a contradiction of the precept that denationalization—the divorce of Africans from their ancestral lineages—was to be avoided.

Probably the simplest explanation is provided by the government's fear of another rebellion, witchcraft having been credited with a seminal role in the Maji Maji War of 1905–1906. The British government, as late as 1957, argued that the revolt was not motivated by opposition to foreign domination, as Julius Nyerere claimed, but "was touched off and spread by witchdoctors who duped the people with 'magic water' and when this failed to protect them from the German bullets, drove them again to their deaths by lies and excuses. The Germans were certainly ruthless, but the high casualties during the revolt were in no small measure due to the deceit of the witchdoctors" (Government of Tanganyika 1957:7).

Behind the defensive position of a government confronted by nationalist demands for independence there may have been a realization that traditional medical practice in some cases involved the active participation of the community in the healing process. This communal participation was different from the individualistic practice of bourgeois liberal medicine, with its one-to-one relationship between physician and patient, in which the patient passively submits to the active intervention of the physician. From the government's explanation cited above, it would seem that the rejection of traditional medicine was motivated by the threat of collective action that its practice entailed.

Western medical practice, on the other hand, could provide the government with an instrument of social control by placing in its hands the power to define ill health and label certain conditions as illnesses. The "sick" label places a problem in a medical context, effectively removing it from a political context, because the label locates the source and treatment of the problem in an individual, thereby obscuring external and underlying causes and isolating people with similar problems from one another. The result is to conceal the need for a collective attack on the problem. Africans, as both patients and practitioners, were conditioned to recognize psychic and physical pain, not as symptoms of oppression and exploitation, but as signs of "schizophrenia" and "hepatitis," diagnostic labels that belied the impotence of clinical medicine. The diseased and dying were conditioned to submit passively to medical procedures in alienating hospital environments, while African concepts of active communal resistance were denigrated. Since traditional medicine was believed to be implicated in rebellion, the government wished to substitute Western medicine and thereby gain that measure of control over the subject population.

In general, however, individual practitioners of traditional medicine who were not involved in any mass movement carried on in rural areas and were not prosecuted unless there were serious cases of iatrogenesis. Since caring for the sick is one of the forms of social security provided by African society, the preservation of traditional medicine was in the interest of both the government and private enterprise. The government left to traditional healers and missions the provision of medical care in the rural areas that supplied the migrant labor force. European medical facilities were built instead in centers of employment.

Curative Medicine for the Labor Force

For those Africans who, deprived of their customary source of sick care, turned to their colonial rulers to provide alternative care, the only services offered were curative. Up to 72 percent of the health budget was spent on expensive curative facilities, as late as 1961. This is in part the origin of the "demand for curative medicine" identified by European physicians. But there were also factors connected with the wage-earning population that helped to determine the type of health care offered. The government adapted colonial medical services to the needs of private enterprise for a productive labor force. First, it made sense to rehabilitate the recruits at their place of work, which entailed curative rather than preventive services. Second, the health problems likely to have required attention during the work period called for a curative approach. These problems included illnesses that interfered with work and accidents, which necessitated first aid and eventually hospital facilities. (Accident prevention would have required costly outlay by capitalists for new machinery, guards, and so on; it was cheaper to pay for care of accident victims.) Men with chronic diseases were likely to be dropped from the labor force or, if discovered on recruitment, not hired. This was especially true of tuberculosis, for which recruits were x-rayed routinely. Third, the concentration of population at a work site made the provision of facilities more economical there than in labor supply areas, where the population was often widely scattered. Fourth, public health measures might have shown workers that colonial private enterprise was the source of their medical problems and spur them to strike or rebel. Thus it was to be expected that the government would continue to emphasize the expansion of curative facilities; even in years of financial stringency following the economic crisis of the 1930s, it continually cut the public health budget first and most drastically.

A focus on labor also calls attention to the government's use of health services to placate discontented workers and to avoid making the more fundamental changes needed to improve their living and working conditions. Although formal demands by striking workers for welfare benefits did not arise in Tanzania before the 1940s, the threat of unrest was a preoccupation of the colonial government. A 1937 nutrition survey promised that improvement in nutrition would mean "more contented labor on plantations and in the mining industry," which would bring "the best type and an adequate supply of workers" (Tanganyika Territory 1937a:8).

Concern with the wage-earning population also suggests an explanation for the low priority assigned to nutrition in the health budget. Despite government recognition of the magnitude, gravity, and significance of malnutrition, at least after World War II, only 0.1 percent of the health budget was spent on nutrition programs in 1961. Laborers were, for the most part, male adults; few women or children were employed. While men, women, and children are all affected, though not equally, by severe famine (for which the government did provide relief), male adults are less vulnerable to malnutrition and its complications than are women and children (World Health Organization 1972). The government was able to meet the nutritional needs of male workers by requiring employers to provide an adequate diet. Hence it was not considered necessary to make a larger provision in the budget for nutrition (Tanganyika Territory 1936, 1937a, 1938b). The government made no direct attempt to care for malnourished women and children in the interwar period. Indirect efforts were made through health education and maternal and child health clinics, though the clinics had such low priority that maternal and child health never appeared as a separate line in the health budget. The one public health area in which the missions played an important role was the provision of maternal and child care. The government was spared this expense by the expedient of missionary medicine. The implicit purpose of providing such services in the rural areas that supplied migrant workers was to ensure the reproduction of the labor force.

Official reports indicate the government's concern with the low productivity of African labor and its conviction that medical care and nutrition would improve output. In 1936 a survey of African food habits was published, in part to aid employers in providing acceptable rations to their workers. The introduction notes:

> There is not the slightest doubt that a large percentage of ill-
> ness suffered by natives employed on estates can be traced to
> inadequate and unbalanced dietaries. Food deficiency nearly
> always plays a part in the . . . wastage of labour. . . . The
> physique of the labourer if properly fed will improve
> greatly, so that the cost to the employer would be more than
> repaid by the increased daily turnout and working capacity
> of his labourers; under-nourished natives cannot be ex-
> pected to, and are not capable of, working really efficiently.
> (Tanganyika Territory 1936:1)

These explanations are consistent with data for Kilosa
and Songea districts. Kilosa, a plantation area with a large
influx of migrant labor, was better served with health facilities in the colonial period than was Songea, a labor reserve,
and most of Songea's facilities were sponsored by missions
rather than the government.

The foregoing analysis provides a number of plausible explanations for the growth of an unevenly distributed and
technically inappropriate health care system, but it does
not fully explain the persistence of the curative approach,
especially after cheaper and more efficient techniques in
preventive medicine became widely available. To understand why this system persisted, it is necessary to examine
the regulation of health policy and the administrative responsibility and decision making behind that policy.

When Britain took over Tanzania from German rule, full
responsibility for the medical services and complete authority were placed in the hands of the medical director, a
post that was always filled by a member of the medical profession. The powers of the director, as described by George
Maclean (1950), who was sleeping sickness officer for the
territory, are impressive: from 1921 to 1938 the director
virtually controlled the medical department, subject only
to financial limitations and the provisions of infectious
disease and other relative ordinances. He had his own
administrative and executive staff (including by 1938 specialists in medicine and surgery) available to advise him,
but there was no standing advisory committee or board of
health to assist him.

The effect of investing professionals with the control of
policy is nicely illustrated in the controversies over quality
versus quantity of health care—for example, in arguments
over the network of services, between the consolidators,

who wished to restrict the dispensary system to limited areas where an efficient service could be built and supervised by the government medical service, and the expansionists, who wanted to extend the scope and activities of the system to full coverage of the rural population. A. McKenzie, acting director of the Tanzanian colonial medical service in 1948, found the expansionists to "represent the civil administration and the people themselves, who not unreasonably desire to see some sort of medical care available to the largest number of people possible, with little thought of the end result or the quality of the treatment given," while the consolidators consisted of "the medical service itself, whose members are anxious that such treatment as they are able to provide shall be of real value and produce permanent effect among the few for whom it is available" (1948:274).[8] Given the low level of medical technology available at the time (few vaccines or antibiotics were developed and there were no known medical remedies for diarrhea and malnutrition, which were the most common conditions), this position was both elitist and self-serving. McKenzie, who described himself as a "staunch upholder of consolidation," believed it was a mistake to encourage the local African authorities to develop their own services; he argued that the professionals of the medical department, not the civil administration, should retain control of the system.

This pattern of vesting medical policy decision-making in the medical profession was well established in Britain and elsewhere. But while professional control may account for the so-called demand for curative services, it does not explain why the medical profession itself was dominated by the concept of curative medicine. That explanation lies in the profession's subjection to capitalist demands and pressures.

Klein (1972) described the medical profession's position within the British National Health Service as a monopoly of technical know-how and control of entry. Freidson (1971: 330) attributed this monopoly to a professional autonomy

8. It is interesting that in this example of the medical profession making decisions about the rate of expansion of the dispensary system, the definition of quality is also medically determined. Since quality is a relative concept, it is open to redefinition by the profession.

he supposed arises when an occupation serves some need or demand of the lay community and subsequently succeeds in becoming a profession. In this teleological explanation, the function enables the profession to become self-sustaining by turning back and shaping, even creating, needs and by defining, selecting, and organizing the way they are expressed in social life. But that autonomy is spurious, as a historical analysis of the development of medicine in Britain reveals: the profession lacked autonomy in determining its own scientific development in the face of capitalist demands and pressures (Turshen 1977). And in the United States, Navarro (1974:20) has shown, control by the medical profession is secondary to that by financial and corporate communities, exercised through, among other means, the "reproductory" health institutions, that is, the medical faculties and other teaching institutions, which perpetuate and legitimize the patterns of control. Control is also exercised through governing bodies such as boards of trustees and directors and through funding agencies such as foundations, which guide the policies of the teaching institutions.

This analysis has important implications for any attempt by young professionals (including young Tanzanians) to change the system, since the medical profession is ultimately not autonomous but controlled by the corporate classes. Older professionals, who make up the faculty of teaching institutions, are often inextricably involved in the capitalist economy and resistant to change. They have a seminal influence on the attitudes and aspirations of the next generation of practitioners. John Robson (1973) has shown how in England, medical students are socialized into the ideology of the profession, which is divorced from the social experience of most patients, and how professional concerns take precedence in any conflict of interests.

An effective African challenge to colonial control of medical policy by a cadre of Tanzanian health workers did not materialize because their training did not place them in a position to question professional medical decisions, and because their identification with the mass of Africans living in rural areas was weakened by their colonial education, which disparaged African culture and extolled the superiority of Western civilization.

9

COLONIAL EDUCATION

olonial education influenced health standards indirectly, especially the health of women, who were largely excluded from formal schooling and thereby deprived of information that would have enabled them to adapt as workers, wives, and mothers to the new capitalist system. General educational policies determined medical care indirectly by controlling the entry of Africans into the professions, while medical educational policy had a direct impact on the type and distribution of medical services.

Tanzania was one of the last territorial acquisitions of the British Empire: in one sense it benefited from being governed by experienced colonial administrators, but in another sense it suffered. The experience of India and, more pertinently, of the colonies in West Africa had persuaded colonial administrators that mass education would produce unrest in Tanzania. According to Thompson (1968:25), government officials were constantly aware of the major social problems created by the expansion of academic education in India and Ceylon.

Colonial Policies

After World War I, colonial governments took the responsibility previously shouldered by missions for African education. Like the mission schools, government schools offered a limited range of subjects: they emphasized religious training and moral instruction rather than social or physical sciences (United Kingdom Colonial Office 1925). Frederick Lugard, who formulated the doctrines of indirect rule, argued that "the diffusion of education throughout the colony, and especially the education of the sons of native rulers, is particularly desirable in order to avoid the present danger of a separate educated class (in West Africa chiefly confined to the Coast cities) in rivalry with the accepted rulers of the people" (1923:426). The purpose of education of the elite was to perpetuate local African authority and thereby British rule. African rulers had to learn to perform colonial duties and to see that their interests were identical to those of government.

For Donald Cameron, the governor who introduced Lugard's policy of indirect rule in Tanzania, "the policy of the Government is to maintain and support native rule. . . . Our aim should be to maintain and develop all that is best in the indigenous methods and institutions of native rule, to avoid as far as possible everything that has a denationalizing tendency, and to inculcate respect for authority, self-respect, and fair treatment of the lower classes, the weak and the ignorant" (Tanganyika Territory 1931a:6).

Because education, particularly secondary and higher education, would have a denationalizing tendency, an extensive educational system would be contrary to the government's interests. As late as 1957/1958, Tanzania had the lowest rate of primary school enrollment among British colonies in Africa: only 27 percent of Tanzanian children received any education as compared with 71 percent of Zimbabwean children (UNESCO 1961, 3:37). The debate over education that took place in Tanzania in the 1920s should be understood in this perspective. The debate was about what type of education should be provided (academic or vocational), by whom it should be provided (government or missions), and to which level (primary, secondary, or intermediate).

In the 1890s, Christian missions started a number of schools in Tanzania, and the German administration also played a part, especially in the north, in training artisans and clerks: in this way a small number of elite families benefited from an educational tradition. Though an effort was made by African staff to keep some of these schools going during and after the East African campaign of World War I, by 1918 education had almost come to a halt, and Tanzania, like Kenya, had to start virtually from scratch in the 1920s (Goldthorpe 1965:3). The British educational system, like the medical services, was racially segregated, and there were substantial differences in the per caput expenditures on each race. In 1960, per caput expenditure on education in Tanzania was about U.K.£12 for Africans, £25 for Asians, and £150 for Europeans.

African education commissions organized by the American Phelps-Stokes Fund[1] and backed by the British Church Missionary Society and the British Colonial Office visited West Africa in 1920/1921 and East Africa in 1923/ 1924. The Phelps-Stokes report recommended that the government issue grants-in aid to subsidize educational work by the missions (Jones 1924). These grants were approved in 1925. Influenced by the report, which was in accord with the aims of indirect rule, the Advisory Committee on Native Education in British Tropical African Dependencies— created in 1923 by the secretary of state for the colonies to advise the Colonial Office on educational policy—issued a white paper declaring that the government should maintain control of educational policy but stressing the importance of religious training; the committee agreed to aid mission schools that provided the required standard of educational efficiency. It stated that religion should be substituted for "superstitious beliefs" because it would act as a buffer in the African's first contact with "civilization," and that education should be adapted to African mentality, aptitudes, occupations, and traditions, conserving as far as possible "all sound and healthy elements" in the fabric of African social life (United Kingdom Colonial Office 1925). According to Thompson (1968:17), this memorandum dictated educational policy in Tanzania until independence.

The Phelps-Stokes report had also recognized the potential conflicts of interest in African education:

> There has been a very unfortunate divergence in the attitude of the missionaries, settlers and government officials toward Native education. The attitude of the missionaries has been determined by their desire to impart their religious ideas to the Native people and to win them to a Christian way of life. The government officials have naturally thought of the colonial administration and have felt the necessity for clerical help and such skilled workers as are needful for the survey-

---

1. The Phelps-Stokes Fund sent Thomas Jesse Jones of the Hampton Institute in Virginia on these missions. The Hampton Institute was founded after the Civil War to educate Afro-Americans, and Jones had a lifetime of experience working with the American rural black population.

ing of roads and other means of transportation. Settlers and traders have been concerned for the various needs of their special occupations. The traders have joined with Government in a demand for clerks. The settler's demand has been primarily for laborers to till the soil and to carry on the varied activities of the farms. These diversities of view have been further intensified by the attitude taken toward the Native people. Some have recognized the principle of trusteeship and desire to assist the Natives to realize their full capacities as human beings; others have thought of them as economic assets to be exploited for the satisfaction of the party in control. (Jones 1924:25)

Conflict erupted a few years later over language policy. The missions taught in the vernacular, whereas the government wanted Swahili or English as the medium of instruction (Marcia Wright 1971:166, 173). Probably too much has been made of this debate between the missions and government; some of it may well have been for the benefit of the League of Nations Permanent Commission of Enquiry, which was pressing for rapid expansion of the educational system and the provision of academic education (Leubuscher 1944:82–89). It is difficult to see a real conflict between the missionaries' belief that secondary and higher education would create denationalized and irreligious elites, a belief that led them to emphasize mass literacy and Bible instruction, and the concerns of government as described by the director of education in his annual report for 1926:

Probably the greatest pitfall and yet one which is so seldom anticipated and guarded against in educational schemes is over-production, or the law of supply and demand. In examining the results of education in different parts of the Empire one wonders whether those responsible for launching schemes 50 years ago tried to visualise the economic needs of today: and no educationist is justified in . . . saddling an unsuspecting posterity with a top-heavy social system. It is an easy matter to organise a system of elementary vernacular schools leading on to secondary and higher schools and thereby to create channels to enter the professions. This, while excellent in itself, developed with circumspection, may prove one of the greatest obstacles to economic development and a source of embarrassment to the administrative authorities of future generations. (Tanganyika Territory 1927a:20)

In the event, both government and missions probably underestimated the denationalizing effect of any type of education and overestimated the extent to which they could control the spread of ideas or the course of events. At the end of the 1930s, Africans were demanding secondary and higher education and, after World War II, the economy required more educated Africans. Under these combined pressures, colonial educational policy was eventually modified; but it would take years to make good the lack of trained cadres and the result was a severe personnel shortage at independence.

Ideology and Instruction

The amount of money available for education was subject to numerous restrictions. From about thirty thousand pounds in 1925 (Leubuscher 1944:83), allocations increased markedly after World War II, reaching about four hundred thousand pounds by 1949 (United Kingdom Colonial Office 1950).

Colonial education was no doubt limited by a lack of funds, but a paucity of relevant ideas may also have been a restriction. Ehrlich (1968:344) argues that because their own system was elitist—fine in quality, deficient in quantity—and export models tended to be caricatures of the domestic product, the British were poorly qualified to provide education suitable for a developing society. This inadequacy was most evident at the university level where costs, standards, and curricula were ill adapted to East Africa's long-term needs.

In the final analysis educational systems reflect the values of society at large. It is not the elitist attitudes to be found in schools that are to be faulted, but the position the educational system occupies in the economy and broader social environment. As Cliffe states, "Until political and social mobility are demonstrably based on criteria other than mere academic performance, the elitist attitudes of the educated merely reflect the realities of life" (1971:64). These attitudes reflect the ideology of the dominant class, and that class determines educational content by virtue of the control it exercises. The educational system is but a part of the superstructure of society, serving to reproduce the organization of production by transmitting attitudes and skills to the next generation.

Nyerere has written an eloquent critique of colonial education, emphasizing that the values transmitted were inappropriate to the needs of Tanzania:

> the educational system introduced into Tanzania by the colonialists was modelled on the British system, but with even heavier emphasis on subservient attitudes and on white-collar skills. Inevitably, too, it was based on the assumptions of a colonialist and capitalist society. It emphasized and encouraged the individualistic instincts of mankind, instead of his cooperative instincts. It led to the possession of individual material wealth being the major criterion of social merit and worth. (1968b:269)

Hirji (1973) points out that the colonial educational system was subservient to the colonial economic system and, in Tanzania, the demand for labor was basically for two kinds of men—workers and bureaucrats. Workers were needed for low-paid jobs requiring little skill or training on farms, in mines, in transport and construction, and in the few existing industries. Hirji notes that formal education is not necessary to train productive workers for these sectors: any requisite skill is acquired within the production process itself. White-collar workers were needed to staff the comparatively large and unproductive administrative apparatus, and it was to meet this demand that the educational establishment was geared. Furthermore, most workers and bureaucrats employed by government and private enterprise were males, and the educational system was subject to the economic system's sexual bias as well. This is clearly reflected in—and partially accounts for—the enormous differentials in educational opportunities for males and females (Mbilinyi 1973).

Hirji's view that the colonial education system was geared to meet the demands of a large bureaucracy is supported by employment statistics. Over the period of colonial rule, from 1930 to 1961, government employment grew both in absolute numbers—from 20,000 to 108,000 workers—and in relation to total employment—from 18 percent to 29 percent (Stephens 1968:179). The medical department also grew and by 1958 had become one of the largest government departments in Tanzania (Tanganyika Territory 1958:145).

Colonial educational policy in the interwar period, with its emphasis on manual skills for most Africans, secondary schooling for the sons of chiefs, and academic education for Asians and Europeans, created a social structure in which Europeans were at the top, Asians and African chiefs were in the middle, and the African masses were at the bottom. After World War II and increasingly as independence approached, more Africans were admitted to secondary and higher educational facilities, but this did not immediately change the social structure. It initiated a process of Africanization of the bureaucracy, though at independence less than 25 percent of all higher and middle level government posts were held by Tanzanians.

Medical Education

The medical services, in particular, suffered from a lack of trained personnel at independence as a consequence of short sighted, racist educational policies. Makerere College in Kampala, Uganda, was the only East African facility available for medical training in the colonial period. Ten or fewer students were enrolled annually before 1930 in an elementary medical course. From 1930 the school was open to Tanzanians, Kenyans, and Ugandans, and the training became more advanced after 1931. The annual enrollment rose rapidly to a pre–World War II peak of fifty-three. It dropped back to an annual average of thirty-one during and after the war and did not reach prewar levels again until 1955 (Goldthorpe 1965:88–89). The first Tanzanians to take a full medical course went to Makerere in the late 1930s. Only ten Tanzanian physicians had qualified by the end of 1952, and only fourteen were in government service by the end of 1960. Another three Tanzanians received their training abroad, making a total of seventeen Tanzanian physicians at independence (Titmuss 1964:12).

In the 1930s and early 1940s, nursing schools were established to train Africans, usually men, as auxiliaries; from 1943 this course was upgraded to a certificate program requiring three to four years of training. Rural medical aids were also trained (World Bank 1978:19).

From 1922 to 1928, Makerere College was administered by the colonial government of Uganda. Control of the college was then transferred from the Ugandan Education De-

partment to a council and assembly, including members
nominated by the governments of Uganda, Kenya, Tanganyika, and Zanzibar, under a constitution resembling that
of an English provincial university. In the late 1940s, a time
of much reorganization, further constitutional changes concentrated authority in a small college council (Goldthorpe
1965:11–12).

From the first, medicine was the most advanced training
available to Africans. The medical course was extended
from four to six years in 1936, and later from six to seven
years. The original certificate in medicine issued by
Makerere College was replaced by the East African diploma
in medicine, granted by the Joint East African Examining
Board in Medicine. This diploma was in turn replaced in
1952 by the licentiate in medicine and surgery (East
Africa), which was later—and retrospectively—recognized
by the General Medical Council of Great Britain. Over the
years, the title of the graduates also changed—from senior
native medical asistant, unlicensed (1923), to senior African medical assistant, with the full responsibility of a medical practitioner though licensed to practice only in government medical departments (1931); this title was in turn
changed to African assistant medical officer and, finally,
in 1952, the title became assistant medical officer (Williams 1952).

These changes in length of training and in title reflected
the increasingly high entrance qualifications demanded of
candidates. The effect of this shifting definition of a
qualified candidate was to ensure that few people would be
eligible for training and even fewer would be graduated.
This method of limiting competition is common under capitalism. In England competition was restricted by the Medical Act of 1858, which permitted only physicians registered
by the professionally controlled General Medical Council to
practice, and by the system of royal colleges, which controlled appointments and career advancement. The economic purpose of such regulation is to increase the exchange value of physicians' skills in a capitalist economy
in which medical care is a commodity.

Another effect of these changes was to turn rural health
workers away from service in remote areas and toward
training for higher qualifications, which would enable them
to progress up the hierarchy. This centripetal force, a char-

acteristic of capitalist economy, deprived rural areas of trained medical personnel, an effect still felt in 1971/1972 (United Republic of Tanzania 1972).

In 1939, the Joint East African Examining Board in Medicine published a set of regulations relating to certification in medicine, surgery, and obstetrics and gynecology. It is remarkable that, despite the different conditions of practice and the diseases encountered in England and East Africa, the curriculum was identical in the two places.[2] It was clinically oriented, adapted to the needs of a northern, industrial, and urban society. Lacking emphasis on public health, tropical diseases, and social medicine, the curriculum was ill adapted to the needs of the mass of Africans living in rural areas, and the few Tanzanian physicians who were graduated from this course were ill prepared to practice in rural Africa. It is not surprising, therefore, that they preferred to work in European-style hospitals, in the clinical environment in which they had been trained.

It is interesting to compare the Makerere curriculum of 1939 with a more recent curriculum of the Medical Faculty of the University of Dar es Salaam (1973). The teaching hours allocated to preventive medicine were 5 percent of the total course in 1939 at Makerere and 19 percent in 1971/1972 at Dar es Salaam. The continued emphasis on clinical and curative medicine seems to confirm the expectation that, in the absence of certain other changes, African assumption of control of medical policy does not necessarily entail radical change in the medical system created by the colonial regime.

The very small number of Tanzanian physicians trained

2. Certification in medicine required six months of clinical work on the wards; three concurrent months of clinical work in an out-patient department; 200 hours of lectures in clinical medicine; 150 hours of lectures; and instruction in vaccination. Surgery required six months of surgical work on the wards; three concurrent months of surgical work in an out-patient department; 100 hours of clinical surgery; 160 hours of lectures; and instruction in dentistry, anesthetics, and ophthalmology. Obstetrics and gynecology called for six months of clinical work on the wards and in an out-patient department; 80 hours of obstetrics and 40 hours of gynecology lectures; and twenty deliveries. Forensic medicine required 40 hours of lectures. Preventive medicine took 40 hours of lectures plus 30 hours of practical demonstrations (for example, mosquito control, infectious diseases, hospitals, and meat inspection) (Joint East African Examining Board in Medicine 1939).

at Makerere invites further comment. Obviously, the supply of candidates with sufficient general education to qualify for the course was limited. Moreover, the medical services had competitors for the few Africans who were eligible. This problem was recognized early in colonial rule: in 1927 the medical department reported that it was difficult to obtain candidates with a thorough knowledge of English and a good general education, and that "an English-speaking native with a fair general education has no difficulty in obtaining a post either in government employment, with a commercial firm, or on a plantation. It is not surprising, therefore, that the majority prefer to take a clerical post immediately rather than undergo a further period of training with an examination to pass" (Tanganyika Territory 1928a:36).

In addition, the prevailing racist attitude toward Africans led to an underestimation of their intellectual capacity and to the expectation that few Africans could ever become fully qualified medical practitioners. This attitude is evident in an unsigned, undated memorandum sent with a letter from the acting district officer of Musoma to the medical officer of Musoma on 2 November 1936:

> The "Pocket Doctor" is taught diagnosis in the widest sense and this requires a knowledge of all branches of medicine and their scientific adjuncts with the intelligence to know what use to make of these aids, and thereafter by the use of the faculties of deduction and reason to arrive at a conclusion, faculties of the intelligence which are lacking except in the unusual native. . . .
>
> Modern civilization has been evolved slowly over the course of many years and it is suggested that the evolution of the native should be taken step by step, that he should creep before he walk or even run after medical truth. (Middleton papers, Mss. Afr. S. 1079)

This widely held attitude influenced colonial policy in every sphere, from peasant agriculture to the Africanization of the bureaucracy.

Finally, the acuity of need for Tanzanian physicians was blunted somewhat by the availability of Asian physicians. Of the 520 registered physicians (as many as 100 of them no longer resident or practicing) in Tanzania in 1960, 194 were Asians. While 158 of these Asian physicians were in private practice, 36 did enter government service and were posted to government hospitals and dispensaries. Similarly, 75 European missionary physicians also helped meet the need for trained personnel in 1960. The missionaries offered the government two advantages—they were willing to work in remote areas and they accepted lower salaries than were paid to physicians in government service.

The expansion of medical care was impeded by colonial policy on African education, which was eventually forced to change by the economy's expanded needs for more educated recruits. Medical training consisted of a simplified version of the curriculum formulated in England, thus perpetuating the attitudes and values as well as the clinical orientation brought by the Europeans who provided the first medical care in the country. The organization of medical services in Tanzania came to mirror the hierarchies of the metropolis: prestige and power were vested in physicians while nursing and public health personnel were subordinate. Tanzania did differ from England in some respects. The tendency to employ women in low-paid unskilled jobs, characteristic of the system in England, was less marked in Tanzania, where the wage employment sector was small and men were likely to fill even unskilled jobs before women. And unlike England, which discriminated against female doctors, Tanzania had few female candidates for any job requiring literacy since discrimination against women in the educational system was so thoroughgoing. There was no question of female applicants for training as physicians, and men were trained even for such traditionally female occupations as nursing.

Colonial medicine was institutionalized in a bureaucracy and reproduced in medical schools. The bureaucrats (colonial medical officers) blurred the distinction between health and health care, as if the former were a product of the latter or as if health care and medical care were synonymous. Medical educators were convinced a priori of the ineducability of African students. As the pool of eligible candidates increased the medical diploma became more difficult to attain so that by 1961 only seventeen Tanzanians had qualified. At independence Africans found themselves ill prepared to fit the colonial medical system to new uses.

10

THE RURAL ECONOMY
AFTER INDEPENDENCE

On 9 December 1961 Tanzania gained independence from Great Britain in a peaceful manner under the auspices of the United Nations trusteeship system. Few changes were made in the system of government initially, although as early as 1962 Nyerere (who assumed the presidency in December of that year) articulated his socialist political philosophy in a paper entitled "Ujamaa—The Basis of African Socialism" (Nyerere 1966). The one-party state adopted a socialist policy in 1967 with the publication of the Arusha Declaration.

A consistent objective of socialism in Tanzania is equity. Nyerere's goal is "to build a society in which all members have equal rights and equal opportunities; in which all can live at peace with his neighbours without suffering or imposing injustice, being exploited, or exploiting; and in which all have a gradually increasing basic level of material welfare before any individual lives in luxury" (1968a:340). Some progress appears to have been made in achieving the goal of equity. One indicator of equality is income distribution. A study by van Ginneken (1976:41) showed little inequality as measured by the distribution of household expenditure and only slightly more in the distribution of landholdings by farm size in rural areas.[1] The average expenditure of the richest group was only ten times greater than that of the poorest; the expenditures of the richest group in urban areas were about the same as those of their counterparts in the rural areas; and, not unexpectedly, the proportion of poor households was much larger in rural than in urban areas (ibid.:11, 15, 37).

1. Gini indices were 0.313 for expenditure in 1969 and 0.484 for landholding in 1972. The Gini coefficient is a measure of equity for distribution: 0 equals perfect equality and 1 equals perfect inequality.

The twin objectives of equity and improved standards of living imposed tasks of great magnitude and difficulty on a largely unskilled and poorly educated population, with few resources and almost no wealth. Tanzania's poverty is well documented. It has been measured in terms of food intake and household expenditures. The Food and Agriculture Organization's recommended minimum calorie intake is 2,300 kilocalories, the Tanzanian daily average in 1972 was 2,009; the safe level of protein intake is 60 grams daily, the Tanzanian average was 52 (ibid.:32). If defined according to the minimum wage law of 1969, poverty includes households whose annual expenditure fell below 1,920 Tanzanian shillings in urban areas and below 1,440 shillings in rural areas: 65 percent of rural and 20 percent of urban households were living in poverty in 1969 (ibid.:37).

Poverty was identified as one of the broad determinants of ill health and malnutrition in the colonial period. This chapter examines the policies the independent government adopted to eradicate poverty in the rural areas and, more specifically, its attempt to restructure the food system. This review is not a comprehensive survey of the rural economy; sectors and programs that affect health and nutrition are singled out.

Food and Agriculture

At the time of independence, commercial agriculture was the mainstay of the economy: agricultural and livestock products together contributed about 80 percent of export earnings, while minerals contributed 13 percent. Four products—cotton, coffee, sisal, and diamonds—accounted for 67 percent of total exports and 28 percent of monetary gross domestic product. Plantations owned and managed by Europeans or Asians, while occupying only 1 percent of the land, were important producers of export crops: they furnished virtually all the sisal and tea, the greater part of tobacco, wheat, pyrethrum, seed beans, peas, and some of the coffee. Livestock were almost entirely African-owned, and African peasants produced around 55 percent of crop exports. African peasants contributed over 80 percent of the country's total crop production (this figure includes a fair valuation of food grown for home consumption) (World Bank 1961:13–16).

At independence, only 3 percent of the population was in wage employment, one-third on sisal plantations alone. The industrial sector consisted of some three hundred small-scale private companies managed by Europeans or Asians. Given this picture of the economy, the World Bank, in the report of a 1959 mission undertaken for the colonial government on the eve of independence, recommended that the main development effort concentrate on African agriculture (ibid.:16).

With this legacy of dependency on the export of a few raw materials and primary commodities subject to world market price fluctuations, virtually no industry, and the problems of poverty, malnutrition, and growing inequality described earlier, the newly independent state set about restructuring the economy.

In the reorganization of agriculture, land is usually the first problem dealt with. In Latin America land reform typically entails a program of breaking up *latifundia* (large estates) and the distribution of land to peasant producers. This was not the case in Tanzania, where large estates never existed. With only 1 percent of the land alienated, the need for agricultural reorganization after independence was based on a very different set of circumstances, namely, a growing internal differentiation among regions. Those regions most suited to production of cash crops for export were becoming richer than those that had served as de facto labor reserves, and within the richer regions, income inequalities were appearing among Africans. Land scarcity was developing in the most densely populated mountainous areas, and rich farmers were buying up the land of poor farmers who were forced to work as wage laborers for them. The first priority, however, was to make credit available to farmers, rather than to reallocate land. Because land scarcity was assumed to be the exception and low population density the rule, coping with low population density became a second priority. Given the country's history of sporadic famine, which the colonial experience had transformed into chronic malnutrition, one might expect that increased food production would be a third priority, but in fact greater emphasis was placed on cash crops.

At independence, the Land Bank, which was the sole source of government credit for agriculture in the colonial era, was replaced by the Agricultural Credit Agency, whose major objective was the extension of its services to Africans farming small plots of land. In 1964, the National Development Credit Agency was established to provide credit to peasant farmers for cultivation and development through cooperatives.

All public land was nationalized in 1967. This action gave the government a general oversight of all dealings in land; the purpose was to ensure maximum use of land, the main resource of a poor country, for the benefit of the entire population. But customary land tenure rules still obtained, and no laws had been passed to regulate contrary practices. As a result absentee ownership, speculation, and land hoarding were not unknown in the area west of Lake Victoria and in Kilimanjaro Region (Sawyers 1969:77).

In a detailed study of Ismani (Iringa District), Rayah Feldman (1974:307) found rights in land to be totally separated from community membership as a result of the intermixing of many ethnic groups, itself caused by technical and economic changes in agriculture. The simultaneous disappearance of nationalities and maintenance of customary land law meant that the social justifications for land tenure rules were no longer valid. Village development committees, responsible for allocating land to those who requested it, did not have the same interest as village elders formerly had in seeing that all members of the community were granted land.

The commercial value of land became a more significant factor in regulating land transfers than the maintenance of group ties through the protection of common interests in land. Feldman maintained that gross inequalities in land ownership were growing, without controls, because government policy retained customary law for most rural land. Commercial land transactions were carried out secretly and were consequently subject to cheating and insecurity. Because land tenure in Ismani, as in many other commercially developed areas, was actually individual tenure, the duty of the Village Development Committee to guard group interests in land was irrelevant. Thus there was no agreed institutional procedure for land allocations. In the context of a land shortage arising from agricultural development within an incipient capitalist framework, there was both license and incentive to cheat. Because the modern version of customary law did not allow or actively discouraged land rent, exploitation took the form of evictions and the insecurity of tenure rather than high prices or rents.

Sawyers (1969) pointed out that, until recently, few Africans commanded sufficient resources to invest in land on any large scale. But since independence, Africans have held well-paying jobs in the government, party, and business, and they have had increased access to loan capital. He noted that this emerging class had the economic power and political influence to dispossess and dominate less fortunate and less able community members.

The other Tanzanian particularity that influenced post-colonial agricultural policy was the dispersed pattern of settlement. It is not certain when or why Tanzanians decided on scattered hamlets rather than the village life that is typical of agricultural societies the world over (Kimambo 1969). The pattern had persisted, in part because it enabled Africans to avoid colonial control and exploitation. Living in villages would have increased their chances of being called for forced labor, assessed for tax, and subjected to a myriad of irksome regulations (Raikes 1975:41).

A policy of resettling hamlet inhabitants into larger villages dates back to colonial days, and several rationales have been offered. The difficulty of providing services to a dispersed population is one reason for urging Tanzanians to relocate.[2] Another motive, cited by Mwapachu (1976:4), then district development director of Shinyanga District, is that participation in development is too limited when people are physically isolated: established forums had to be within reach of a larger segment of the population, if the majority of the people were to participate in their own development. But these justifications were not the only grounds for the policy: resettlement has its roots in British administration of agriculture in the colonial period.

At the very end of British rule in the late 1950s, colonial administrators tried to create a new farming system through closely supervised settlements. The experts argued that, if

2. Coulson (1977:94) finds two difficulties with this argument that do not invalidate it but do show its limited relevance to the problem. First, the government could not afford to maintain the services it was providing before villagization, and by promising more it was creating impossible demands it could not fulfill. Second, in some areas population density was already high enough for this purpose.

they could get some of the more maleable farmers physically away from their homes and culturally away from the
restraining influence of African society, these farmers could
be made to cultivate under more modern conditions, providing there were adequate controls. Only a few such
schemes got off the ground before independence, but the
underlying concept of planning agricultural advance largely
through the introduction of modern farming systems in
areas of new settlement, coupled with the emphasis on ex-
pert management and control as the key components, was
available as the basis for postindependence agricultural
planning (Cliffe 1972:96–98).

The supervised approach received endorsement from the
World Bank (1961) in the report of its mission to Tanzania,
and the bank's recommendations were embodied in the
three-year development plan adopted immediately after independence. This plan gave high priority to the "transformation approach" whereby, through village settlement
schemes, new technical, social, and legal systems would be
developed. At the same time, more orthodox extension and
credit services would be the basis for a separate "improvement approach" aimed at gradual but progressive
improvement of the farmers' methods of crop and animal husbandry.

Programs under the improvement approach—pest control, storage, seed improvement, extension advice—
contributed to increased production of cash crops in the
1960s, although it is not possible to work out the precise
amount. Cliffe (1972:101) argues that increased production
did little to change either the technologically backward
character of agriculture or its fragmented individual structure; on the contrary, the change in the nature of rural society was in the direction of individualization and the growth
of regional, class, and gender differences, and this change
was propelled by the government's improvement activities.

Under the transformation approach of the Village Settlement Programme eight villages were created. Because a
wide range of services was provided for them in advance,
thus making them capital intensive and expensive, and because there was little capital available, the program could
touch only few people. It also created a danger of bur-
dening the settlers with excessive amounts of debt. The Rural Settlement Commission (1966:40) concluded in 1965
that the schemes were not economically viable and that so-

cial relations in the villages led to an undesirable gap between members and staff.

But while the scheme was rejected, the form survived. The problem of agricultural advance continued to be thought of in terms of projects, new settlements, and physical and social boundaries. In this environment control and management were easier, but what the Tanzanians call "commandism," meaning the tendency for managers to order workers around and for workers to wait for orders, was also more likely to develop, along with an attitude among workers of dependence on the government.

The continuity in government agricultural policy from colonial times through independence is well documented by Coulson (1977). He found an uninterrupted policy line, beginning with the post–World War II groundnut scheme; through the focal point or improvement approach (1956–1967), which concentrated on progressive farmers, and various settlement schemes (settlement under close supervision, 1953–1962; spontaneous settlement, 1962–1963; planned settlement, 1963–1966); to the *ujamaa* villages (1967–1969) and villagization (1969–1976) discussed below.

There was no improvement in most socioeconomic fields in the years immediately after independence. In some years the situation worsened: between 1960 and 1966 wage employment dropped by 20 percent, prices rose by 15 percent, and individual consumption rose by a mere 1 percent annually. To most rural dwellers the worsening terms of trade for raw materials meant that their incomes remained stationary (Tabari 1975:90–91). While commercial agriculture grew fairly rapidly in the early 1960s, food production did not, and the government was importing maize, rice, and wheat to meet domestic needs (World Bank 1977c:8–10).

It is against this background that the Arusha Declaration was proclaimed in 1967. Clearly a new approach was called for, and there is no doubt that President Nyerere was impressed by what he had seen during his visits to China in the 1960s, particularly by the promise of increased productivity that collectivization offered.

Collective Farming and Village Formation

In 1967 Nyerere issued a policy statement entitled "Socialism and Rural Development." In it he advocated his conception of *ujamaa* (Swahili for extended family or community) as cooperative living and working for the good of all: "This means that most of our farming would be done by groups of people who live as a community and work as a community. They would live together in a village; they would farm together; market together; and undertake the provision of local services and small local requirements as a community" (1968b:351).

Such communities would need managers, treasurers, and governing bodies, but these people would come from within the community, not outside. All members of the community would be equals and would govern themselves in all matters that concern their own affairs. The distribution of returns in an *ujamaa* village would be made on the basis of shares according to the work done; at the same time, a proportion of the total return would be set aside to help the sick, the crippled, the old, and orphaned children. Another part would be set aside for expansion or investment. These decisions would be made by all participants through the established structures of village democracy.

The collectivization drive began after the publication of Nyerere's statement (a small number of collective villages had been formed spontaneously after independence). By 1969, both the government and the party, the Tanganyika African National Union (TANU),[3] had established organizations to promote the creation of *ujamaa* villages. By 1973 more than two million peasants had joined these villages, but no more than 10 percent of the villages had actually attained full collectivization (McHenry 1976).

While the policies enunciated in the presidential circular of 1969 and the second five-year development plan implied a completely new departure in planning perspectives, in practice the changes in method and organization were not so dramatic. Administrators tended to regard *ujamaa* villages as another on the list of rural projects. By 1972 the policy was almost exclusively identified with new settlements and villagization, that is, the relocation of people in villages, generally in the poorer, more sparsely populated

---

3. Tanzania has been a one-party state since 1965. In 1977 TANU joined with the Afro Shirazi party of Zanzibar; under the name Chama Cha Mapinduzi, the Party of Revolution, it became the single legal party of Zanzibar, Pemba, and mainland Tanzania.

parts of the country. From 1973 the goal of collectivization was abandoned, and the resistant peasantry was compelled to live in villages. By 29 December 1976, as reported in the Dar es Salaam *Daily News*, there were 13,076,220 people in 7,684 villages, representing 85 percent of mainland Tanzania's estimated population of 15,378,140.

The impact of *ujamaa* policy on rural planning was in general very limited at the outset. Tea and tobacco were to be farmed cooperatively rather than individually; and dairy cattle were to be kept collectively, although the cooperative activity was limited to marketing and such services as providing feed and did not deal with the problem of improving the stock of poorer peasants. There were specialized programs to expand agricultural training, to provide credit, and to create thirty state farms, although from the beginning President Nyerere said that state farms, which paid workers a wage and therefore represented the proletarianization of the peasantry, were not a solution to be adopted on a broad scale. Proposals for regional specialization, however, were not put forward, although agricultural planners spent much time on crop priorities.

While Nyerere did not single out women as a group for whom the *ujamaa* system would be especially advantageous, he was mindful of the need to improve their lot. In "Socialism and Rural Development" he cited two inadequacies of the precolonial African system that a socialist society would correct: poverty and the inequality of women. He argued that "women in traditional society were regarded as having a place in the community which was not only different, but was also to some extent inferior. It is impossible to deny that the women did, and still do, more than their fair share of the work in the fields and in the homes. . . . within traditional society ill-treatment and enforced subservience could be their lot. This is certainly inconsistent with our socialist conception" (Nyerere 1968b:339).

Where kinship systems of mutual security have broken down, *ujamaa* villages may provide what the modern welfare state does in advanced capitalist countries. In a report that appeared in the *Daily News* on 17 September 1972, a widow, none of whose three children was living, said that *ujamaa* was the solution for her—it offered her security and a community. She was not originally from the village where she was then living, and not a member of the group predominant in that area.

In the Uluguru mountains of Morogoro Region, however, Brain (1976:275) found that women, both legal and common-law wives, were significantly worse off in a settlement than they had been in their traditional societies, where they had held considerable rights in land: by contrast, in the settlements all rights in land were vested in the husband and, as a corollary, all proceeds were handed over to him. Women had no rights whatsoever, and the government scheme made no provision in the event of the husband's death. It was assumed that the woman would leave the settlement and go home. But, as Brain pointed out, going home would have been difficult, for the women would have returned to nothing; custom dictated that a person must forfeit rights to uncultivated land, and it was unlikely that women would have found workers to farm their land or had the money to pay them. Even more revealing of the second-class treatment of women was the derision with which Brain's findings were greeted when he presented them at a week-long seminar on settlement in East Africa held at the University of Dar es Salaam in April 1966. In the audience were many senior African civil servants who argued that common-law wives had no claim to a man's income, while proposed regulations disbursing a statutory amount of farm income to legal wives would disrupt the relationship between husbands and wives. Apparently even in matrilineal areas the new villages were adopting the more conservative patrilineal customs, which are predominant in Tanzanian society. According to Bryceson and Mbilinyi (1978:54), the marriage law of 1971 crystallized patrilineal organization, perpetuating the oppressed position of women as minors that had been legislated by the colonial regime.

Cliffe argued that the identification of the collective aspect of ujamaa policy with new settlements at the first stage of village formation meant that in practice only a single strategy—one appropriate to only some areas of the country—was tried; yet at least a third of the rural areas, including some of the most developed parts, required another approach. If cooperative production activities were to accompany villagization or be introduced in areas where the formation of villages was unnecessary (that is, in the most developed areas, which were the most densely populated), then plans must stress the benefits of specific forms of socialist modes of production (Cliffe 1972:108). It was relatively easy to see the advantages of more readily available social services, but that did not touch the issue of relinquishing individual peasant farms, which collectivization entailed. Resistance by kulaks (rich peasants) centered on this issue of losing ownership or control of their profitable commercial farms.

In the early 1970s, a spate of reports of resistance to the *ujamaa* policy began to appear. Chale (1973) described how emergent large farmers controlled the TANU party organization in Usangu (Mbeya District) and were therefore well placed to obstruct the implementation of the policy. Van Hekken and Thoden van Velzen (1970) showed that because government staff responsible for executing policy hesitated to interfere with local power relations in Rungwe District, only peasants who could offer a minimum resistance were asked to comply with unpopular measures—for example, a widow was told that she must forfeit her fallow land unless she cultivated it, whereas the richest farmer in the area had several acres of fallow riverland that the authorities never touched. Half a dozen case studies of *ujamaa* villages covering the effect of traditionalism, the problem of land tenure, administrative problems, and leadership structure in a number of districts, were collected by university students (Proctor 1971); these studies generally confirmed the observations of Chale and van Hekken and Thoden van Velzen. In Kilosa District in 1973, of ten *ujamaa* villages, I saw only one that was a truly collective effort. The others usually set aside one plot of land to farm collectively or "block farm," and the degree to which this land was worked varied; the purpose of declaring a village collectivized was clearly to qualify for some form of government assistance.

Raikes categorized the different approaches to sidestepping *ujamaa* policies as "*ujamaa* through sign-painting," that is, changing the name of a village without substantively changing its relations of production; "villagization through material inducement," persuading a village to go *ujamaa* by promising services like health care, schools, and water supplies; "kulak *ujamaa*," which meant rich farmers using *ujamaa* to gain access to land, making those villages rather like joint stock companies; the use of coercion (before villagization was made compulsory); and the "frontal approach," in which whole areas or districts were enrolled in ujamaa villages in a series of major collectivization campaigns (1975:43–46).

Von Freyhold (1979:117) concluded, on the basis of case studies of ujamaa villages in Tanga Region, that the party, which had called for collectivization, was to blame for the little progress made by the communal villages, and that ultimately the ujamaa policy failed because the party did not support poor and middle peasants against kulaks, did not uphold democratic village structures against the authoritarian bureaucracy, and did not force technical staff to serve villagers loyally and intelligently.

Coulson believed that the outcome of the ujamaa policy was decided in 1969, when the Ruvuma Development Association (RDA), located in Songea District and the most advanced ujamaa organization in the country (Ibbott 1966), was declared illegal and its assets confiscated by TANU. (For a full description of the experience see Coulson 1982:263–271.) The party destroyed the RDA because it was so advanced, fearing that it would create a new form of differentiation between committed socialists and the rest. According to Coulson (1977:91) Nyerere rejected calls for a vanguard party, or for cadres such as the Social and Economic Revolutionary Army of the RDA. The dismantling of RDA was one of several policy changes in 1969 that legitimized the use of force against the peasantry, a decisive factor in the evolution of class relations in Tanzania. In Coulson's view, the ultimate objective of village formation was to raise agricultural productivity, a goal that cannot be attained by the use of force, judging by past experience in the Soviet Union and elsewhere.

Another aspect of collectivization and village formation is the link between agriculture and industry. Most economists believed that Tanzania's crucial problem was to raise low levels of agricultural production (van Ginneken 1976:54), rather than to industrialize. The World Bank (1977) has proposed to increase agricultural output by extending cultivated areas, expanding crop yields, and improving farming systems. Shivji (1976:104) argued that this policy by itself could not succeed because productivity, in his view, was basically a function of the level of industrial development. Productivity in agriculture was not likely to rise substantially in the absence of an industrial sector that provided producer goods and consumer necessities for the agricultural sector.

One government strategy was to promote small-scale industries in rural areas, for which the Small Industries Development Organization was created. Its purpose was to help *ujamaa* villages, cooperatives, agricultural producers, and other rural people to start such projects as food processing so as to add value to the commodities they produced and to receive those profits that previously went to traders. But there is no evidence that this program met the agricultural sector's needs for industrial supports.

There is yet another issue in the debate on *ujamaa* policies: the role of foreign aid in the development of Tanzanian agriculture. Shivji (1976:107), a severe critic of *ujamaa* villages, expected that in the long run the policies would succeed only if they really transformed agriculture and built a nationally integrated economy as part of an overall strategy of disengagement from the world capitalist system. This strategy involves political struggle against the internal and external classes with vested interests in maintaining and perpetuating existing relations of production.

The role of foreign aid in subsidizing internal classes that support the status quo has been the subject of lively debate in Tanzania. As part of the Arusha Declaration, TANU issued a policy statement on self-reliance that specifically drew attention to the links between foreign aid and agricultural development: "It is therefore obvious that the foreign currency we shall use to pay back the loans used in the development of the urban areas will not come from the towns or the industries [but] . . . from the villages and from agriculture. . . . The largest proportion of the loans will be spent in, or for, the urban areas, but the largest proportion of the repayment will be made through the efforts of the farmers" (TANU 1967:12).

In an analysis of links between national and international bourgeoisies, Coulson (1977:91) showed that bureaucrats in Tanzanian ministries were dependent on foreign aid donors. Without gifts and loans from abroad, production shortfalls in the mid 1970s would have had much greater and more destabilizing effects than they did. The acceptance of gifts and loans was in direct contravention of the

Arusha Declaration, which warned that external finance would endanger Tanzanian independence: "Independence cannot be real if a Nation depends upon gifts and loans from another for its development" (TANU 1967:9). Only self-reliant development was held to be real. Despite this declared policy Tanzania has been successful in attracting foreign aid, according to Coulson, because of its strategic importance in southern Africa and its ideals, which conform with the views of social democrats.

Tandon (1978) is even more cynical than Shivji and Coulson as regards the motives of foreign donors and the effect of multinational aid on food production and the villagization program. In an analysis of the national maize project—begun in 1976 with World Bank support to increase maize production—Tandon showed that the goal of food self-sufficiency was actually subverted by the World Bank,[4] not only to produce food for the world market, but also to cheapen the cost of production for the imperialist monopolies and to seek openings for the export of capital. Tanzania's dependence on external finance has grown tremendously, especially since the 1973 drought, when international aid came to its rescue. The *New African* (March 1979:67) reported that from 1961 to 1972 Tanzania had received a total of U.S. $200 million in foreign aid (excluding the Tanzam railway); the amount received in the three-year period from 1974 to 1976 was U.S. $244 million. Tanzania's debts may be written off periodically (as they were by Sweden and Britain in 1978), but loans are not a lasting solution to balance-of-payments problems. In 1977, the payment deficit was U.K. £120 million, leading to a cycle of requiring more aid just to repay previous loans.

Cooperatives and Marketing

The modern cooperative movement was born in England in the mid nineteenth century as a response to the new problems and conditions presented by the industrial and agricultural revolutions. There are three main types of cooperative—marketing, credit, and consumer. The institution, mostly in the form of marketing cooperatives, was trans-

---

4. For a critique of the World Bank's agricultural policy in the Third World see Payer 1982, especially ch. 8.

planted to Tanzania by the British in the period between the two world wars.

Marketing (or producer) cooperatives enable their members to sell their crops together and thus bargain for higher prices than any individual grower could negotiate. Under capitalist conditions of agriculture, marketing cooperatives are sometimes successful, particularly when the state is supportive and passes favorable legislation (Worsley 1975: 134). In colonial East Africa, the ostensive reason for introducing marketing cooperatives was to protect the peasants from the exploitive activities of unscrupulous traders, who were usually non-African. But as Brett (1973:237-262) has shown, the effects were to reduce the returns and therefore the incentive to African producers; to eliminate competition among buyers, thus closing an avenue of capital accumulation and advancement into industrial processing, which effectively barred Africans from the modern economy; and to centralize control in an economic system based upon state bureaucracy on the one hand and the large capitalist firm on the other.

This cooperative system, introduced to rationalize control and eliminate competition, was eventually used by Africans to create primary growers cooperative societies affiliated in regional cooperative unions and thereby to gain a material base and political control. In the 1940s and 1950s the cooperatives were at the center of the nationalist movement, but after independence the movement was often less progressive. Shivji (1976:115) believed the cooperative societies in Kilimanjaro were virtually controlled by African kulaks. Kulak control of such organizations was one way of stalling the implementation of *ujamaa* policy.

Consumer cooperatives, which usually deal in household goods for daily consumption, provide collective benefits to members in the form of lower prices, dividends, or improved services. Credit cooperatives encourage people to save in credit unions; they can borrow money from the credit unions at low interest rates, in proportion to the savings they have invested (Worsley 1975:134). Both consumer and credit cooperatives existed in Tanzania, but on a much smaller scale than marketing cooperatives.

In 1971 the government created the Tanzania Rural Development Bank to support the cooperative movement and *ujamaa* village development programs. At the same time it encouraged the creation of district development corporations, designed to initiate commercial development projects and control small-scale commercial enterprises purchased from the private sector. In most cases the shareholders were the district and town councils, but in a few cases the local cooperative unions were also participants. Eligibility for Rural Development Bank assistance extended to cooperative unions, cooperative societies, district development corporations, *ujamaa* villages, and registered associations (Tanzania Rural Development Bank 1972).

The Rural Development Bank was described as one of the government's key institutions for achieving an increase in rural incomes as well as the equitable distribution of that increase. It was a secondary institution, in the sense that it was designed to support primary structures, among which the cooperatives figured prominently.

The goal of the government was to establish a cooperative union in each region to which most cooperative societies would affiliate (ibid.:4). By 1975 Tanzania was covered by a network of twenty-four cooperative unions and about a hundred cooperative marketing societies. Cooperatives generally operated under compulsory marketing orders that ruled out alternative channels for selling one's crops.[5] They could help an area realize its full productive potential by making quality marketing service available. The quality of the marketing service depended in part on the size of the cooperative. The largest, the Nyanza Cooperative Union, was probably the largest nonpublic enterprise in East Africa (Cliffe and Saul 1972:84–85).

Like other aspects of agricultural policy, cooperative marketing can be traced back to colonial policy. From 1953 to 1974, marketing cooperatives purchased farm produce through primary growers societies and sold it to government marketing boards. The marketing boards gradually extended their activities to include extension services, provision of agricultural supplies and equipment, and processing, so that eventually they made cooperative unions redundant (Coulson 1977:100).

The aim of government policy was to integrate the coop-

---

5. Under compulsory marketing orders only cooperatives could purchase certain crops; frequently there was no other legal outlet (Coulson 1982: 149).

erative movement closely with the *ujamaa* program, and in 1974, the primary societies' function of purchasing crops was taken over by *ujamaa* villages. In 1976, when the cooperative marketing services had deteriorated drastically and the cooperatives were deeply in debt, the government nationalized them and replaced them with government corporations (ibid.; Coulson 1982:180, 341).

Where cooperatives are introduced into situations already marked by strong inequalities, these disparities tend to be reinforced rather than reformed (Apthorpe 1977:6). Cooperatives may create inequalities if they are imposed by the state or if they favor one group of producers over another. Although nothing in the requirement for membership in marketing societies—which was to be a *bona fide* farmer, agricultural producer, or farmer who occupied land —excluded women, it was interpreted in the colonial era to mean male landowners, who were designated "head of household" (Maro 1974). When men were so designated, women were more often than not excluded from the societies, even though they were responsible for productive activities (Apthorpe 1977:6). For Maro "it is still a dream to admit women" to some types of cooperative (1974:23). She suggested an amendment to allow membership of families, so that women could vote in the absence of their husbands. In the case of consumer cooperatives, Maro proposed a separate membership for men and women. The issue did not arise with credit societies since husbands and wives could maintain separate accounts; the problem was rather whether women earned any cash to save.

The cooperative is not so much a socialist solution as a socialist defense against the wider capitalist society. It does not equalize, for each member retains what she or he owns and each benefits in proportion. Cooperatives do not eliminate private property in land, capital, or equipment; they do not collectivize the means of production. They are a compromise between private ownership (or consumption) and collectivism. Cooperatives remain federations of small producers, some of whom are "big men" (important government or party officials) with the necessary material assets and social skills to dominate. Although economies can be made in purchasing and sharing, the private ownership of wealth—land, capital, and equipment—sets limits upon what can be jointly achieved. To step beyond these limits requires bringing society's assets into common ownership (Worsley 1975:135).

The failures of the cooperative, collectivization, and villagization movements are most telling in the declining productivity of agriculture. Tanzania has not met its goal of self-sufficiency in food production. Dependence on imports of food grains grew from 42,000 metric tons in 1965/1966 to 94,000 metric tons in 1975/1976. The years 1973 to 1975 were critical because of widespread drought: in 1973/1974 net imports totaled 240,000 metric tons and in 1974/1975 490,000 metric tons (World Bank 1977c:10). But the trend toward increasing dependence began in the 1960s and has continued: estimates for 1980/1981 were 385,000 tons (United States Department of Agriculture 1981:45). Another indicator, per caput food production indices, showed the same decline—from 115 in 1976 to 105 in 1980 (1969/1971 = 100) (ibid.:84).

African women, as we saw in chapter 4, play a central role in food production and processing. One must ask what their experience was in the restructuring of Tanzanian society after independence and what impact declining agricultural productivity has had on their health.

The Mobilization of Women

Women are conspicuously absent from nationalist histories of Tanzania, nor has there been a Tanzanian novelist of the stature of Senegal's Sembene Ousmane to celebrate women's role in anticolonial struggles (see his God's Bits of Wood). All the more reason, one would think, for paying attention to women after independence. The motive for mobilizing women, if not to redress past neglect, might be the expected economic and social returns to society. A strong women's movement in the rural areas might, for example, have made headway toward a more equitable distribution of tasks between men and women, so that men participated in both child care and household work, as well as food production.

TANU's socialist program promised that reorganization would improve conditions for women and children in the rural areas. The collective organization of production was to assure an even distribution of labor. Instead of carrying babies on their backs while they hoed and weeded, for example, women might be assigned work near crèches where they could leave their unweaned infants and still breastfeed them. Day care centers would offer care and regular meals to preschool children whose mothers were at work in the fields, and communal kitchens would relieve women of the burdens of meal preparation in the periods of peak labor demands. Collective production would increase output and ensure that food surpluses were stockpiled so that supplies were available throughout the year. In the agricultural off-peak season, collective labor could construct conduits to bring water supplies within easy reach of every home, so that water collection was not a burden at any time of the year, and sufficient water was always at hand for cooking, cleaning, and bathing. To implement socialist reorganization, women's participation was essential.

Several women's groups, including the Tanganyika Council of Women, were started by British women before independence to offer African women classes in homecraft (Ladner 1971). Staudt (1977) suggests that one function of such groups was to introduce African women to their role as consumers in capitalist society. Home economics courses furthered the commercialization of the economy by creating demands for purchasable items. Far from offering training to modernize and transform subsistence farm work, colonial projects for African women reinforced and extended domesticity in the Victorian mode.

An African women's organization under the leadership of Bibi Titi Mohamed developed alongside the male-dominated nationalist movement (Geiger 1982:47). As the women's section of the nationalist party, its task was to mobilize rural women for political independence. In 1962 it was renamed *Umoja wa Wanawake wa Tanzania* (UWT), United Women of Tanzania, and became an affiliate of TANU; its founding objectives were to bring together all the women of mainland Tanzania to think, speak, and act together; to promote the unity of the nation; to foster women's participation in economic, educational, political, cultural, and health activities; to cooperate with the government and the party on women's issues; and to uphold the rights and dignity of women. The organization sought to achieve these objectives through cooperation with other organizations having similar aims, without regard to the color, creed, or race of the members and provided that their policies were rooted in socialism, equality, and self-reliance (Kokuhirwa n.d.). Membership in the UWT was opened to Tanzanian women aged sixteen years and over; groups of women as well as individuals could join. By 1979 there were reportedly three thousand branches on the mainland, with 180,000 members, though Geiger (1982:50) warns that membership figures are unreliable because it is difficult to keep track of women who fail to pay monthly dues.

The administrative structure of the organization follows the pyramidal shape of government (Kokuhirwa n.d.). A national chairwoman is elected by the national UWT conference and holds this post for five years. She is assisted by a vice chairwoman, who is also elected by the national conference. A general secretary is appointed by the president of Tanzania, who also chairs the national executive committee. A national treasurer is appointed by the national executive committee.

This structure is repeated on the regional level. Since August 1974 the regional chairwoman and her secretary have been paid workers, earning a modest salary. The regional secretaries assisted by the government and by UNICEF, which provide transport, coordinate UWT activities down to the district level; the district structure is similar to that of the regions. On the divisional level and below, the leaders are volunteers; most of them are retired teachers, nurses, mission workers—in principle women with a good level of literacy. In practice UWT branches are understaffed at all levels, in part for lack of trained personnel, a problem that has its roots in the colonial neglect of girls' education (Geiger 1982:51).

The UWT has its own institute for training women—the Pungemba Leaders Training Center in Iringa Region—which was given to the UWT by the government (Kokuhirwa n.d.). Training, which covers leadership skills, home economics, child care, income and budgeting, needlework, home management, nutrition, hygiene, and agriculture, lasts three months and is open to nonmembers as well. There are also women's sections at the Cooperative College and the International Cooperative Alliance, both in Moshi (Kilimanjaro District), where women are trained in household management and farm-related activities (Geiger 1982:54).

The Dar es Salaam *Daily News* (21 December 1976) reported that the UWT, in collaboration with the Ministry of Labour and Social Welfare, had established day care centers throughout the country to enable women to participate more fully in development activities. The UWT had set up a special fund to run the centers and had distributed part of it to each region. The quality of day care varied from "a place under a tree where ill-trained and poorly-paid girls watched or didn't watch too many children" (Geiger 1982: 52) to community-built centers with educational programs and midday meals, which I observed in Lushoto District in 1973.

Some UWT projects received international as well as government assistance. UNICEF assisted women who were producing clothing and underwear. *Ujamaa* villages helped young women set up small businesses by training them in management and accounting. Tanzania's Small Industries Development Organization helped women obtain credit from wholesalers, working capital from the Tanzania Rural Development Bank, and machinery under a hire-purchase scheme. The sponsorship of *ujamaa* villages and UWT ensured that women received assistance in building premises and other support under self-help schemes (United Nations Economic Commission for Africa 1976:78–79).

Other ventures were set up to generate income: the UWT helped establish small-scale industries, cooperative shops, cooperative handicraft groups, vegetable gardens and farms, poultry units, hotels, beer stores, and restaurants. Geiger (1982:50, 59) points out that these projects do not challenge convention on the sexual division of labor; to do so, she argues, would provoke fierce resistance from village men. For her the central question not addressed by UWT development projects is whether women control their own labor.

In an editorial on 20 December 1976, the *Daily News* acknowledged that the UWT had provided the women of Tanzania with a forum to air their grievances, to organize production, and to campaign against sexually discriminatory and exploitive laws and traditional practices. It went on to say, however, that "UWT has been criticised for being largely an organization of the big men's wives. This criticism may not be fair but the big men's wives certainly form a large percentage of its leadership. Its activities reflect to some extent the preoccupations of well-placed ladies." Another accusation was that the UWT, despite its rural origins, had become an urban phenomenon with offices at district headquarters and an almost exclusively urban membership (Nduru 1974).

Reports from local areas were also critical of UWT. One report from Moshi, in Kilimanjaro District, indicated both the great need for a protective society that would serve women's interests and the failure of UWT to play this role:

> There is no sign of a woman's movement designed to improve women's position at home and in society. Women do not know or cannot defend their most elementary legal rights (on rape, on maintenance of children, etc.), they work for half of the male wage (for the same work) on private estates, and tolerate oppression and neglect at home without ever considering any way of organizing to find a solution to any of these problems. If they do unite, it is usually to run a beer club, while every single one of them will complain about male alcoholism. . . . Organized women's groups are of two kinds: There are Christian women's groups run by the missions and there are Umoja wa Wanawake (UWT) groups. Both are normally in heavy competition with each other and usually with the same primary objective: to gather women for learning and practice of homecrafts. Sewing groups and cooking instructions are quite popular. (von Freyhold, Sawaki, and Zalla 1973:204–205)

The same study reported that, on paper, 8 percent of the women in Kilimanjaro District were members of UWT. They were recruited during official campaigns run by TANU party officials, when women often registered out of a sense of civic duty rather than any particular interest. The Kilimanjaro UWT had a sewing group, beer stores, snack bars, consumer cooperatives, and day care centers (some helped by other institutions). The conclusion of local rural development workers was that the UWT seemed to mirror women's weaknesses and lack of unity instead of improving their position (ibid.:206–207).

The mention of beer shops deserves an explanation. The British colonial government ruled that beer could be sold only on licensed premises. Licenses cost the equivalent of U.S. $2.50 per day; four gallons of beer cost $.20 to $.50 to brew and might sell for $.75 to $1.00. In 1957/1958 the colonial government forbade all brewing during the cultivating season except on weekends. The regulation was invoked to prevent neglect of cultivation and depletion of

grain reserves before harvests were in. Officials did not recognize that beer sales were the main source of cash for
many people at that season. During the legal beer-brewing
season in Kilosa District before independence, a few men
purchased licenses and invited local women to make beer
and sell it at their clubs. In return they collected a small
payment from each woman. The profit from such clubs was
large by local standards: the total sales for one day might be
larger than the annual cash income of most individuals. Because of government regulations and the ways these were
enforced, a large share of the profits went to headmen and
male entrepreneurs with political connections rather than
to the women brewers (Beidelman 1971:26).

According to Swantz, Henricson, and Zalla (1975:67),
this practice has not changed much since independence. In
Kilimanjaro, men still own the beer clubs and control the
price of beer brewed by women, keeping them in competition with each other. Because it would be controlled by
women who could retain the profits, a cooperative enterprise of beer brewing is seen as a positive advance. In this
sense the UWT beer stores were a positive measure, though
von Freyhold, Sawaki, and Zalla's question about male al-
coholism remains unanswered.

One wonders whether women would fare better if UWT
were stronger and independent of TANU, or whether UWT
would be more effective if it were financed by TANU, or
whether the party would be more responsive if more women
held official positions. The data are lacking for more than
an impressionistic check on this last speculation.

Few women appear to be active in government or party
ranks (Kjekshus 1975). In 1972, shortly after elected local
government was replaced by a decentralized civil service
under the prime minister,[6] a UWT conference in Morogoro
town noted that not a single woman had been appointed
to regional or district level jobs. The following year Kilosa
District in Morogoro Region did have a woman district director, and in 1976 the Morogoro regional party secretary
was a woman. In the 1975 general elections, only nineteen

6. A similar reorganization of TANU strengthened salaried party officials at the expense of elected representatives, creating a strong, well-
paid party bureaucracy at regional, district, divisional, and ward levels
(Coulson 1977:93).

female members of Parliament were elected or nominated; two female ministers were appointed and two others were elected to represent Tanzania at the East Africa Legislative Assembly.[7] Fifteen years after independence that was a poor showing.

Reynolds (1975:26) believed there was better integration at higher levels of the national government and administration: one judge, six state attorneys, one first secretary, and two third secretaries were women. The Ministry of Health employed sixty women in professional positions and the Ministry of Education twenty-seven. There were also women in the police force and immigration service, for which they received training in the National Service Corps —a paramilitary unit open to all eighteen year olds (Ladner 1971).

While we have no national statistics on women's participation in the lowest ranks of the party, reports scattered in the literature give the overall impression that there were few women. The unit at the lowest level of the party is the ten-house cell, which elects a leader, an unpaid voluntary position. From Iringa District Kawago reported, "there is a conspicuous absence of women in leadership positions; only one female leader is to be found in Ulula" (1971:58). Similarly, a report on cells in Dar es Salaam and Bukoba noted, "It is clear that there was a strong preference for men as cell leaders for none of those interviewed in either area belonged to a cell with a female leader" (Kokwebangira 1971:46). In Lushoto District Mshangama found "not a single female cell leader in the areas surveyed, for to the Shambalas politics is purely a business for men" (1971:25). Finally, in Ulanga District, Njohole noted, "The impact of traditionalism on the cell system in the country-side can be seen further in the fact that none of the cell leaders (at least none in the author's home area) is a woman" (1971:10).

In Pare District, however, O'Barr (1972:461) found that fifteen of sixty-six cell leaders of the Kighare ward of

7. Parliament consists of the president and the National Assembly, which has 218 members—116 elected by popular ballot from mainland Tanzania and 102 nominated by the president of Tanzania or the Revolutionary Council (the governing body of Zanzibar). The East Africa Legislative Assembly consists of members elected by the national parliaments of Tanzania, Kenya, and Uganda.

Usangi were female. According to O'Barr, women in Usangi had a long history of political activism and were proud of their accomplishments in politics. This situation is especially interesting as these women tended to be older, Muslim, less educated, less involved in the cash economy (as measured by cash cropping), and more active as cell leaders (as measured by the frequency of cell meetings) than their counterparts in the Mshewa ward of Mbaga, who were almost uniformly young Christian male cash croppers.

If women's participation in the political life of their country reflects the power and authority of Tanzanian women, then this review suggests that their position is not much improved since independence. The same conclusion emerges from the review of food and agriculture: falling productivity, especially of food crops for domestic consumption, indicates that women, who are the principal farmers, have not improved their situation. The experiments with collectives and cooperatives, which promised so much and excited such optimism in world socialist circles, were terminated prematurely by party bureaucrats unwilling to relinquish their newfound power to women and men of the working classes. *Ujamaa,* which had become the slogan of African socialism, degenerated into forced villagization, the forcible removal of peasants from their isolated hamlets into rural settlements. Though the present assessment of the food system and, in particular, of women's position in the social system is pessimistic, perhaps there is reason to be hopeful about the future. There are lessons to be learned even from negative experiences and, as we shall see in the next chapter, other programs, especially the extension of health services to the entire population, have accomplished far more.

11

HEALTH CARE REORGANIZED

Since independence there has been a great increase in the health services available to Tanzanians: curative and preventive services are not only more numerous and more equitably distributed around the country, but also more accessible because government services are free and voluntary agencies' fees are kept low by arrangement with the government, which subsidizes some of them.[1] In 1960 there were 425 physicians including 12 Tanzanians, 99 hospitals and 11,160 hospital beds, 22 rural health centers, and 990 dispensaries (United Republic of Tanzania 1972:124); by 1977 there were 727 physicians including 400 Tanzanians, 141 hospitals and 19,970 beds, 161 rural health centers, and 2,088 dispensaries (Akerele, Dhalla, and Qhobela 1978:59–61). This expansion is astonishing, the more so as most of the effort in the rural areas to extend services not based on hospitals dates from 1972.

Health Care at Independence

Expenditure on hospital services accounted for nearly three-quarters of total health expenditures in the last year of British rule. Facilities were concentrated in urban areas: Dar es Salaam, which in 1961 had a little over 1 percent of the country's population, received 20 percent of the government's health care budget. Over 16 percent of all government general hospital beds were in Dar es Salaam, while some districts lacked a hospital and had no physicians in residence. Specialist services were also concentrated in the

---

1. In 1978 almost half of all hospital services were provided by voluntary (primarily religious) agencies. The government designated fifteen voluntary hospitals, for which it assumes full operating costs, to provide free services and to supervise and coordinate all other services in the districts in which they are located (Akerele, Dhalla, and Qhobela 1978:42).

capital city, and more than 25 percent of the total expenditure on medical staff salaries attributable to the hospital and dispensary services was paid to staff attached to the Dar es Salaam hospitals (Titmuss 1964:40–41).

This colonial legacy of urban, hospital-based, curative medical services was criticized by Richard Titmuss, a consultant from the London School of Economics engaged by the Ministry of Health in 1961 to review the organization of medical care. Titmuss advocated an expansion of preventive services to the rural population, but his recommendations, published in 1964, do not appear to have affected more than the rhetoric of the first five-year plan. The plan stated that the aim of medical development is to improve the standard of health through a coordinated health service in which "an increasing emphasis will be placed on the *preventive aspects of medicine* and on the urgent need to extend health services into the rural areas" (United Republic of Tanzania 1964, 1:68; emphasis in the original).

These aims were not realized. During the plan period (1964–1969) urban medical facilities were developed, while rural health services received little attention. In the middle of this period, the Arusha Declaration was published, giving a new impetus to the redirection of health resources. The second five-year development plan reflected the new philosophy in its criticisms of the health ministry's accomplishments to date: "During the First Plan effort was directed towards the development of physical medical facilities, mainly located in urban centers. New foundations were laid and others were strengthened in medical education, and in regional and district hospital services. However, there was little significant vertical development in health, and no break-through was achieved towards solving many of the major health problems facing Tanzanians" (United Republic of Tanzania 1969, 1:62).

The effect of continuing the curative medical care system that developed under colonialism was to deprive the rural population of services, because, in the first place, hospitals are expensive institutions to build, equip, supply, maintain, and staff. Muhimbili, the largest hospital in Tanzania, is located in Dar es Salaam; it was opened in 1960 at a cost of U.K. £918,000. In 1967 it had 792 beds and by 1970 the number had increased to 921 beds (Gish 1972). In 1970/ 1971 over U.K. £330,000 was spent on services and supplies (recurrent costs) for this one hospital alone (Segall 1972:164). Tanzania was too poor to afford enough hospitals to serve the entire population. It was so large, with a population so widely scattered (before compulsory villagization) and a communication network so rudimentary, that many people lived far from the few existing hospitals. Only a small proportion of the population was able to benefit from hospital medical services. Furthermore, hospital services were becoming more and more expensive: the Regional Consultant Hospital in Mwanza with 450 beds, completed in 1971, cost U.K. £2,778,000 (Magome 1973). Part of the higher cost was attributable to the installation of expensive modern equipment.

Segall makes a second point: a "predominantly curative approach to the diseases of the country continues to allow people to fall ill. It does not reduce the *occurrence* of disease in the country; it does not improve the people's *health*. It merely provides treatment, which may or may not be effective" (1972:151; emphasis in the original). Thus, even if the hospital system could have been expanded to all parts of Tanzania, it would not have had a lasting and beneficial impact on African health. Hospital treatment is an inappropriate response to the major health problems of Tanzania: for example, the control of the major communicable diseases demands mass public health efforts as the main medical strategy rather than individual treatment of the sick.

Despite these arguments, raised in national debates about what type of health care system would be suitable in a socialist country, the government's *Economic Survey 1971–72* noted continuing imbalances in favor of curative services in the urban areas, a shortage of adequately trained medical personnel in the rural areas, and weakness in current communicable disease control program. The government survey identified four specific problems: "the lack of effective machinery for the administrative control of development; a continuing shortage of manpower in almost all cadres; an inadequate capacity for planning; and difficulties in the rural areas" (United Republic of Tanzania 1972:124).

Beginning in 1972, the government began to record the distribution of medical services by district. A unique study was undertaken by the Bureau of Resource Assessment and Land Use Planning (BRALUP) of the University of Dar es

Salaam to calculate the rural population's proximity to health facilities. The criterion used for accessibility was ten kilometers, based on a lack of transport in the rural areas and on the observation that a healthy adult on foot may cover that distance in two hours, while a sick person, a pregnant woman, or a child may need twice as long. Thomas and Mascarenhas (1973) found that, on average, 75 percent of Tanzanians lived within ten kilometers of some health facility, but in some remote districts the figure dropped as low as 54 percent. Proximity to a hospital was much less common: on average only 7.5 percent of rural Tanzanians lived within five kilometers and 20.4 percent lived within ten kilometers of a hospital.

Although the exact dimensions of the problem of unevenly distributed health services were not known before this study was published, it was generally assumed that the dispersal of health resources followed the same pattern as the spread of economic resources: given the colonial legacy of unequal development and regional differentiation, the expectation was that commercially developed districts would have more resources than the former labor reserves (Turshen 1975). The BRALUP study confirmed this prediction: in Songea, a labor reserve in the colonial era, 65 percent of the total population lived within ten kilometers of any health facility, while in Kilosa, a plantation economy in colonial times, 86 percent lived within ten kilometers of any facility.

Medical Bureaucracy

Why did the health sector lag behind others in implementing the Arusha Declaration of 1967? One answer lies in the bureaucratic structure of colonial medicine, which persisted after independence.

The case for regarding medical services as a bureaucracy is especially strong in Tanzania. Western medical practice took on a bureaucratic structure when it was first introduced in the country as a government service. Though there were a few medical missionaries in the nineteenth century before the Germans established colonial rule, individual practitioners did not set up private practice much before government medical services were established. The organization of the colonial medical service exhibited some of the classic characteristics of bureaucracy: institutionalization through posts, grades, appointments, contracts, salaries, pensions, and so on; hierarchical ordering of executive and administrative authority; specialization of functions at any given level; and the routinization of those functions (Albrow 1970:44).

The study of bureaucracy is also useful for a better understanding of the independent government's medical service and its resistance to change. Weber (1968:956–1005) wrote that as bureaucratization increases, the power of bureaucrats tends to increase, making it progressively more difficult for anyone outside the bureaucracy to control it. Thus bureaucratic organization reinforces the tendency of physicians to resist attempts by nonmedically trained personnel to direct or control medical affairs. Moreover, Weber points out that politicians cannot dispense with or replace the bureaucratic apparatus once it exists without risking chaos.

After independence the government was faced with the problem of providing health care to the nation. The means were slender, and the bureaucracy was large, although there were few fully trained Tanzanian physicians to replace colonial bureaucrats. The medical services continued to offer curative care in hospitals even though the development plans called for more emphasis on rural health care. Ten years after independence it was abundantly clear that this emphasis had been ignored. An article in the Dar es Salaam *Daily News* accused the Ministry of Health of "relying overwhelmingly on curative services; what is more, it is allowing a highly expensive, Western-style of medicine to develop. It is centralizing the scant resources available for health in large hospitals in the towns, while the rural health services (for 94% of the population) remain grossly underdeveloped" (reprinted in Segall 1972:151).

Lenin's statement that bureaucracy and socialism are irreconcilable sheds light on the government's difficulty in reorienting health services. Lenin (1919) wrote that the bourgeois state apparatus, of which the bureaucracy is a part, cannot be reconciled with the aims of socialism: socialism requires the complete destruction of bourgeois state institutions because bureaucratic organization makes mass participation impossible. Nyerere described his vision of mass participation: "a really socialist village would elect its own officials and they would remain equal members with the others, subject always to the wishes of the people. Only in relation to work discipline would there be any hierarchy, and then such officials would be merely acting for the village as a whole" (1968:353). But he ignored entrenched power in the medical bureaucracy just as he had overlooked the strength of the kulaks in the villages.

Despite real attempts to curb the power of the bureaucracy in 1967 with the adoption of the Arusha Declaration, Nyerere was forced to call attention to the persistence of old ways in his address to the sixteenth TANU biennial conference on 24 September 1973:

> In the Ten Year Report to TANU in 1971 I said that the Ministry of Health should put more emphasis on rural services and on preventive work. As I have already explained, this change is taking place. We must determine to maintain this national policy and not again be tempted by offers of a big new hospital, with all the high running costs involved—at least until every one of our citizens has basic medical services readily available to him.
>
> But planning for the next five years is now being initiated in towns, villages, and districts of the country, and it appears that the reason for this stress, and its implication, need to be more widely understood. For practically every district is indicating that demands will be coming forward for new or enlarged curative services, for better hospitals or for large health centres. Virtually no area has so far proposed that new preventive medical services should be established, or stressed the need for large numbers of small dispensaries and first aid posts! (Daily News, 26 September 1973)

Shivji's (1976) class analysis of the bureaucracy explains the mechanisms by which petit bourgeois physicians and their subordinates maintain control of health policies and shape medical services to satisfy their professional and class interests. Since independence, he argues, some members of the petit bourgeoisie (which includes physicians and other professionals, as well as higher officials and prosperous traders and farmers) have obtained power through the state and have split off to form the bureaucratic bourgeoisie,[2] while remaining linked to the petit bourgeoisie by

---

2. For a discussion of the application of this term to Africa see Cohen 1981:94–98; for the Tanzanian debate see, among others, Coulson 1982: 320–331 and von Freyhold 1977.

familial, marital, and cultural ties. Together the two groups constitute the new ruling class of Tanzania; they rule by virtue not of ownership of the means of production but of access to those means through the state. Coupled with their technocratic control, the state power of the bureaucratic bourgeoisie enables it to direct resources to itself.

Thus physicians in the government medical services (bureaucratic bougeoisie) allied with physicians in private practice (upper level of the petit bourgeoisie) and were able to dominate health policy for ten years after independence, ignoring the Arusha Declaration. Once President Nyerere put his prestige behind the reform issue in 1972, however, the party bureaucrats gained the upper hand and a nonmedical policy was formulated.

The period from 1962 to 1972 was also dominated by foreign contributions to Tanzanian health services, despite the injunction of the Arusha Declaration on foreign aid. Switzerland and West Germany helped expand Muhimbili Hospital to accommodate a new faculty of medicine,[3] and the West German government (through Catholic and Protestant missions) funded the hospitals at Mwanza and Moshi (Coulson 1982:208). This domination by foreign contributions continued after 1972: although the type of health service receiving assistance changed, the amount of aid did not; if anything it increased. In 1977, bilateral and multilateral, governmental and nongovernmental aid agencies provided 70 percent of the total national and regional health development budget (Akerele, Dhalla, and Qhobela 1978: 67). The flexibility of foreign aid—both the willingness of capitalist governments to assist socialist Tanzania and the ability of the medical-industrial complex to adapt to low-cost preventive approaches to health care (Turshen 1976) —is evident in this twenty-year period.

---

3. The trend to longer training, higher entrance requirements, and more advanced certificates continued in Tanzania after independence. A training program for Tanzanian medical practitioners with less than full university qualifications and destined to work in rural health centers was started in 1963 at the newly created Dar es Salaam School of Medicine. But, as Sharpston observed, "the school could not persist in the face of the internationally recognized medical school at Makerere, Uganda, and the proposed new medical faculty of full professional standard for Kenya at Nairobi. Within five years it became a medical school of comparable standard within the University of East Africa" (1973:459).

Current Patterns of Health Service Delivery

From 1972 the government began to allocate one-third of the health budget to rural health services. Health centers and dispensaries were emphasized as the basic rural health institutions, as part of a policy of reforming the country's hospital-based health care structure, and a new system was introduced to cater especially to health needs in the *ujamaa* villages, in which nonprofessional staff would provide simple medical and public health care.

To bring about this redistribution of expenditures, new mechanisms were developed. Under the old system, to qualify for grants to build new health centers, district councils had to put up 50 percent of the total capital costs, which few could afford to do (van Etten 1976:40). Under a new plan, the vertical authority of individual ministries was abandoned in favor of integrated district development councils and planning committees at the local level. Functional officers were to replace ministerial representatives and were to be part of a new district development team. This change meant the transfer of responsibility for local health facilities, personnel, and training to the central government, which in turn could reallocate resources on the basis of need to ensure equitable distribution. "A fair share for all" became the motto, and the new planning unit in the Ministry of Health was dedicated to spreading additional expenditures thinly, in keeping with the realities of population distribution, transport possibilities, and disease patterns (Gish 1975:77). The result was a very real redistribution of expenditure within the health budget, shifting the emphasis away from hospital services and toward rural health care and training.

The new structure has at its base the village health service, which aims at providing simple medical and health care in *ujamaa* villages. Run by part-time personnel known as village medical helpers, who are recruited from within the village on the recommendation of villagers, the system is consciously patterned after the Chinese commune health scheme staffed by "barefoot doctors." Above the village health service is the dispensary, the primary unit for medical treatment under the colonial regime, which remains the foundation of the health care delivery system; most Tanzanians rely upon it for their health care. Ideally run by rural medical aides, dispensaries are still often staffed by hospital-trained auxiliaries, called "dressers" in colonial times. Gish (1975:77) estimated that over three-quarters of the nation's dispensaries were still staffed by them in 1975.

At the next level is the health center, which provides in-patient as well as out-patient curative treatment and midwifery services and, in principle, is responsible for such preventive work as maternal and child health, immunization, health education, and environmental sanitation. These centers are staffed by medical assistants, nurses, and health auxiliaries, who perceive their function to be predominantly curative (van Etten 1976:119). Next is the general hospital, which is usually located in the district capital and is staffed by a physician, who is usually the district medical officer. As a result of this location and combination of duties, the district medical officer often neglects public health work in the face of the overwhelming clinical workload and the physician's personal preference for clinical care. Finally, there are regional and consultant hospitals, which provide specialist services and are not considered part of the basic health service structure. They were intended to serve large populations, but for the most part they draw patients from the urban centers in which they are located. Although the 1972 reorientation of health care pledged a halt to the construction of expensive establishments that consume a large part of the health budget in recurrent costs, the government accepted a British offer in 1979 to build another consultant hospital in the south of the country.

Since independence the number of general hospitals has increased more slowly than the number of dispensaries or health centers and, in fact, rural health centers have increased rapidly. Health personnel have also increased steadily. A nutrition unit was created in 1974 to monitor and correct the nutritional status of the Tanzanian population (Akerele, Dhalla, and Qhobela 1978:41). Its establishment is an important step toward reducing malnutrition in the country, especially as its activities include oft-neglected research on the nutritional values of locally grown foods. But without a productive agricultural base in the country, it cannot succeed in correcting poor diets, which are ultimately determined by food availability and purchasing power.

By shifting the emphasis from hospital treatment to rural

health care, the government hoped to cut costs. Another way it attempted to reduce expenses and at the same time to increase revenues available for other services was by centralizing purchases of pharmaceuticals. A study by Yudkin (1980) concluded that such a policy could save an estimated U.K. £1.6 million a year. The National Pharmaceutical Company was established in 1973 as a parastatal, that is, a public, profit-making corporation with responsibility for importing and distributing drugs to the private medical sector. At the same time the Central Medical Stores was created to import and distribute drugs to the public sector. In theory these institutions cooperate; in practice they exercise little control over the situation. Tanzania is behind Algeria (Helali et al. 1983), Sri Lanka (Lall and Bibile 1978), and even India (Lall 1974) in controlling its relations with the multinational pharmaceutical industry.

About 22 percent of the health budget was allocated to the purchase of drugs in 1977 (Honey 1977:1070–1071). This proportion is low in comparison with many underdeveloped countries where it is as high as 60 percent, but the value of drug distribution in Tanzania is growing at an annual rate of 33 percent (World Bank 1978) and total purchases of drugs amount to an estimated 40 percent, that is, almost twice as much as the health budget allocation (Honey 1977:1070). Although drug buying and distribution are centralized, each physician has the authority to order any drug deemed necessary, and voluntary agencies are free to import any drug they want. Multinational pharmaceutical companies are allowed free access to physicians, and with 147 sales representatives in the country in 1976, there was one salesperson for every four physicians in the country (World Bank 1978:29). Their target was the annual fund of U.K. £11,786 that each physician controlled for the purchase of drugs (Honey 1977:1070).

The way out of this dilemma has been pioneered by other countries. The steps are relatively simple, in principle and at the macrolevel: (1) adapt to national needs the list of two hundred essential drugs proposed by the World Health Organization (1977), adopt it as the national formulary, and limit all imports and prescriptions to it; (2) substitute generics for brand names in the public and private sectors; (3) establish a national buying agency to purchase and supply all drugs, disallow imports by any other route, and consolidate orders to facilitate bulk purchasing (thereby enabling the agency to exert bargaining power); (4) supply the medical profession with adequate and objective information on drugs and their prices from sources other than drug manufacturers; (5) control patent licensing for drug production; and (6) extend local pharmaceutical production, preferably in cooperation with neighboring countries, to create regional production and technology centers (Lall 1975).

The problems encountered in implementation at the microlevel are not to be underestimated. First of all, the national bourgeoisie will oppose strict limitations of the list of essential drugs because it does not supply their wants. Second, it is difficult to control the private sector, which may include, for example, medical missions receiving shipments of drugs as gifts. Third, the multinational pharmaceutical industry, which has shown its ability to act in concert when faced with national legislation of this type (Muller 1982), will exert extreme pressure on the state buying agency through its control of local subsidiaries or its monopoly on needed preparations that cannot be produced locally. Fourth, this program requires a local expertise that national governments may not possess. And fifth, national production puts the state in the position of selling drugs at home and abroad, introducing a profit-making motive to government medical services. This position may create a drug-dependent population because the government has a vested interest in producing and dispensing as many drugs as possible. Despite these caveats, there is no question but that Third World governments should undertake to control the operations of multinational pharmaceutical firms within their borders.

Tanzania's failure to control drugs is symptomatic of what one is tempted to call systemic dependency in the health sector. For example, even though the number of Tanzanian physicians nearly doubled between 1972 and 1977 (when it reached 400), the number of foreign physicians increased slightly in the same period, from 397 in 1972 to 425 in 1977 (Akerele, Dhalla, and Qhobela 1978: 64). The dependence on foreign physicians to staff the medical services, the reliance on foreign voluntary agencies (mainly Christian missions) to run nearly half of the country's hospitals, and the recourse to foreign aid to fund 70 percent of the national and regional health budget raises a number of political issues.

First, it is clear that Tanzanians have exchanged a measure of independence for a health care system. Given the extensive external financing and management of the Tanzanian health care system, its dependency—one might even say its neocolonial character, as this situation has existed since independence—cannot be disputed. Normally dependency in the health sector is associated with the construction of expensive urban hospitals, which characterized Tanzania to 1972, rather than low-cost rural health centers, which characterize the system today (see page 199).

Second, President Nyerere appears to have accepted foreign aid for the health care system because it conformed with his belief that it is the function of the state to provide social services.[4] His belief coincided with the desires of the bourgeoisie to enjoy health and other social services formerly the prerogative of the colonials. But as this group lives in the cities, a transformation of the urban medical services into a rural health care delivery system was not in its interests. The solution was to invite foreign agencies to fund primary health care for the rural areas while leaving the urban structures intact. Thus foreign aid has allowed the bourgeoisie to maintain its privileges and, at the same time, respond to political demands for rural health care. One would like to know specifically how many of the nearly one hundred Cuban and Chinese physicians working in Tanzania are posted to the remote districts, and what proportions of Tanzanian physicians are working in urban versus rural areas.

Third, the employment of foreign physicians reinforces dependency by delaying progress toward a socialist health service run by the people and responsive to their needs. It is doubtful whether popular participation in health care can have any real meaning when staff and patients do not speak the same language. The users of health services cannot contribute to the reform of the system, or to their own recovery, when they are unable to communicate with health service personnel. This exclusion of workers and

4. For a critique of Nyerere's ideology, see Couslon 1982:317–331.

peasants from the management of their health care delays reform of the system and reinforces the power of the bourgeoisie, prolonging its rule.

The employment of foreign personnel also foils attempts by the Ministry of Health to control costs and improve health care by, for example, standardizing treatment. When nationals do not control the system, they cannot impose efficient, low-cost, uniform regimens for the treatment of common conditions. For example, in tuberculosis control, low-cost protocols that standardize treatment (diagnosis with microscopic examination of sputum rather than chest x-rays, and the prescription of inexpensive generics rather than expensive name-brand antibiotics) are often ignored or rejected by those foreign personnel with habits acquired in more affluent societies where cost is no object.

Some foreign physicians may also set a bad example for national health personnel in their attitudes toward coworkers, clients, and clinical medicine. Because many were trained in hierarchical systems, they may be unprepared to adopt democratic practices with their national counterparts. Because a common language is lacking, they may be patronizing in their relations with health service users and think of them as ignorant and superstitious. They will almost certainly be of a higher social class than the people they treat and, if they are not of the same culture, their behavior may be offensive or, worse, racist. Because they are clinicians, they may have little appreciation of the value of public health work in an underdeveloped country. Van Etten (1976) surveyed students at the Mwanza Medical Assistants Training Center and found that many of these attitudes already exist among Tanzanians.

Finally, reliance on foreign aid fosters technological dependency. When scientific and technical knowledge are not produced nationally, dependence on scientific progress abroad is more or less permanent. This progress can be neither directed nor controlled, which incurs the risk of financial and intellectual as well as technical dependence (Aberkane 1983). Financial dependence arises because technology does not come as a gift, and loans must eventually be repaid with scarce foreign exchange. In Tanzania, as we have seen, foreign aid has engendered a cycle of indebtedness. Intellectual dependence arises because the development of national capabilities in research and development is delayed, with the result that research conducted in the country by foreign agencies does not address national priorities. In Tanzania, the little medical research currently being carried out focuses on tropical diseases rather than the most common causes of death, which are diarrheal diseases and respiratory infections (World Health Organization 1980: 41). Technical dependence arises when the innovations come from the capitalist economies of advanced industrial nations; in that case there is little chance that they will be appropriate or beneficial to underdeveloped socialist countries. When innovations are developed by private corporations in those nations, socialist governments will pay dearly for licenses to patented technologies, if they can be bought at any price. The long-term effect of this dependency is blocked development in health as in other sectors.

The lack of information on disease—little more is known now than at the end of the colonial period—is a final indicator of Tanzania's dependency. It is peculiar that extensive data should be available on health services while almost no statistics exist on the health status of the population or on the types, incidence, and prevalence of disease. A nation in charge of its health care system would be likely to devote substantial resources to uncovering the fundamental causes of disease in order to eradicate them. It would not confuse health with health care or view health as a commodity that can be given to people by their government. Better health is not the product of medical treatment or even of health care, but rather a political choice embodied in national development strategies. Health is the fruit of people's labor and, like all other work products, it can be kept only if the social organization of production returns it to them.

Health and Development

Many health planners assume with economists that development—which is implicitly equated with capitalism—will solve problems of poverty, ill health, and "overpopulation" in the Third World. This assumption is embedded in accepted theories: the dual model of economies supposes that development creates wealth in modern enclaves, while lack of development explains the poverty of the hinterland; and demographic transition theorists believe that development brings down birth rates. Even when these theories are disproved, they continue to influence policy, often in the guise of new variations on old themes.

Public health has its counterpart to economic models in disease models that embody the capitalist vision of development. In the nineteenth century, English sanitary reformers such as Edwin Chadwick (1965) acted on the premise that disease was a cause of poverty. Their project was not, however, to eliminate disease by erasing poverty, but to sanitize the environment and thereby enrich the nation. To a degree their hypothesis proved correct: sanitary reform did contribute to improved health conditions in England, but many of us would argue that the rising living standards attributable to an expanding empire contributed more.

Engels (1969) stood Chadwick's proposition on its head and suggested instead that working-class poverty was a cause of disease. Engels together with Marx analyzed the causes of poverty, rather than disease, and found early industrial capitalism at the source. In the *Communist Manifesto* they proposed that the working classes use industrialism for the proletariat's benefit to eradicate poverty and improve health. In the communists' view, capitalism could raise the forces of production to such high levels that the needs of the entire population could be satisfied. In this sense there is some truth in the equation of capitalism with development: the capitalist mode of production is capable of producing goods and services at levels far above what precapitalist economic formations could achieve. Capitalist relations of production, although efficient in the use of materials, are wasteful of human life and health. As Marx wrote in *Capital*, capitalism squanders human lives, not only blood and flesh, but also nerves and brains.

In twentieth-century Tanzania (as in nineteenth-century England), poverty was a cause of disease, and the roots of poverty have been traced in this book to capitalism. But capitalist development was blocked in Tanzania, and the forces of production did not rise to levels high enough to meet human needs. Tanzanian workers and farmers have never fared as well as their British counterparts. Initially this blockage could be attributed to colonialism— shorthand for the very complex economic, social, and political processes described in the book. But after independence, and especially after the commitment to socialism with the Arusha Declaration of 1967, the hindrances to development require a different analysis. The colonial legacy accounts for some of the difficulty: the problem was how to reform colonial institutions and adapt them to new uses without creating chaos in the process. Moreover, the British forestalled rapid change. On the eve of independence they appointed commissions and consultants to review every sector of society and to propose detailed plans and programs to the new government.

Tanzania's unequal place in international markets and trade is a another part of the explanation. While not a British neocolony, Tanzania has suffered in the world capitalist economy. In the way of many Third World countries, Tanzania is disadvantaged in the unequal exchange of low-priced raw materials for high-cost manufactured goods. This analysis was proffered by Nyerere in an address to the Ministerial Conference of the Third World alliance known as the Group of 77 in Arusha in 1979: "Whatever the economic philosophy of our nations, we had all found that individual efforts to develop our own national economy kept running into a solid wall of power—the power of the rich nations and the rich transnational corporations. . . . The so-called neutrality of the world market place turned out to be a neutrality between the exploiter and the exploited, between a bird of prey and its victim" (Nyerere 1979:2). But this analysis does not tell us why Tanzania is not able to feed itself; in other words, it does not account for all of the issues of internal development. At least some of those issues are products of national policy and priorities.

Nyerere, in the same speech, considered that there are unavoidable pressures for compromise within individual countries—the inclination to take offers of special treatment, or special representation, and then, instead of using these as a base for further Third World advance, to lose interest in the wider struggle: "Those forces have not yet won within any country, but it would be stupid to pretend that they do not exist. For they will not just disappear" (ibid.:6). The same pressures created disunity within the Group of 77 and Nyerere noted the links between internal and external forces: "In all our countries there are groups which identify themselves with the powerful and privileged of the world and who aim only to join them—regardless of the poor in their own nation and elsewhere" (ibid.:9).

In formulating Tanzanian policies and priorities, Nyerere

has consistently identified with the poor and the weak. Acting in the democratic socialist tradition, he concentrated on redistributive policies to redress the inequalities created by capitalism in the colonial era. His program emphasized equal access to such services as health care, education, urban housing, and so on. But in the absence of levels of production sufficient to create the wealth needed to build and staff those services, the government could not provide them without mortgaging the country's future. The government's preoccupation with services rather than production is manifest in recurrent scarcities. By turning to foreign donors to finance social services, the government sacrificed independence for a kind of equity. Some would call the government's program an exercise in the management of poverty. I would argue that a network of basic services is now in place, and it remains for Tanzanian women and men to take control.

BIBLIOGRAPHY

Aall-Jilek, L. M.
1965   "Epilepsy in the Wapogoro Tribe in Tanganyika." *Acta Psychiatrica Scandinavica* 41:57–86.

Aberkane, A.
1983   "Réflexion sur les Critères de Dépendance du Système National de Santé." Paper presented at the *Séminaire sur le Développement d'un Système National de Santé: l'Expérience Algérienne*, Algiers, 7–8 April. Mimeo.

Ackernecht, E. H.
1946   "Natural Diseases and Rational Treatment in Primitive Medicine." *Bulletin of the History of Medicine* 19(5):467–497.

Akerele, O., A. Dhalla, and Q. Qhobela
1978   "Country Health Profile: United Republic of Tanzania." Dar es Salaam: World Health Organization. Photocopy.

Albrow, M.
1970   *Bureaucracy*. London: Pall Mall Press.

Alpers, Edward A.
1967   *The East African Slave Trade*. Historical Association of Tanzania Paper no. 3. Nairobi: East African Publishing House.
1969   "The Coast and the Development of the Caravan Trade." In *A History of Tanzania*, edited by I. N. Kimambo and A. J. Temu, 35–56. Nairobi: East African Publishing House.
1975   *Ivory and Slaves in East Central Africa*. New York: Harper and Row.

Amin, Samir
1981   "Underdevelopment and Dependence in Black Africa—Origins and Contemporary Forms." In *Political Economy of Africa: Selected Readings*, edited by Dennis L. Cohen and John Daniel, 22–44. London: Longman Group.

Anderson, O. W.
1972   *Health Care: Can There be Equity? The United States, Sweden, and England*. New York: Wiley.

211

Anker, Richard, Marya Buvinic, and Nadia Youssef
1982   Women's Roles and Population Trends in the Third
        World. London: Croom Helm.
Apthorpe, R.
1977   "The Cooperatives' Poor Harvest." New Internationalist,
        no. 48:4–6.
Arrighi, Giovanni
1970   "Labour Supplies in Historical Perspective." Journal of
        Development Studies 6(3):197–234.
Barakat, M. R.
1976   "Nutritional Anaemias." In Nutrition in Preventive Med-
        icine, edited by G. H. Beaton and J. M. Bengoa, 55–82.
        Geneva: World Health Organization.
Barnes, J. A.
1951   Marriage in a Changing Society. Rhodes Livingstone Pa-
        pers no. 20. Capetown: Oxford University Press.
Bauer, P. T. and B. S. Yamey
1968   Markets, Market Control and Marketing Reform. Lon-
        don: Weidenfeld and Nicolson.
Beck, Ann A.
1970   A History of the British Medical Administration of East
        Africa, 1900–1950. Cambridge: Harvard University
        Press.
Beckford, G. L.
1973   "The Economics of Agricultural Resources and Develop-
        ment in Plantation Economies." In Underdevelopment
        and Development: The Third World Today, edited by
        Henry Bernstein, 115–151. Harmondsworth: Penguin
        Books.
Beidelman, T. O.
1967   The Matrilineal Peoples of Eastern Tanzania. London:
        International African Institute.
1971   The Kaguru. New York: Holt, Rhinehart and Winston.
Berneria, Lourdes
1981   "Conceptualizing the Labor Force: The Underestimation
        of Women's Economic Activities." Journal of Develop-
        ment Studies 17:10–28.
Bernstein, Henry
1977   "Notes on Capital and Peasantry." Review of African Po-
        litical Economy 10:60–73.
Berry, L. and E. Berry
1969   Land Use in Tanzania by Districts. University of Dar es
        Salaam, Bureau of Resource Assessment and Land Use
        Planning Research Notes no. 6.
Blacker, J. C. G.
1963   "Population Growth and Natural Increase in Tanganyika

and Uganda." In *Population Characteristics of the Commonwealth Countries of Tropical Africa*, edited by J. C. G. Blacker and T. E. Smith. London: Athlone Press.

1971   "Economics of Health." In *Health and Diseases in Africa*, edited by G. C. Gould, 352–358. Kampala: East Africa Literature Bureau.

Boserup, Ester
1970   *Woman's Role in Economic Development*. London: Allen and Unwin.

Boyden, S. V., ed.
1970   *The Impact of Civilization on the Biology of Man*. Canberra: Australian National University.

Brain, James L.
1976   "Less Than Second-class: Women in Rural Resettlement Schemes in Tanzania." In *Women in Africa*, edited by Nancy J. Hafkin and Edna G. Bay, 205–282. Stanford: Stanford University Press.

Brass W., and A. J. Coale
1968   *The Demography of Tropical Africa*. Princeton: Princeton University Press.

Brenner, R.
1977   "The Origins of Capitalist Development: A Critique of Neo-Smithian Marxism." *New Left Review*, no. 104: 25–92.

Brett, E. A.
1973   *Colonialism and Underdevelopment in East Africa*. London: Heinemann.

Brewer, Anthony
1980   *Marxist Theories of Imperialism*. London: Routledge and Kegan Paul.

Brooke, C.
1967   "Types of Food Shortage in Tanzania." *Geographical Review* 108(3):333–357.

Bryant, John
1969   *Health and the Developing World*. Ithaca: Cornell University Press.

Bryceson, Deborah Fahy
1980   "Changes in Peasant Food Production and Food Supply in Relation to the Historical Development of Commodity Production in Pre-colonial and Colonial Tanganyika." *Journal of Peasant Studies* (3)7:281–311.

Bryceson, Deborah Fahy and Marjorie Mbilinyi
1978   "The Changing Role of Tanzanian Women in Production: From Peasants to Proletarians." University of Dar es Salaam, Bureau of Resource Assessment and Land Use Planning Service Paper no. 78/5.

Bursell, E.
1955   "Experiments in Tsetse Control in Southern Tangan-
         yika." *Bulletin of Entomological Research* 46:589–597.
Burton, Richard F.
1860   *The Lake Regions of Central Africa.* New York: Harper
         and Row.
Caldwell, J. C.
1981   "The Mechanisms of Demographic Change in Historical
         Perspective." *Population Studies* 35(1):5–27.
Cameron, Donald
1939   *My Tanganyika Service.* London: Allen and Unwin.
Cameron, Verney Lovett
1877   *Across Africa.* 2 vols. London: Daldy, Isbister and Co.
Chadwick, Edwin
1965   *Sanitary Condition of the Labouring Population,* edited
         by M. W. Flinn. Edinburgh: Edinburgh University Press.
         First published 1842.
Chale, H. F.
1973   "Emergent Large Farmers and the Problems of Imple-
         mentation of Ujamaa Vijijini Policy in Usangu (Mbeya
         District)." University of Dar es Salaam, Political Science
         Paper, 7(a).
Chidzero, B. T. G.
1961   *Tanganyika and International Trusteeship.* London: Ox-
         ford University Press.
Chipindulla, D. C.
1968   "The Maji Maji Rising in Kilosa Town." Maji Maji Re-
         search Project Collected Papers. Dar es Salaam: Univer-
         sity College, Research Project no. 2/68/1/1.
Chisholm, B.
1952   "The Work of WHO, 1951." Geneva: World Health
         Organization.
Cliffe, Lionel
1971   "Socialist Education in Tanzania." In *Education and Po-
         litical Value: An East African Case Study,* edited by
         K. Prewitt, 53–67. Nairobi: East African Publishing
         House.
1972   "Planning Rural Development." In *Towards Socialist
         Planning,* 92–118. Dar es Salaam: Tanzania Publishing
         House.
Cliffe, Lionel and John S. Saul
1972   "The District Development Front in Tanzania." *African
         Review* 2(1):65–104.
Clyde, David F.
1962   *History of the Medical Services in Tanganyika.* Dar es
         Salaam: Government Printer.
1967   *Malaria in Tanzania.* London: Oxford University Press.

Cohen, Dennis L.
1981   Introduction to "The Internal Structures of Depen-
          dency." In *Political Economy of Africa: Selected Read-
          ings*, edited by Dennis L. Cohen and John Daniel,
          75–77. London: Longman Group.
Cohen, Dennis L. and John Daniel, eds.
1981   *Political Economy of Africa: Selected Readings.* Lon-
          don: Longman Group.
Comité Information Sahel
1974   *Qui se Nourrit de la Famine en Afrique?* Paris: Maspero.
Cordell, Dennis D.
1983   "Low Fertility in Africa: An Evaluation of the Bio-medi-
          cal Approach of Anne Retel-Laurentin." Paper presented
          at the Canadian Association of African Studies, Quebec,
          15–18 May.
Coulson, Andrew
1977   "Agricultural Policies in Mainland Tanzania." *Review of
          African Political Economy* 10:74–100.
1982   *Tanzania: A Political Economy.* Oxford: Clarendon
          Press.
Coupland, R.
1939   *The Exploitation of East Africa, 1856–1890: The Slave
          Trade and the Scramble.* London: Faber and Faber.
Crosby, A. W.
1972   *The Colombian Exchange: Biological and Cultural Con-
          sequences of 1492.* Westport, Conn.: Greenwood Press.
Darwin, Charles
1904   *On the Origin of Species.* New York: J. A. Hill and Com-
          pany. First published 1859.
Davies, J. N. P.
1959   "James Christie and the Cholera Epidemics of East Af-
          rica." *East African Medical Journal* 36(1):1–6.
De Wilde, J. C., ed.
1967   *Experience with Agricultural Development in Tropical
          Africa.* 2 vols. Baltimore: Johns Hopkins University
          Press.
Dobson, E. B.
1954   "Comparative Land Tenure of Ten Tanganyikan Tribes."
          Journal of African Administration 6:80–91.
Dos Santos, T.
1970   "The Structure of Dependence." *American Economics
          Review*, Papers and Proceedings, 60:231–236.
Draper, Patricia
1975   "!Kung Women: Contrasts in Sexual Egalitarianism in
          Foraging and Sedentary Contexts." In *Toward an An-
          thropology of Women*, edited by Rayna R. Reiter,
          77–109. New York: Monthly Review Press.

Dubos, René
1959   Mirage of Health. New York: Harper and Row.
1968   Man, Medicine, and Environment. Harmondsworth: Penguin Books.
Durkheim, Emile
1938   The Rules of Sociological Method. Glencoe: Free Press. First published 1895.
1951   Suicide: A Study in Sociology. Glencoe: Free Press. First published 1897.
East Africa Royal Commission
1956   1953–1955 Report. London: Her Majesty's Stationery Office.
East African Statistics Department
1949   East African Economic and Statistical Bulletin, nos. 3 and 5.
1950   East African Economic and Statistical Bulletin, no. 10.
1951   East African Economic and Statistical Bulletin, nos. 11, 12, and 13.
1952   East African Economic and Statistical Bulletin, no. 15.
Ehrlich, C.
1968   "Economic and Social Development before Independence." In Zamani: A Survey of East African History, edited by B. A. Ogot and J. A. Kieran, 334–348. Nairobi: East African Publishing House.
Engels, Frederick
1969   The Condition of the Working Class in England. London: Panther Books. First published 1845.
Enzensberger, Hans Magnus
1974   "A Critique of Political Ecology." New Left Review, no. 84:3–31.
Etienne, Mona and Eleanor Leacock
1980   "Introduction." In Women and Colonization: Anthropological Perspectives, edited by Mona Etienne and Eleanor Leacock, 1–24. New York: Praeger.
Fei, J. C. H. and G. Ranis
1964   Development of the Labour Surplus Economy. Homewood, Ill.: Irwin.
Feierman, Steven
1979   Health and Society in Africa: A Working Bibliography. Waltham: Crossroads Press.
Feldman, Rayah
1974   "Custom and Capitalism: Changes in the Basis of Land Tenure in Ismani, Tanzania." Journal of Development Studies 10(3 and 4):305–306.
Ferguson, D. E.
1980   "The Political Economy of Health and Medicine in Colonial Tanganyika." In Tanzania under Colonial Rule, ed-

ited by M. H. Y. Kaniki, 307–343. London: Longman Group Limited.

Fimbo, G. M.
1974   "The Right of Occupancy in Tanzania: The Political Economy of an African Land Tenure System." *East Africa Law Review* 2:121–156.

Fine, B.
1978   "On the Origins of Capitalist Development." *New Left Review*, no. 109:88–95.

Flint, John
1983   "Planned Decolonization and Its Failure in British Africa." Paper presented at the Canadian Association of African Studies, Quebec, 15–18 May. Photocopy.

Ford, John
1971   *The Role of Trypanosomiasis in African Ecology.* London: Oxford University Press.

Foster-Carter, A.
1978   "The Modes of Production Controversy." *New Left Review*, no. 107:47–77.

Frank, Andre Gunder
1969   *Latin America: Underdevelopment and Revolution.* New York: Monthly Review Press.
1971   *Capitalism and Underdevelopment in Latin America.* Harmondsworth: Penguin Books.

Frankel, S. H.
1953   *The Economic Impact on Under-developed Societies.* Cambridge: Harvard University Press.

Freedman, Ronald
1979   "Theories of Fertility Decline: A Reappraisal." *Social Forces* 58(1):1–17.

Freidson, E.
1971   *Profession of Medicine: A Study of the Sociology of Applied Knowledge.* New York: Dodd, Mead.

Fuggles-Couchman, N. R.
1964   *Agricultural Change in Tanganyika, 1945–1960.* Stanford: Stanford University, Food Research Institute.

Gallagher, J. T.
1974   "The Emergence of an African Ethnic Group: The Case of the Ndendeuli." *International Journal of African Historical Studies* 7(1):1–27.

Geiger, Susan
1982   "Umoja wa Wanawake wa Tanzania and the Needs of the Rural Poor." *African Studies Review* 25(2 and 3):45–65.

Gelfand, M.
1961   *Northern Rhodesia in the Days of the Charter.* Oxford: Blackwell.

Gerlach, L. P.
1965   "Nutrition in Its Sociocultural Matrix: Food Getting and
          Using along the East African Coast." In *Ecology and Eco-
          nomic Development in Tropical Africa*, edited by D.
          Brokensha, 245–268. Berkeley: University of California
          Press.
Gish, Oscar
1972   "The Supply and Demand for Hospital Beds in Tanza-
          nia." Dar es Salaam: Ministry of Health. Mimeo.
1975   *Planning the Health Sector: The Tanzanian Experience.*
          London: Croom Helm.
Goddard, D.
1969   "Limits to British Anthropology." *New Left Review*, no.
          58:79–89.
Goldthorpe, J. E.
1952   "Attitude to the Census and Vital Registration in East
          Africa." *Population Studies* 6(2):163–171.
1956   "The African Population of East Africa." In *East Africa
          Royal Commission 1953–55 Report.* London: Her Majes-
          ty's Stationery Office, appendix 7.
1965   *An   African   Elite: Makerere   College   Students,
          1922–1960.* Nairobi: Oxford University Press.
Good, C. M.
1971   "Market Development in Traditionally Marketless Socie-
          ties: A Perspective on East Africa." Ohio University Cen-
          ter for International Studies, Africa Series Paper no. 12.
Gould, Carol C.
1981   *Marx's Social Ontology.* Cambridge: MIT Press.
Gray, R. and D. Birmingham
1970   "Some Economic and Political Consequences of Trade
          in Central and Eastern Africa in the Pre-colonial Pe-
          riod." In *Pre-colonial African Trade*, edited by R. Gray,
          and D. Birmingham, 1–23. London: Oxford University
          Press.
Great Britain Colonial Office
1930/31   *East African Agricultural Research Station, Amani, An-
          nual Report.* London: His Majesty's Stationery Office.
1931   *Report on Tanganyika Territory for the Year 1930.* Lon-
          don: His Majesty's Stationery Office.
1932   *Report on Tanganyika Territory for the Year 1931.* Lon-
          don: His Majesty's Stationery Office.
1939   *East African Agricultural Research Station, Amani, An-
          nual Report.* London: His Majesty's Stationery Office.
1941   *East African Agricultural Research Station, Amani, An-
          nual Report.* London: His Majesty's Stationery Office.
1942   *East African Agricultural Research Station, Amani, An-
          nual Report.* London: His Majesty's Stationery Office.

1943   *East African Agricultural Research Station, Amani, An-
          nual Report.* London: His Majesty's Stationery Office.
1944   *East African Agricultural Research Station, Amani, An-
          nual Report.* London: His Majesty's Stationery Office.
1949   *Report on Tobacco.* London: His Majesty's Stationery
          Office.
1950   *Grain Storage in East and Central Africa.* London: His
          Majesty's Stationery Office.
Gulliver, P. H.
1955   *Labour Migration in a Rural Economy.* Kampala: East
          African Institute of Social Research.
1956   "History of the Songea Ngoni." *Tanganyika Notes and
          Records* 41:16–30.
1960   "The Population of Arusha Chiefdom." *Rhodes-Living-
          ston Journal,* December.
Gulliver, P. H., ed.
1969   *Tradition and Transition in East Africa.* Stanford: Stan-
          ford University Press.
Gwassa, G. C. K.
1969   "The German Intervention and African Resistance in
          Tanzania." In *A History of Tanzania,* edited by I. N.
          Kimambo and A. J. Temu, 85–122. Nairobi: East African
          Publishing House.
Gwatkin, Davidson R. and Sarah K. Brandel
1982   "Life Expectancy and Population Growth in the Third
          World." *Scientific American* 246(5):57–65.
Hackett, C. J.
1971   "Diagnosis of Diseases in the Past." In *Modern Methods
          in the History of Medicine,* edited by E. Clarke, 99–111.
          London: Athlone Press.
Hailey, Malcom
1938   *An African Survey.* London: Oxford University Press.
1950   *Native Administration in the British African Territories.*
          Part 1. London: His Majesty's Stationery Office.
Hawkins, H. C. G.
1965   *Wholesale and Retail Trade in Tanganyika.* New York:
          Praeger.
Hayter, Teresa
1971   *Aid as Imperialism.* Harmondsworth: Penguin Books.
Helali, A., M. Benmiloud, M. Hartani, and D. Saiki
1983   "Maîtrise des Ressources Matérielles." Paper pre-
          sented at the Séminaire sur le Développement d'un
          Système National de Santé: l'Expérience Algé-
          rienne, Algiers, 7–8 April. Mimeo.
Henin, R. A. and B. Egero
1972   "1967 Population Census of Tanzania: A Demographic
          Analysis." University of Dar es Salaam, Bureau of

Resource Assessment and Land Use Planning Research Paper no. 19.

Heussler, R.
1971 *British Tanganyika: An Essay and Documents on District Administration.* Durham: Duke University Press.

Hirji, K. F.
1973 "School Education and Underdevelopment in Tanzania." *Maji Maji* (Dar es Salaam) 12:1–22.

Hirst, M. A.
1969 "Net Migration Patterns over Tanzania." *East Africa Geographical Review* 7:25–36.
1970 "Patterns of Population Growth in Mainland Tanzania, 1948–57." In *Studies in Population Geography of Uganda and Tanzania,* edited by M. A. Hirst et al., 1–20. Department of Geography, Occasional Paper no. 14. Kampala; Makerere University College.

Hobsbawm, Eric J.
1962 *The Age of Revolution, 1789–1848.* New York: New American Library.

Hodder, B. W.
1965 "Some Comments on the Origins of Traditional Markets in Africa South of the Sahara." *Transactions of the Institute of British Geographers* 36:97–105.

Honey, Martha
1977 "Multinational Drug Scandal in Tanzania." *New African,* November.

Horn, Joshua
1969 *Away with All Pests.* London: Paul Hamlyn.

Hudson, E. H.
1965 "Treponematosis and Man's Social Evolution." *American Anthopologist* 67:885.

Hughes, J. P.
1972 "Economic Development and the Health Planner: Opportunity or Handicap?" In *Health Care for Remote Areas,* edited by J. P. Hughes. Oakland, Calif.: Kaiser Foundation International.

Hurst, H. R. G.
1959 "A Survey of the Development of Facilities for Migrant Labour in Tanganyika during the Period 1926–1959." *Bulletin of the Inter-African Labour Institute* 6:50–91.

Huxley, Thomas
1959 *Man's Place in Nature.* Ann Arbor: University of Michigan Press. First published 1863.

Ibbott, R.
1966 "The Ruvuma Development Association." *Mbioni* 3(2)3–43.

Iliffe, John
1967   "The Effects of the Maji Maji Rebellion of 1905–1906
          on German Occupation Policy in East Africa." In *Brit-
          ain and Germany in Africa*, edited by P. Gifford
          and R. Louis, 557–575. New Haven: Yale University
          Press.
1969   *Tanganyika under German Rule, 1905–1912*. Cam-
          bridge: Cambridge University Press.
1971   *Agricultural Change in Modern Tanganyika*. Historical
          Association of Tanzania, Paper no. 10. Nairobi: East Af-
          rican Publishing House.
1979   *A Modern History of Tanganyika*. Cambridge: Cam-
          bridge University Press.
Ingham, K.
1958   "Tanganyika in the Twenties: The Era of Byatt and Cam-
          eron." *Makerere Journal* 1:11.
Jalée, P.
1974   *Le Tiers Monde en Chiffres*. Paris: François Maspero.
Joint East African Examining Board in Medicine
1939   *Regulations Relating to Certification in Medicine, Sur-
          gery, Obstetrics and Gynaecology*. Entebbe: Government
          Printer.
Jones, T. Jesse
1924   *Education in East Africa*. New York: Phelps-Stokes
          Fund.
Jones, William O.
1968   "Plantations." In *International Encyclopedia of the So-
          cial Sciences*, edited by D. L. Sills, 12:154–159. Paris:
          UNESCO.
Kaniki, M. H. Y., ed.
1980   *Tanzania under Colonial Rule*. London: Longman
          Group.
Kawago, K. S.
1971   "The Operation of TANU Cells in Iringa." In *The Cell
          System of the Tanganyika African National Union*,
          edited by J. H. Proctor, 57–66. Dar es Salaam: Tanzania
          Publishing House.
Kimambo, I. N.
1969   "The Interior before 1800." In *A History of Tanzania*,
          edited by I. N. Kimambo and A. J. Temu, 14–33. Nai-
          robi: East African Publishing House.
Kimambo, I. N. and A. J. Temu, eds.
1969   *A History of Tanzania*. Nairobi: East African Publishing
          House.
Kjekshus, Helge
1975   "The Elected Elite: A Socioeconomic Profile of Can-
          didates in Tanzania's Parliamentary Election, 1970."

Scandinavian Institute of African Studies Research Report no. 29. Uppsala.

1977   *Ecology Control and Economic Development in East African History.* London: Heinemann.

Klein, R.

1972   "Participation and the Health Service: The Case for a Counterbureaucracy." London: Fabian Society. Mimeo.

Kokuhirwa, Hilda

n.d.   "Towards the Social and Economic Promotion of Rural Women in Tanzania." Dar es Salaam: Institute for Adult Education. Photocopy.

Kokwebangira, R. M.

1971   "Cells in Dar es Salaam and Bukoba." In *The Cell System in the Tanganyika African National Union,* edited by J. H. Proctor, 42–49. Dar es Salaam: Tanzania Publishing House.

Komba, B. M. L.

1968   "The Maji Maji Rising in Mkuvumusi." Maji Maji Research Project Collected Papers, Project no. 6/68/8/1, Appendix. Dar es Salaam: University Library.

Kozak, I. G.

1968   "Two Rebellions in German East Africa and Their Study in Microcosm." M. A. thesis, Howard University.

Kreysler, Joe

1973   "Nutrition." In *The Young Child Study in Tanzania,* 12–40. Dar es Salaam: UNICEF.

Kuczynski, R. R.

1949   *Demographic Survey of the British Colonial Empire.* Vol. 2. London: Oxford University Press.

Kuper, H.

1965   *An African Aristocracy: Rank among the Swazi.* London: Oxford University Press.

Ladner, Joyce

1971   "Tanzanian Women and Nation Building." *Black Scholar* 3(4):22–28.

Lall, Sanjaya

1974   "The International Pharmaceutical Industry and Less Developed Countries, with Special Reference to India." *Oxford Bulletin of Economics and Statistics* 36(3):143–172.

1975   "Major Issues in the Transfer of Technology to Developing Countries: A Case Study of the Pharmaceutical Industry." Geneva: United Nations Conference on Trade and Development. Mimeo.

Lall, Sanjaya and Senaka Bibile

1978   "The Political Economy of Controlling Transnationals: The Pharmaceutical Industry in Sri Lanka, 1972–1976." *International Journal of Health Services* 8(2):299–327.

Lambert, Jacques
n. d.   *Os Dois Brasis.* Rio de Janeiro: Ministerio da Educacao e
           Cultura.
Langlands, B. W.
1965   *Bibliography of the Distribution of Disease in East
           Africa.* Kampala: Makerere University College Press.
Lapeysonnie, L.
1963   "La Méningite Cérébrospinale en Afrique." *Bulletin of
           the World Health Organization* 28, supplement.
Large, J. W.
1938   "Notes." In Tanganyika District Books, Songea District.
           Dar es Salaam: Tanzania National Archives.
Layrisse, M., M. Roche, and S. J. Baker
1976   "Nutritional Anaemias." In *Nutrition in Preventive Med-
           icine,* edited by G. H. Beaton and J. M. Bengoa, 55–82.
           Geneva: World Health Organization.
Lazonick, William
1974   "Karl Marx and Enclosures in England." *Review of Radi-
           cal Political Economics* 6(2):1–59.
Lee, R. B. and I. DeVore, eds.
1968   *Man the Hunter.* Chicago: Aldine.
Lenin, V. I.
1919   *The State and Revolution.* London: George Allen and
           Unwin.
Leubuscher, C.
1944   *Tanganyika Territory: A Study of Economic Policy un-
           der Mandate.* London: Oxford University Press.
Lewis, W. Arthur
1954   "Economic Development with Unlimited Supplies of La-
           bour." *Manchester School of Economic and Social Stud-
           ies* 22(2):139–191.
1955   *The Theory of Economic Growth.* London: Allen and
           Unwin.
Lewontin, R. C.
1983   "The Corpse in the Elevator." *New York Review of
           Books,* January 20, 34–37.
Lomas, P. K.
1966   "A Study of the Raisman Commision Report." In *Read-
           ings on Economic Development and Administration in
           Tanzania,* edited by H.E. Smith, 513–521. London: Ox-
           ford University Press.
Lorenz, Konrad
1966   *On Agression.* New York: Harcourt Brace Jovanovich.
1971   *Studies in Animal and Human Behaviour.* 2 vols. Lon-
           don: Methuen and Co.
Lorimer, F. and M. Karp
1960   *Population in Africa.* Boston: Boston University Press.

Lugard, Frederick
1923   *The Dual Mandate in British Tropical Africa.* Edin-
         burgh: Blackwood.
Luttrell, William L.
1972   "Location Planning and Regional Development in Tan-
         zania." In *Towards Socialist Planning*, edited by
         Uchumi Editorial Board, 119–148. Dar es Salaam: Tanz-
         ania Publishing House.
McHenry, Dean E.
1976   "The Ujamaa Village in Tanzania: A Comparison with
         Chinese, Soviet and Mexican Experiences in Collectivi-
         zation." *Comparative Studies in Society and History*
         18(3):347–370.
McKelvey, J. J.
1973   *Man against Tsetse.* Ithaca: Cornell University Press.
McKenzie, A.
1948   "The Native Authority System in Tanganyika Territory."
         East African Medical Journal 7:273–280.
McKeown, Thomas
1976   *The Role of Medicine.* London: Nuffield Provincial Hos-
         pitals Trust.
Maclean, George
1929   "The Relationship between Economic Development and
         Rhodesian Sleeping Sickness in Tanganyika Territory."
         Annals of Tropical Medicine and Parasitology 23:
         37–46.
1950   "Medical Administration in the Tropics." *British Medi-
         cal Journal* 1:756–761.
Maclean, Una
1974   *Magical Medicine: A Nigerian Case Study,* Harmonds-
         worth: Penguin Books.
McMichael, Joan K., ed.
1976   *Health in the Third World: Studies from Vietnam.* Lon-
         don: Spokesman Books.
Mafeje, Archie
1972   "The Fallacy of Dual Economies." *East Africa Journal*
         7(9):30–34.
1973   "The Fallacy of Dual Economies Revisited." In *Dualism
         and Rural Development in East Africa*, edited by R.
         Leys, 27–52. Copenhagen: Institute for Development
         Research.
Magome, G.
1973   "The Mwanza Regional Consultant Hospital: An Ap-
         praisal." Dar es Salaam *Daily News*, January, 25.
Maji Maji Research Project
1966   Collected Papers. Dar es Salaam: University Library.

Mapunda, O. B. and Mpangara G. P.
1969   *The Maji Maji War in Ungoni.* Maji Maji Research Paper
          no. 1. Nairobi: East African Publishing House.
Maro, E.
1974   "Woman Participation versus Cooperative Legislation."
          Report on the Proceedings of the Regional Women's Co-
          operators Seminar, International Cooperative Alliance,
          Kampala, 14–18 January. Photocopy.
Marx, Karl
1967   *Capital.* New York: International Publishers. First pub-
          lished 1867.
1973   *Grundrisse.* New York: Vintage Books. First published
          1857–1858.
1974   *The German Ideology.* London: Lawrence and Wishart.
          First published 1846.
Mathias, M. E.
1965   "Medicinal Plant Hunting in Tanzania." In *Ecology and
          Economic Development in Tropical Africa,* edited by D.
          Brokensha, 83–92. Berkeley: University of California
          Press.
May, Jacques M.
1958   *The Ecology of Human Disease.* New York: MD
          Publications.
Mbilinyi, Marjorie J.
1973   "Education, Stratification and Sexism in Tanzania: Pol-
          icy Implications." *African Review* 3(2):327–340.
Mechanic, David
1962   "The Concept of Illness Behavior." *Journal of Chronic
          Diseases* 15:189–194.
1963   "Some Implications of Illness Behavior for Medical
          Sampling." *New England Journal of Medicine* 269:
          244–247.
Meillassoux, Claude
1972   "From Reproduction to Production." *Economy and Soci-
          ety* 1(1):93–105
1974   "Development or Exploitation: Is the Sahel Famine
          Good Business?" *Review of African Political Economy*
          1:27–33.
Merton, R. K.
1957   *Social Theory and Social Structure.* Glencoe: Free
          Press.
Mettan, R. W. M.
1937   "A Short History of Rinderpest with Special Reference
          to Africa." *Uganda Journal* 5(1):22–26.
Mhlongo, Sam
1981   "An Analysis of the Classes in South Africa." In *Politi-
          cal Economy of Africa: Selected Readings,* edited by

Dennis L. Cohen and John Daniel, 130–154. London: Longman Group.

Middleton, J. C.
n. d.   Donated Papers. Oxford University, Rhodes House. Mss. Afr.s.1079.

Millar, J. D.
1970   "Epidemiological Characteristics of Measles in West and Central Africa." Paper presented at Seminar on Small-pox Eradication and Measles Control in Western and Central Africa, Atlanta, National Communicable Disease Center.

Mkunduge, G. L.
1973   "The Ukaguru Environment: Traditional and Recent Responses to Food Shortages." *Journal of the Geographical Association of Tanzania* 8:63–85.

Molohan, M. J. B.
1959   *Detribalization*. Dar es Salaam: Government Printer.

Montagu, Ashley
1956   *The Biosocial Nature of Man*. New York: Grove Press.

Mshangama, A. H.
1971   "TANU Cells: Organs of One-Party Democratic Socialism." In *The Cell System of the Tanganyika African National Union*, edited by J. H. Proctor, 20–31. Dar es Salaam: Tanzania Publishing House.

Muller, Mike
1982   *The Health of Nations: A North-South Investigation*. London: Faber and Faber.

Mullings, Leith
1976   "Women and Economic Change in Africa." In *Women in Africa*, edited by Nancy J. Hafkin and Edna G. Bay, 239–264. Stanford: Stanford University Press.

Mwapachu, J. V.
1976   "Operation Planned Villages in Rural Tanzania: A Revolutionary Strategy for Development." *African Review* 6(1):1–16.

Mzingi, M.
1969   "Nutritional Problems in the Weaning Period and Nutrition Services in Tanzania." Alexandria, Egypt: World Health Organization. Mimeo.

Navarro, Vicente
1974   "Social Policy Issues: An Explanation of the Composition, Nature and Functions of the Present Health Sector of the United States." Paper based on a presentation at the Annual Conference of the New York Academy of Medicine, 25–26 April. Photocopy.

Nduru, C. T.
1974   "Tanzania—the Politics of Participation: TANU and

Popular Participation after Decentralization; the Case of Mbinga District." University of Dar es Salaam, Department of Political Science, Dissertation Paper 307.

Njohole, B.
1971   "Building Party Cells in Tanzania." In *The Cell System of the Tanganyika African National Union*, edited by J. H. Proctor, 1–19. Dar es Salaam: Tanzania Publishing House.

Nyerere, Julius K.
1966   "Ujamaa—The Basis of African Socialism." In *Freedom and Unity: A Selection from Writings and Speeches 1952–65*. Dar es Salaam: Oxford University Press.
1968a   "Education for Self-reliance." In *Freedom and Socialism: A Selection from Writings and Speeches 1965–1967*, 267–290. Dar es Salaam: Oxford University Press.
1968b   "Socialism and Rural Development." In *Freedom and Socialism: A Selection from Writings and Speeches 1965–1967*, 337–366. Dar es Salaam: Oxford University Press.
1979   "Unity for a New Order." Opening address to the Ministerial Conference of the Group of 77. Arusha, 12 February.

O'Barr, J. F.
1972   "Cell Leaders in Tanzania." *African Studies Review* 15(3):437–465.

O'Keefe, Phil, Ken Westgate, and Ben Wisner
1976   "Taking the Naturalness Out of Natural Disasters." *Nature* 260:565–566.

Oliensis, D.
1967   "East African Psychological Patterns." *Journal of the American Academy of Child Psychiatry* 6:551–572.

Oliver, R.
1952   *The Missionary Factor in East Africa*. London: Longmans.

Omari, C. K.
1972   "The Mganga: A Specialist of His Own Kind." *Psychopathologie Africaine* 8(2):217–231.

Omran, A. R.
1971   "The Epidemiological Transition—A Theory of the Epidemiology of Population Change." *Milbank Memorial Fund Quarterly* 49(4):1, 509–538.

Orde-Browne, G.
1946   *Labour Conditions in East Africa*. Colonial 193. London: His Majesty's Stationery Office.

Orley, J. H.
1970   *Culture and Mental Illness*. Nairobi: East African Publishing House.

Pala, Achola O.
1977   "Definitions of Women and Development: An African
        Perspective." In Women and National Development:
        The Complexities of Change, edited by the Wellesley
        Editorial Committee, 9–13. Chicago: University of Chi-
        cago Press.
Parsons, Talcott
1952   The Social System. London: Tavistock.
1963   Social Structure and Personality. Glencoe: Free Press.
Patterson, K. David
1978   "Bibliographic Essay." In Disease in African History: An
        Introductory Survey and Case Studies, edited by Gerald
        W. Hartwig and K. David Patterson, 238–250. Durham:
        Duke University Press.
Paul, Jim
1977   "Medicine and Imperialism in Morocco." MERIP Re-
        ports 60:3–12.
Payer, Cheryl
1982   The World Bank: A Critical Analysis. New York:
        Monthly Review Press.
Post, Ken
1972   "Peasantisation and Rural Political Movements in West-
        ern Africa." Archives of European Sociology 13:
        223–254.
Powles, John
1973   "On the Limitations of Modern Medicine." Science,
        Medicine and Man 1(1):1–30.
Pradervand, Pierre
1970   Family Planning Programmes in Africa. Paris: Organiza-
        tion of Economic Cooperation and Development.
Proctor, J. H., ed.
1971   The Cell System of the Tanganyika African National
        Union. Dar es Salaam: Tanzania Publishing House.
Puffer, R. R. and C. V. Serrano
1973   "Patterns of Mortality in Childhood." Pan American
        Health Organization, Scientific Publication no. 202.
        Washington, D.C.
Raikes, P. C.
1975   "Ujamaa and Rural Socialism." Review of African Politi-
        cal Economy 3:33–52.
Rald, J. and K. Rald
1975   Rural Organization in Bukoba District, Tanzania. Upp-
        sala: Scandinavian Institute of African Studies.
Ranger, Terence O.
1969   "The Movement of Ideas, 1850–1939." In A History of
        Tanzania, edited by I. N. Kimambo and A. J. Temu,
        161–188. Nairobi: East African Publishing House.

1981   "Godly Medicine: The Ambiguities of Medical Mission
        in Southeast Tanzania, 1900–1945." *Social Science and
        Medicine* 15B:261–277.
Read, Margaret
1956   *The Ngoni of Nyasaland.* London: Oxford University
        Press.
Redmond, P. H.
1972   "Political History of the Ngoni of Songea District, Tanza-
        nia, from the Mid-Nineteenth Century to the Rise of
        TANU." Ph.D. dissertation, University of London,
        School of Oriental and African Studies.
Reining, Priscilla
1970   "Social Factors and Food Production in an East African
        Peasant Society: The Haya." In *African Food Production
        Systems,* edited by P. F. M. McLoughin, 41–89. Balti-
        more: Johns Hopkins University Press.
Review of African Political Economy
1974   Editorial. No. 1.
Reynolds, D. R.
1975   "An Appraisal of Rural Women in Tanzania." Study for
        the Regional Economic Services Office, United States
        Agency for International Development, Washington,
        D.C. Photocopy.
Richards, Audrey
1939   *Land, Labour, and Diet in Northern Rhodesia.* London:
        Oxford University Press.
Rigby, Peter
1969   *Cattle and Kinship among the Gogo.* Ithaca: Cornell Uni-
        versity Press.
Roberts, A., ed.
1968   *Tanzania before 1900.* Nairobi: East African Publishing
        House.
Robson, J. R. K.
1962   "Malnutrition in Tanganyika." *Tanganyika Notes and
        Records,* nos. 58–59:259–267.
1974   "The Ecology of Malnutrition in a Rural Community in
        Tanzania." *Ecology of Food and Nutrition* 3:61–72.
Robson, J. R. K., G. A. Carpenter, M. C. Latham, R. Wise, and
    P. G. Lewis
1962   "The District Team Approach to Malnutrition: Maposeni
        Nutrition Scheme." *African Child Health,* December,
        60–75. Reprinted in *Journal of Tropical Paediatrics*
        8(1962):68.
Robson, J. R. K., F. A. Larkin, A. M. Sandretto, and B. Tadayyon
1972   *Malnutrition: Its Causation and Control.* 2 vols. New
        York: Gordon and Breach.

Robson, John
1973   "The NHS Company Inc.? The Social Consequences of
          the Professional Dominance in the National Health Ser-
          vice." International Journal of Health Services 3:3,
          413–426.
Rodney, Walter
1980   "The Political Economy of Colonial Tanganyika, 1890–
          1930." In Tanganyika under Colonial Rule, edited by
          M. H. Y. Kaniki, 128–163. London: Longman Group.
Rogers, L.
1954   "Leprosy Incidence and Control in East Africa, 1924–
          1952, and the Outlook." Leprosy Review 25:
          41–59.
Rosa, Franz W. and Meredeth Turshen
1970   "Fetal Nutrition." Bulletin of the World Health Organi-
          zation 43:785–795.
Rose, Steven, ed.
1982a   Against Biological Determinism. London: Allison and
          Busby.
1982b   Towards a Liberation Biology. London: Allison and
          Busby.
Rural Settlement Commission
1966   A Report on the Village Settlement Programme from the
          Inception of the Rural Settlement Commission to 31 De-
          cember 1965. Dar es Salaam: Government Printer.
Ruthenberg, Hans
1964   Agricultural Development in Tanzania. Berlin: Springer
          Verlag.
Rweyemamu, Justinian
1974   Underdevelopment and Industrialization in Tanzania:
          A Study of Perverse Capitalist Industrial Development.
          Nairobi: Oxford University Press.
Sacks, Karen
1979   Sister and Wives: The Past and Future of Sexual Equal-
          ity. Westport: Greenwood Press.
Sanday, Peggy Reeves
1981   Female Power and Male Dominance: On the Origins of
          Sexual Inequality. Cambridge: Cambridge University
          Press.
Santos, Milton, Phil O'Keefe, and Richard Peet, eds.
1977   Antipode 9(3).
Saunders, Lyle
1954   Cultural Differences and Medical Care. New York: Rus-
          sell Sage Foundation.
Sawyers, G. F. A.
1969   "Discriminatory Restrictions on Private Dispositions of
          Land in Tanganyika: A Second Look." In Land Law Re-

form in East Africa, edited by J. Obol-Ochola, 59–88. Kampala: Milton Obote Foundation.

Schapera, I.
1947   *Migrant Labour and Tribal Life*. London: Oxford University Press.

Scofield, Sue
1974   "Seasonal Factors affecting Nutrition in Different Age Groups and Especially Preschool Children." *Journal of Development Studies* 11(1):22–40.

Segall, Malcolm
1972   "The Politics of Health in Tanzania." In *Towards Socialist Planning*, edited by Uchumi Editorial Board, 149–165. Dar es Salaam: Tanzania Publishing House.

Seidman, Ann
1972   *Comparative Development Strategies in East Africa*. Nairobi: East African Publishing House.

Sharpston, M. J.
1973   "Health and Development." *Journal of Development Studies* 9(3):455–460.

Sheriff, Abdul M. H.
1971   "The Rise of a Commercial Empire: An Aspect of the Economic History of Zanzibar, 1770–1875." Ph.D. dissertation, University of London.

Shields, N. G.
1976   "The Relevance of Current Models of Married Women's Labor Force Participation in Africa." Paper presented at the Seminar on Household Models of Economic Demographic Decision Making, Mexico City, 4–6 September. Photocopy.

Shivji, Issa G.
1976   *Class Struggles in Tanzania*. London: Heinemann.

Sidel, Ruth and Victor W. Sidel
1982   *The Health of China*. Boston: Beacon Press.

Siskind, Janet
1973   *To Hunt in the Morning*. London: Oxford University Press.

Smartt, C. G. E.
1956   "Mental Maladjustment in the East African." *Journal of Medical Services* 102:441.

Special Issue Editorial Collective
1978   "Uneven Regional Development: An Introduction to This Issue." *Review of Radical Political Economics* 10(3):1–12.

Spies, E.
1943   "Observations on Utani Customs among the Ngoni of Songea District." *Tanganyika Notes and Records* 16:49–53.

Stark, Evan
1977   "The Epidemic as a Social Event." *International Journal of Health Services* 7:681–705.
1982   "What Is Medicine?" *Radical Science Journal* 12:46–89.

Stauder, J.
1974   "The Relevance of Anthropology to Colonialism and Imperialism." *Radical Science Journal* 1:51–70.

Staudt, K.
1977   "Victorian Womanhood in British Colonial Africa: the Role of Social Service Programs." Paper presented at the Conference on the History of Women, Saint Paul, Minnesota. Photocopy

Stephens, R. W.
1968   *The Political Transformation of Tanganyika, 1920–67.* New York: Praeger.

Storgaard, Birgit
1973   "A Delayed Proletariarization of Peasants." In *Dualism and Rural Development in East Africa*, 103–125. Copenhagen: Institute for Development Research.

Svendsen, Knud Erik
1969   "Nature, Climate and Population." In *Self-reliant Tanzania*, edited by Knud Erik Svendsen and Merete Teisen, 1–28. Dar es Salaam: Tanzania Publishing House.

Swantz, M. L.
1975   "Women and Land: Basic Problems." Dar es Salaam *Sunday News*, 17 August.

Swantz, M. L., H. S. Henricson, and M. Z. Zalla
1975   "Socio-economic Causes of Malnutrition in Moshi District." University of Dar es Salaam, Bureau of Resource Assessment and Land Use Planning Research Paper no. 38.

Szentes, Tamas
1971   *The Political Economy of Underdevelopment.* Budapest: Akademiai Kiado.

Tabari, A.
1975   "Review of Freedom and Development by J. K. Nyerere." *Review of African Political Economy* 3:89–96.

Tandon, Yash
1978   "The Food Question in East Africa: A Partial Case Study of Tanzania." *Africa Quarterly* 17:5–45.

Tanganyika
1932   *Census of the Native Population, 1931.* Dar es Salaam: Government Printer.
1953   *Report on the Enumeration of African Employees, July 1952.* Nairobi: East African Statistics Department.
1957   *Explanatory Tables for Census, 1957.* Dar es Salaam: Government Printer.

1963   *African Census Report, 1957.* Dar es Salaam: Government Printer.

Tanganyika, Government of

1957   "Some Comments on Mr. Nyerere's Speech at the Fourth Committee of the United Nations." London: Her Majesty's Stationery Office.

Tanganyika African National Union

1967   *The Arusha Declaration and TANU's Policy of Socialism and Self-reliance.* Dar es Salaam: TANU Publicity Section.

Tanganyika and Zanzibar, United Republic of

1964   *Kampala Agreement.* Dar es Salaam: Information Service.

Tanganyika Territory

1922   *Annual Medical Report for the Year 1921.* Dar es Salaam: Government Printer.

1926   *Annual Medical Report for the Year 1925.* Dar es Salaam: Government Printer.

1927a   *Annual Report of the Department of Education for the Year 1926.* London: His Majesty's Stationery Office.

1927b   *Blue Book for the Year Ended 31 December 1926.* Dar es Salaam: Government Printer.

1928a   *Annual Medical and Sanitary Report for the Year 1927.* London: Crown Agents for the Colonies.

1928b   *Labour Department Annual Report 1927.* London: Crown Agents for the Colonies.

1928c   *Blue Book for the Year Ended 31 December 1927.* Dar es Salaam: Government Printer.

1929   *Blue Book for the Year Ended 31 December 1928.* Dar es Salaam: Government Printer.

1931a   *Principles of Native Administration and Their Application.* Native Administration Memorandum no. 1. Kaduna: Government Printer.

1931b   *Annual Report of the Labour Department for the Year 1930.* Dar es Salaam: Government Printer.

1931c   *Annual Report of the Provincial Commissioners for the Year 1930.* Dar es Salaam: Government Printer.

1932a   *Annual Report of the Provincial Commissioners on Native Administration for the Year 1931.* Dar es Salaam: Government Printer.

1932b   *Blue Book for the Year Ended 31 December 1931.* Dar es Salaam: Government Printer.

1933   *Blue Book for the Year Ended 31 December 1932.* Dar es Salaam: Government Printer.

1934   *Blue Book for the Year Ended 31 December 1933.* Dar es Salaam: Government Printer.

1936   *The Tribes of Tanganyika, Their Districts, Normal Dietary and Pursuits.* Dar es Salaam: Government Printer.

1937a   Preliminary Survey of the Position in Regard to Nutrition amongst the Natives of Tanganyika Territory. Dar es Salaam: Government Printer.

1937b   Annual Medical Report for the Year 1936. Dar es Salaam: Government Printer.

1937c   Blue Book for the Year Ended 31 December 1936. Dar es Salaam: Government Printer.

1938a   Annual Report of the Provincial Commissioners on Native Administration for the Year 1937. Dar es Salaam: Government Printer.

1938b   Report of the Committee Appointed to Consider and Advise on Questions Related to the Supply and Welfare of Native Labour in Tanganyika Territory. Dar es Salaam: Government Printer.

1938c   Blue Book for the Year Ended 31 December 1937. Dar es Salaam: Government Printer.

1939a   Annual Medical Report for the Year 1938. Dar es Salaam: Government Printer.

1939b   Blue Book for the Year Ended 31 December 1938. Dar es Salaam: Government Printer.

1941   Annual Report of the Provincial Commissioners on Native Administration for the Year 1940. Dar es Salaam: Government Printer.

1942   Annual Report of the Provincial Commissioners on Native Administration for the Year 1941. Dar es Salaam: Government Printer.

1944   Annual Report of the Provincial Commissioners on Native Administration for the Year 1943. Dar es Salaam: Government Printer.

1945   Annual Report of the Provincial Commissioner on Native Administration for the Year 1944. Dar es Salaam: Government Printer.

1947   Blue Book for the Year Ended 31 December 1946. Dar es Salaam: Government Printer.

1948   Blue Book for the Year Ended 31 December 1947. Dar es Salaam: Government Printer.

1949   Blue Book for the Year Ended 31 December 1948. Dar es Salaam: Government Printer.

1954   Review of Development Plans in Southern Province. Dar es Salaam: Government Printer.

1958   Appointments at the Senior Levels in the Civil Service. Dar es Salaam: Government Printer.

1959   Annual Report of the Provincial Commissioners for the Year 1958. Dar es Salaam: Government Printer.

Tanganyika Territory Department of Agriculture
1930   Annual Report 1928/1929. Dar es Salaam: Government Printer.

Tanganyika Territory Legislative Council
1926   *Instructions to Administrative Officers in Regard to Na-
         tive Labour and the Production of Economic Crops.* Ses-
         sional Paper no. 2. Dar es Salaam: Government Printer.
1949   *A Review of the Medical Policy of Tanganyika.* Ses-
         sional Paper no. 2. Dar es Salaam: Government Printer.
Tanganyika Territory Medical Department
1938   *Memorandum on Medical Policy.* Dar es Salaam: Gov-
         ernment Printer.
Tanner, R. E. S.
1960   "Land Rights on the Tanganyika Coast." *African Studies*
         19(1):14–24.
TANU   *See* Tanganyika African National Union
Tanzania, Government of
1967   *Atlas of Tanzania.* Dar es Salaam: Surveys and Mapping
         Division.
Tanzania, United Republic of
1964   *Tanganyika First Five Year Plan for Economic and So-
         cial Development 1964–1969.* Dar es Salaam: Govern-
         ment Printer.
1969   *Second Five Year Plan.* Dar es Salaam: Government
         Printer.
1972   *The Economic Survey 1971–72.* Dar es Salaam: Govern-
         ment Printer.
Tanzania Bureau of Statistics
1971   *1967 Population Census.* Dar es Salaam: Government
         Printer.
n.d.   *1978 Population Census Preliminary Report.* Dar es Sa-
         laam: Ministry of Finance and Planning.
Tanzania Rural Development Bank
1972   *Proposed Investment Plan 1972/73–1978/79.* Dar es
         Salaam.
Taueber, Irene B.
1949   *The Population of Tanganyika.* New York: United
         Nations.
Taute, M.
1939   "A German Account of the Medical Side of the War in
         East Africa, 1914–1918." *Tanganyika Notes and Rec-
         ords* 8:1–20.
Teitelbaum, Michael S.
1975   "Relevance of Demographic Transition Theory for De-
         veloping Countries." *Science* 188:420–425.
Temu, A. J.
1972   *British Protestant Missions.* London: Longmans.
Thomas, I. D. and A. C. Mascarenhas
1973   "Health Facilities and Population in Tanzania." Univer-

sity of Dar es Salaam, Bureau of Resource Assessment
and Land Use Planning Research Paper no. 21.

Thomas, I. D. and C. J. Thomas
1971   *Comparative Population Data for the Divisions of
        Tanzania.* University of Dar es Salaam, Bureau of Re-
        source Assessment and Land Use Planning Research
        Notes no. 10.

Thompson, A. R.
1968   "Ideas Underlying British Colonial Educational Policy
        in Tanganyika." In *Tanzania: Revolution by Education,*
        edited by Idrian N. Resnick. 15–32. Arusha: Longmans
        of Tanzania.

Titmuss, Richard M.
1964   *The Health Services of Tanganyika: A Report to the
        Government.* London: Pitman Medical.

Trowell, H. C., J. N. P. Davies, and R. F. A. Dean
1954   *Kwashiorkor.* London: Edward Arnold.

Turshen, Meredeth
1975   "The Political Economy of Health with a Case Study of
        Tanzania." Ph.D. dissertation, University of Sussex.
1976   "An Analysis of the Medical Supply Industries." *Inter-
        national Journal of Health Services* 6(2):271–294.
1977   "The Political Ecology of Disease." *Review of Radical
        Political Economics* 9(1):45–60.

Turshen, Meredeth and Annie Thébaud
1981   "International Medical Aid." *Monthly Review* 33(7):
        39–50.

UNESCO
1961   *World Survey of Education.* Vol 3. Paris: UNESCO

United Kingdom Colonial Office
1925   *Educational Policy in British Tropical Africa.* London:
        His Majesty's Stationery Office.
1950   *Report on the Administration of Tanganyika.* London:
        His Majesty's Stationery Office.
1956   *Annual Report on Tanganyika to the United Nations.*
        London: Her Majesty's Stationery Office.
1962   *Annual Report on Tanganyika to the United Nations.*
        London: Her Majesty's Stationery Office.

United Nations
1953   "Additional Information on the Population of Tan-
        ganyika." *Population Studies* no. 14. New York: United
        Nations.
1971   *The World Population Situation in 1970.* New York:
        United Nations.

United Nations Economic Commission for Africa
1976   *Report on the Workshop on Food Preservation and Stor-*

age Held 21/7–8/8/75, Kibaha, Tanzania. Addis Ababa: United Nations.

United Nations Trusteeship Council

1952   *Report of the Visiting Mission to Tanganyika, 1951.* New York: United Nations.

1955   *Report of the Visiting Mission to Tanganyika, 1954.* New York: United Nations.

1958   *Report of the Visiting Mission to Tanganyika, 1957.* New York: United Nations.

United States Bureau of the Census

1978   *World Population: 1977—Recent Demographic Estimates from the Countries and Regions of the World.* Washington, D.C.: Government Printing Office.

United States Department of Agriculture

1981   *Agricultural Situation: Africa and the Middle East. Review of 1980 and Outlook for 1981.* Economic Research Service, Supplement no. 7. Washington, D.C.

University of Dar es Salaam

1973   "Teaching Programme, Session 1973–74." Dar es Salaam: Faculty of Medicine. Mimeo.

van de Walle, Etienne

1977   "Trends and Prospects of Population in Tropical Africa." *Annals of the American Academy* 432(1):11.

van Etten, G. M.

1976   *Rural Health Development in Tanzania.* Assen, Holland: Van Gorcum.

van Ginneken, W.

1976   *Rural and Urban Income Inequality.* Geneva: International Labour Organisation.

van Hekken, P. M. and H. U. E. Thoden van Velzen

1970   *Relative Land Scarcity and Rural Inequality.* Afrika Studiecentrum, Rungwe Agro-socio-economic Research Project Technical Paper no. 6. Leiden, Holland.

von Freyhold, Michaela

1977   "The Post-colonial State and Its Tanzanian Version." *Review of African Political Economy* 8:75–89.

1979   *Ujamaa Villages in Tanzania: Analysis of a Social Experiment.* New York: Monthly Review Press.

von Freyhold, Michaela, K. Sawaki, and M. Zalla

1973   "Moshi District." In *The Young Child Study in Tanzania,* 116–240. Dar es Salaam: UNICEF.

Waddy, B. B.

1958   "Frontiers and Disease in West Africa." *Journal of Tropical Medicine and Hygiene* 61:100–107.

1962   "The Present State of Public Health in the African Soudan." *Transactions of the Royal Society of Tropical Medicine and Hygiene* 56(1):95–115.

Waterman, Peter
1975   "The 'Labour Aristocracy' in Africa: Introduction to an
         Unfinished Controversy." *South Africa Labour Bulletin*
         (2(5):10−27.
Watson, William
1978   *Tribal Cohesion in a Money Economy*. Manchester:
         Manchester University Press.
Weber, Max
1968   *Economy and Society*. New York: Bedminster Press.
         First published 1922.
White, C. M. N.
1959   "A Survey of African Land Tenure in Northern Rho-
         desia." *Journal of African Administration* 11(4):
         171−178.
Wilcocks, C.
1932   "The Problem of Tuberculosis in East Africa." *Kenya
         and East Africa Medical Journal* 9:88−98.
Williams, A. W.
1952   "The History of Mulago Hospital and the Makerere Col-
         lege Medical School." *East Africa Medical Journal*
         29:253−263.
Wilson, E. O.
1975   *Sociobiology: The New Synthesis*. Cambridge: Cam-
         bridge University Press.
Wilson, Godfrey and Monica Wilson
1945   *The Analysis of Social Changes Based on Observations
         in Central Africa*. Cambridge: Cambridge University
         Press.
Winteler, J. C.
1949   "Medicine in the Groundnut Scheme." *East Africa Med-
         ical Journal* 26:332−335.
Wisner, Ben
1973   "Global Interdependence, Drought and the Struggle for
         Liberation." *Journal of the Geographical Association of
         Tanzania* 8:86−112.
Wolf, Eric
1969   *Peasant Wars of the Twentieth Century*. London: Faber
         and Faber.
Wolpe, Harold
1972   "Capitalism and Cheap Labour Power in South Africa:
         From Segregation to Apartheid." *Economy and Society*
         1(4):425−456.
World Bank
1961   *The Economic Development of Tanganyika*. Baltimore:
         Johns Hopkins University Press.
1977a   *Economic Memorandum on Tanzania*. Washington,
         D.C.: World Bank.

1977b   "Tanzania Basic Economic Report." Annex 2: "Fiscal
         Implications of Universal Primary Education and Uni-
         versal Rural Water Supply." Washington, D.C.: World
         Bank. Mimeo.
1977c   "Tanzania Basic Economic Report." Annex 6: "Key
         Issues—Agriculture and Rural Development." Washing-
         ton, D.C.: World Bank. Mimeo.
1978   "Tanzania Health Sector Report." Washington, D.C.
         Photocopy.
1980   Health Sector Policy Paper. Washington, D.C.: World
         Bank.
World Health Organization
1972a   Human Development and Public Health." Technical Re-
         port Series no. 485. Geneva: World Health Organization.
1972b   Supplement to the Fourth Report on the World Health
         Situation. Geneva: World Health Organization.
1977   The Selection of Essential Drugs. Technical Report Se-
         ries no. 615. Geneva: World Health Organization.
1980   Sixth Report on the World Health Situation 1973–1977.
         Part 2. Review by Country and Area. Geneva: World
         Health Organization.
Worsley, Peter
1975   Inside China. London: Allen Lane.
Wright, E. O.
1955   African Consumers in Nyasaland and Tanganyika. Lon-
         don: Her Majesty's Stationery Office.
Wright, Marcia
1971   German Missionaries in Tanganyika, 1891–1941. Ox-
         ford: Clarendon Press.
Wrigley, C. C.
1965   "Kenya: The Patterns of Economic Life, 1902–45." In
         History of East Africa, edited by V. Harlow and E. M.
         Chilver, 229–232. Oxford: Clarendon Press.
Wyatt, A. W.
1944   "Notes." In Tanganyika District Books, Songea District.
         Dar es Salaam: Tanzania National Archives.
Young, Kate
1978   "The Social Determinants of Fertility." University of
         Sussex, Institute for Development Studies. Mimeo.
Yudkin, John S.
1980   "The Economics of Pharmaceutical Supply in Tan-
         zania." International Journal of Health Services
         10(3):455–477.

INDEX

Accident prevention, 149
Administration: in colonial era, 31–33. *See also* Indirect rule
Africa: context of Tanzania in East, 37–39; economic development in, 4–5; health status and, 7; imperialism and diseases in, 10–11; social class and, 18; white mortality in, 9, 10. *See also names of individual African countries*
Age: health and, 62–63; marriage and, 127; migration and, 51, 52
Agricultural extension services, 36, 77, 78, 88, 172
Agriculturalists: early Tanzanian history and, 24; infections among, 9; modes of production and, 55–56; nutrition and, 10
Agriculture, 50; colonial economy and, 35, 36; colonial policies and, 72–79; commercial, 79, 173; cooperative, 176; cooperative marketing and, 182; expansion of, 19; food production and, 36–37; independence and, 168–173, 179; lack of investment in, 78, 79, 88–89; migration and, 120–121; modernization of, 65–66; neocolonial exploitation of, 5; peasant, 78; production for export and, 92–93, 94; rainfall and, 22;

reproduction and cycles in, 63–64; transport and, 83–84; use of fire in, 76; village formation and, 178; women and, 56–63, 191. *See also* Crops; Farmers; Food crops; Plantations
Algeria, 202
Alpers, Edward A., 45, 80
Amani agricultral research station, 74
Amin, Samir, 109
Anemia, 63, 120
Animal husbandry. *See* Cattle
Antibiotics, 144, 152. *See also* Medicines
Arab influence, 18, 24, 26, 96, 99, 103; colonial administration and, 31; markets and, 80–81; Omani rule, 24–25
Army: German rule and, 29, 30, 97, 98, 112, 133
Arrighi, Giovanni, 130
Arusha, 143
Arusha Declaration, 173, 179, 180, 194, 196, 198, 199, 207–208
Asian community, 18, 96, 99; markets and, 80–81; medical education and, 164
Authority (local or "native"), 32, 33, 115

Balance of payments problem, 180

Medicines: antibiotics, 144,
152; death rate and modern,
41; ethnography and, 17; of
Europeans in early 1800s, 10;
pharmaceutical industry and,
202–203
Meillassoux, Claude, 5, 55,
128–129
Men: agricultural labor and, 57,
96; demographic trends and,
47, 51; employment opportunities and, 58, 59; hunter-
gatherers and, 56; labor
demand and, 116; land ownership and, 61; marketing
societies and, 183; migration
and, 118, 121; as warriors,
30n
Merton, R. K., 13
Migrant labor. *See* Labor migration
Migration, 43; male and female
demographic trends and, 47;
women's subsistence farming
and male, 62. *See also* Labor
migration
Millar, J. D., 139
Millet, 96, 105, 120
Mill, John Stuart, 13
Minimum wage law of 1969,
168
Mining, 29; labor for European,
109; nutrition and, 150; transport and, 83
Ministry of Health, 200, 205
Missionary efforts: Benedictine
mission and, 121, 130; education and, 155, 156, 157, 158;
medical services and, 140,
141, 142, 193, 196; traditional
medicine and, 145, 146, 147;
UWT and, 188
Mkunduge, G. L., 102, 103
Modes of production, 43, 55–
56, 88; disease causation and,
15; "familial," 42; population
growth and, 107; women and,

55–57, 60, 61, 64. *See also*
Capitalism; Socialism
Mohamed, Bibi Titi, 185
Montague, Ashley, 13
Morbidity, 64, 107; colonialism
and increases in, 137
Morogoro, 100, 176, 189
Mortality: child (in Moshi), 62;
in industrialized countries,
12; infant (in Africa), 44–45,
48, 51; infant (in Europe, late
1800s), 10; labor migration
and, 50–51, 52; malnutrition
and, 139; medical care and
public health and, 53; popu-
lation change and, 43–45;
population growth and, 106,
107; slave trade and, 25–26;
standard of living and, 64;
white (in Africa), 9, 10. *See
also* Death rate
Moshi, 62, 143, 186, 188
Mozambique, 24, 50, 110
Mpangara, G. P., 112
Mpwapwa, 96
Mshope, 110, 124
Mtwara, 83, 114
Mullings, Leith, 54
Muslim influence. *See* Islamic
influence
Musoma, 164
Mwanza, 96, 143, 195
Mwanza Medical Assistants
Training Center, 205
Mwapachu, J. V., 171

National Pharmaceutical
Company, 202
Natural selection, 13
Nature: disease agents and
epidemics and, 15; Marxist
construction of, 16, 21
Navarro, Vicente, 153
Ngoni, 23, 32; labor migration
and, 112; labor reserve analysis and, 110–111, 112, 113,
114, 115, 116, 117–118,